Teaching Sport Concepts and Skills

A Tactical Games Approach

Teaching Sport Concepts and Skills
A Tactical Games Approach

Linda L. Griffin, PhD
PETE Program
University of Massachusetts

Stephen A. Mitchell, PhD
School of Exercise, Leisure and Sport
Kent State University

Judith L. Oslin, PhD
School of Exercise, Leisure and Sport
Kent State University

Human Kinetics

This book is dedicated to Sheila and other teachers who believe that learning to teach is a lifelong career.

—Linda L. Griffin

This book is dedicated to Carolyn, Katie, Matthew, and all other children who like to play games.

—Stephen A. Mitchell

This book is dedicated to teachers like Becky who strive for quality physical education from themselves, their colleagues, and their students.

—Judith L. Oslin

Library of Congress Cataloging-in-Publication Data

Griffin, Linda L., 1954-
    Teaching sport concepts and skills : a tactical games approach /
Linda L. Griffin, Stephen A. Mitchell, Judith L. Oslin.
        p.   cm.
    Includes bibliographical references (p.) and index.
    ISBN 0-88011-478-9
    1. Sports--Study and teaching.   2. Coaching (Athletics)
I. Mitchell, Stephen A., 1959- . II. Oslin, Judith L., 1950- .
III. Title.
GV361.G64   1997
796'.07--dc21   97-2387
                                                                                                                      CIP

ISBN: 0-88011-478-9

Table 2.1 adapted, by permission, from L. Almond, 1986, Reflecting on Themes: A Games Classification. In *Rethinking Games Teaching*, edited by R. Thorpe, D. Bunker, and L. Almond (Loughborough: University of Technology), 71-72.

Acquisitions Editor: Scott Wikgren; **Developmental Editors:** Nanette Smith and Julie Rhoda; **Assistant Editor:** Henry Woolsey; **Editorial Assistants:** Coree Schutter and Jennifer Jeanne Hemphill; **Copyeditor:** Denelle Eknes; **Proofreader:** Erin Cler; **Graphic Designer:** Robert Reuther; **Graphic Artist:** Tara Welsch; **Photo Editor:** Boyd LaFoon; **Cover Designer:** Jack Davis; **Photographer (cover):** Michael Moffett; **Photographer (interior):** CLEO (p. 7), Zoe Perry (pp. 3, 19, 65, 93, 129, 145, 167, 217, and 227), Stephen Mitchell (p. 193); **Illustrator:** Craig Ronto; **Printer:** Braun Brumfield

Human Kinetics books are available at special discounts for bulk purchase. Special editions or book excerpts can also be created to specification. For details, contact the Special Sales Manager at Human Kinetics.

Printed in the United States of America   10 9 8 7 6 5 4

Human Kinetics
Web site: www.humankinetics.com

United States: Human Kinetics, P.O. Box 5076, Champaign, IL 61825-5076
1-800-747-4457
e-mail: humank@hkusa.com

Canada: Human Kinetics, 475 Devonshire Road, Unit 100, Windsor, ON N8Y 2L5
1-800-465-7301 (in Canada only)
e-mail: humank@hkcanada.com

Europe: Human Kinetics, P.O. Box IW14, Leeds LS16 6TR, United Kingdom
+44 (0)113-278 1708
e-mail: humank@hkeurope.com

Australia: Human Kinetics, 57A Price Avenue, Lower Mitcham, South Australia 5062
(08) 82771555
e-mail: liahka@senet.com.au

New Zealand: Human Kinetics, P.O. Box 105-231, Auckland Central
09-309-1890
e-mail: humank@hknewz.com

Contents

Acknowledgments

We wish to acknowledge several people whose interest, support, serious feedback—and skepticism—helped us put this book together. First, a special thanks to Becky Berkowitz, Westerville Middle School, for her significant contributions to the development of a tactical approach to games teaching in real schools. Second, we thank Darlene Lipovic, Shaker Heights Schools; Linda Nickson and Jenn Wolfe, Stow High School; and several other practitioners in Northeast Ohio. Third, we thank Joanne Witek, Marks' Meadow School, and the students at Marks' Meadow School and Stow High School for allowing us to photograph them. We also acknowledge the support we have received from fellow teacher educators Deborah Tannehill, The Ohio State University; Adrian Turner, Bowling Green State University; Celia Regimbal, University of Toledo; Mary Jo Sariscsany, University of Northern Colorado; Susan Peterson, Springfield College; Marsha Mantanin, Youngstown State University; Patt Dodds, Judy Placek, and PETE doctoral students Mike Carney, Klara Gubacs, and Salee Supaporn at the University of Massachusetts.

Preface

If you struggle, as many of us do, with jumping between teaching skills and teaching what to do with these skills in a game, this book is for you. The primary goal of a tactical approach is to improve students' game performance. A tactical approach encourages students to solve tactical problems by providing a concrete link between skills and tactics. This approach to learning games is student-paced and game-centered.

Teaching Sport Concepts and Skills: A Tactical Games Approach addresses the need for improved games teaching in our elementary, middle, and high school settings. We wrote this book because we believe passionately in the effectiveness of a tactical approach to games teaching. Teachers and students have responded enthusiastically to a tactical approach.

This text provides you with a complete model for tactical teaching. We did not want to give you a cookbook of activities or tricks of the trade to teaching tactics in games. Rather, we address the skills and tools you will need to understand, implement, and use this model with the students in your school—using your school's facilities and equipment, and with you as the teacher.

For many students, traditional approaches to games teaching have not stimulated interest or improved ability to play games but often have convinced children that they lack the skills necessary to play games well. For several years we have visited schools as consultants or student teacher supervisors. We found many teachers with problems balancing teaching for skill acquisition and teaching for improved game perfor-

mance. Such problems have led to games lessons that follow one of two formats—one emphasizing isolated skill drills and another revolving solely around game play. Though we *do* sometimes see a combination of skill and game play, we rarely see teachers include tactics associated with the game.

This text presents the theory and practice of teaching games from a tactical perspective, an approach originally proposed in 1982 by David Bunker and Rod Thorpe of Loughborough University, England. Our work involving tactical approaches to games teaching has been for and by practitioners. Practitioners include teachers, teacher educators, and coaches dedicated to improving game performance in students and athletes. The teaching objectives of the tactical approach are for students (a) to acquire competence in games playing by linking games tactics with skill development, (b) to enjoy the activity, and (c) to solve problems and make decisions while playing.

Teaching Sport Concepts and Skills: A Tactical Games Approach provides teachers a rationale for reexamining their philosophies on games education. This teaching model enables students to appreciate the links between games and to improve their game performance. The approach emphasizes game play and places skill learning within its game context, allowing students to see the relevance of skills to game situations. No more will students in elementary and secondary schools ask, "Why are we doing this?" or "When can we play a game?"

Part I

A TACTICAL APPROACH

CHAPTER 1

Introduction to Using This Book

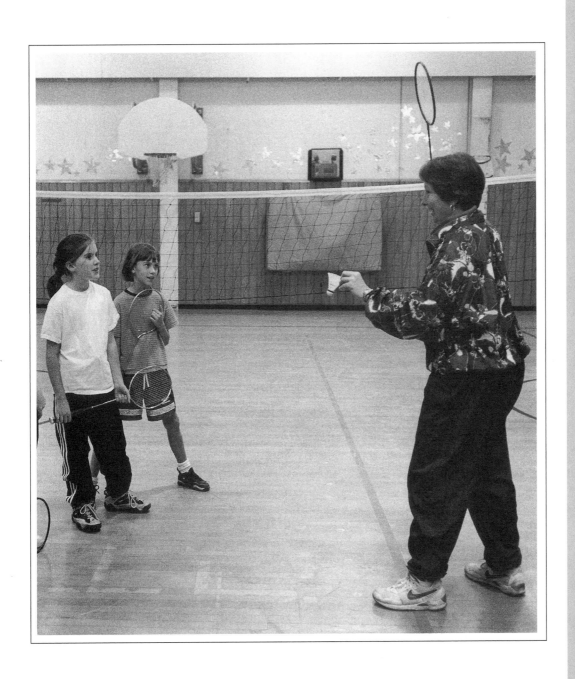

Teaching Sport Concepts and Slills: A Tactical Games Approach is the first text that provides both the rationale for rethinking games teaching and the materials that teachers can use in schools. We organized the book to answer the *why, what,* and *how* of games teaching. In chapter 2 we challenge you as the teacher to (a) rethink how you select and teach games, and (b) address game tactics when planning games units. We present reasons and organizing structures for implementing a tactical approach and introduce frameworks to break each game into tactical problems, on-the-ball skills, and off-the-ball movements. We describe levels of tactical complexity so you can teach games in a developmentally appropriate manner.

In part II (chapters 3 through 9) we provide you with applications of a tactical approach to specific games and sport teaching. We cut across the games classification system and offer tactical applications for the (a) invasion games, soccer and basketball; (b) net games, volleyball, badminton, and tennis; (c) a fielding/run-scoring game, softball; and (d) a target game, golf.

Chapters 3 through 9 address the *how to* question by providing lesson plans and potential units to use in elementary and secondary settings. We have designed each lesson to challenge students to solve a tactical problem.

Lessons begin with a developmentally appropriate game form, followed by skill or movement tasks that lead to the reapplication of these skills in another game. In each lesson we provide you with the tactical problem, lesson focus, and objective. We present each lesson in the tactical format that we advocate and suggest a progression of game-questions-practice-game. In each game we provide you with the goal (e.g., setting up to attack using the forearm pass) and game conditions (e.g., size of playing area and specific rules). After each initial game ask your students the given set of questions addressing what to do and how to do it. Use the practice tasks after the questions to help your students develop their tactical awareness of movements and skills. We provide relevant teaching cues to assist your instruction. We end with a game to reinforce the objective of the lesson.

These chapters are only building blocks for developing your own units. You may choose to review content with your students by using previous levels before moving to the next level of tactical complexity. Each chapter provides you with ideas to enhance your units, but we encour-age you to be creative. For example, you can include aspects of (a) sport education, such as roles of coaches, officials, and managers and organize units into sport seasons, and (b) cooperative learning, such as peer tutoring. We also encourage you to organize different types of tournaments for your units.

We believe a tactical approach provides opportunities for your students to problem solve their physical and cognitive actions in games. This approach places tactical awareness at the heart of games teaching and learning. As you move through the specific games and sport chapters, we encourage you to make it yours (i.e., adapt it for *your* students, *your* school, *your* facilities and equipment).

In part III we discuss strategies related to assessment and implementation. The *authentic assessment* of outcomes in physical education is critical if our subject is to retain standing within the K-12 school curriculum. In an approach to games teaching that emphasizes improved game performance, we must go beyond using isolated skill tests to measure student achievement. Chapter 10 presents an instrument, the Game Performance Assessment Instrument, to measure the components of effective game performance.

Chapter 11 provides suggestions for starting your journey from traditional methods of games teaching to a tactical approach. We have derived these suggestions from questions posed at our teacher development workshops and from feedback offered by physical educators working with a tactical approach in their schools. These teachers have found the approach rewarding for themselves and their students, though their journeys have presented difficulties. We share their suggestions with you to smooth your implementation of a tactical approach. To those practitioners, we are extremely grateful.

The benefits of the book are twofold. First, as a teacher, the book encourages you to rethink your games teaching. It provides actual units and lessons for specific games as well as the tools to create your own units and lesson content. The second benefit is to the learner. Built into a tactical approach is individual instruction rather than class-paced instruction (Jones, 1982). Though instruction might focus on particular tactical problems and skills associated with a level of complexity, you can individualize your instruction by presenting advanced performers with more complex skills related to a specific tactical problem.

The text provides a complete package for teaching games, which links skills with tactics and identifies common elements of games. The games classification system presented in chapter 2 encourages students to identify the similarities between games, which will assist them in transferring understanding from one game to another. This notion of understanding transfer is also true for teachers. The games presented in chapters 3 through 9 represent different game types, classified according to the tactics they employ. This makes game similarities easier to identify for teachers. For example, having used the materials in the soccer chapter, teachers can easily apply the lesson plans to a game such as ultimate Frisbee, which is tactically similar to soccer.

We hope these ideas will open your mind about your own games teaching. As with learning any new method, implementing a tactical approach will challenge you to think differently about games and sport teaching. Believe in your ability as a professional and challenge yourself to grow.

Understanding a Tactical Approach

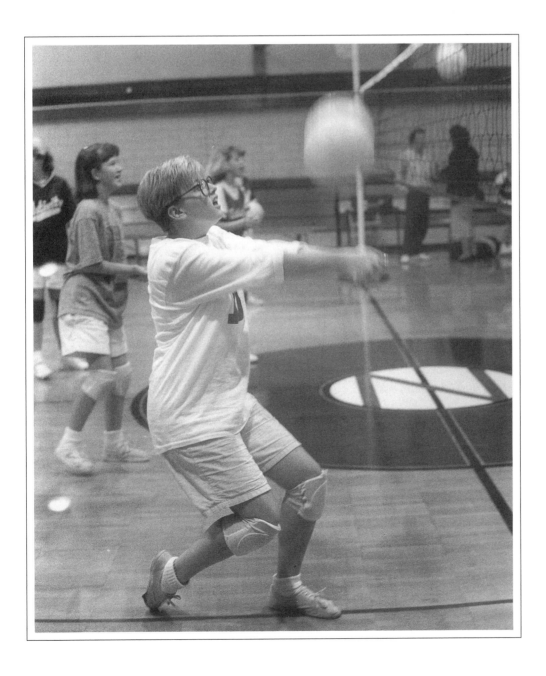

Much of what physical educators teach in schools revolves around sport-related games. About two-thirds of a typical physical education curriculum involves games teaching and learning. We believe that, given this emphasis, teachers must try to teach games effectively. Sports and games have been viewed negatively, particularly by fitness advocates, being labeled as elitist, overly competitive, and not conducive to health and fitness development. This is perhaps because of an emphasis on large-sided, zero-sum games in which winners and losers are obvious and active participation is minimal for many students. We believe that sports and games can be fun, educative, and challenging, and can enhance health and self-esteem. Although we feel games teaching should remain a valuable part of the physical education curriculum, we concede that the way games have traditionally been taught is a problem. This is the reason for our efforts in writing this book.

Many teachers teach both skills and tactics of games, but we often come across those who have problems linking these components. For example, in basketball units that spend several days covering passing, dribbling, and shooting skills, followed by several lessons on game play, skill development is not apparent during game play. Skills have usually been taught in isolation, out of their tactical context. The approach we outline in this book links tactics and skills by emphasizing the appropriate timing of skill practice and skill application within the tactical context of the game.

> The aim of a tactical approach is to improve students' game performance, which involves combining tactical awareness and skill execution.

Tactical awareness, critical to game performance, is the ability to identify tactical problems that arise during a game and to select the appropriate responses to solve them. Responses might be on-the-ball skills, such as passing or shooting, and off-the-ball movements, such as supporting and covering. For example, in soccer a tactical problem is to maintain possession of the ball. Players do this by selecting and executing appropriate passing, ball control, and support skills.

In a tactical approach, students are placed in a game situation that emphasizes maintaining possession *before* identifying and practicing passing, ball control, or support as solutions to the problem. Another tactical problem in soccer is defending space. Players solve this problem by marking opponents, pressuring the player with the ball, covering for teammates, and clearing the ball away from danger areas effectively. We believe the link between skills and tactics enables students to learn about a game and improve their performance, especially because game tactics provide the forum to apply game-related motor skills.

RATIONALE FOR A TACTICAL APPROACH

As suggested earlier, we believe that traditional games teaching in schools has done little to educate students for games playing. The tactical approach we advocate in this book promotes greater interest to learn games, more understanding of game play, and improved ability to play games.

Interest and Excitement

The traditional approach to games teaching is technical and focuses on teaching skills to answer the question, "How is this skill performed?" For example, badminton instruction often develops service, overhead clear, drop shot, and smash by concentrating on specific critical elements of these skills. Though this format *might* improve technique, it has been criticized for teaching skills before students can grasp their significance within the game. As a result, we lose the contextual nature of the skill and games teaching becomes a series of drills conforming to textbook techniques (Pigott 1982).

Commonly used drills often lead students to ask, "Why are we doing this?" or "When can we play a game?" For example, you might hear these questions in a volleyball lesson in which students must pass or set a volleyball against a wall. For many, particularly the less able, the volleyball game is characterized by aimless participation following a breakdown of passing and setting techniques. This situation creates frustration for the student and teacher. It is possible that the only thing many children learn about games is that they cannot perform the necessary complex skills (Booth 1983). In addition, skilled students often perceive isolated drills as tedious and irrelevant to their performance during game play.

We believe that a tactical approach provides an exciting alternative through which students can learn to play games. Our research, and the experience of others, indicates that students find a tactical approach motivational and teachers find it a preferable way to teach games (Berkowitz 1996; Burrows 1986; Griffin, Oslin, and Mitchell 1995; Mitchell, Griffin, and Oslin 1994). Another attractive feature of a tactical approach is its sequential nature, which eliminates redundancy in games teaching for you and your students.

Knowledge as Empowerment

Although motor skill execution is critical to game performance, appropriate decisions concerning *what to do* in game situations are just as important. French and Thomas (1987) state that "mistakes commonly observed in young children in various sports may stem from a lack of knowledge about *what to do* (our emphasis) in the context of a given sport situation" (p. 17). Furthermore, Bunker and Thorpe (1986) propose that the uniqueness of games lies in the decision-making processes that precede the use of appropriate techniques. If your students do not understand the game, their ability to identify the correct technique for a situation is impaired. Bunker and Thorpe (1986) also suggest that an increased understanding of games, achieved through teaching for tactical awareness, will *empower* children to solve the problems each game situation poses more easily and skillfully.

The next time you teach a games lesson observe the differences between the performances of high- and low-ability students. You will see more proficient skill execution by high-ability students, but you will also notice a better quality of game-related decision making and skill selection in response to specific situations. This reflects more knowledge by higher ability performers, an attribute supported by the research of McPherson and her colleagues (McPherson 1994, 1995).

Transfer of Understanding and Performance Across Games

A tactical focus may provide your students with carryover of understanding from one game to another. For example, tactical problems in soccer, field hockey, and basketball, all of which we consider *invasion games*, are similar. In our expe-

rience the best novice soccer players are those with experience of field hockey, ice hockey, basketball, or other invasion games, because these players already understand the spatial aspects of soccer. Tactically these games are similar even though the skills used are completely different. We can make a similar case for commonly taught *net games* (e.g., badminton, tennis), *fielding games* (e.g., softball, cricket), and *target games* (e.g., golf, bowling) (Werner and Almond 1990). These similarities enable us to group games for instruction according to the tactics they employ. We define invasion games as games in which the goal is to invade an opponent's territory to score. Net and wall games involve propelling an object into space so an opponent is unable to make a return. In fielding and run-scoring games the goal is to strike an object, usually a ball, so it eludes defenders. We define target games as games in which the performer propels an object, preferably with a high degree of accuracy, at a target. Table 2.1 presents the classification system suggested by Almond (1986).

The premise for developing this classification system was that teachers could select from several game types to expose children to a variety of activities (Almond 1986). The weakness of this approach is its unlikeliness to lead to depth of tactical learning and improved game performance within any category. Lack of depth is an important issue because performance enhancement in any game will probably not result from a typical unit of six to eight lessons. We propose an alternative use for this system, involving selection from within rather than across game categories. This provides students with a deeper understanding of what constitutes effective game performance by identifying similarities between games within each category.

Table 2.1 emphasizes game tactics rather than skills. This suggests that if your students are well versed in tactics, the carryover of performance from one game to another within a category will be more effective than skills emphasized in isolation. To clarify, the skills used in soccer, basketball, and field hockey are different, and if these skills become the focus of instruction there will be little carryover from one game to another. Nevertheless, the games have much in common tactically, and instruction focusing on tactical problems can lead to positive transfer from one game to another. Several teachers have found this transfer effect to be the greatest benefit derived from using a tactical approach to games teach-

Table 2.1
A Classification System for Games

Invasion	Net/wall	Fielding/run-scoring	Target
Basketball (FT)	Net	Baseball	Golf
Netball (FT)	Badminton (I)	Softball	Croquet
Team handball (FT)	Tennis (I)	Rounders	Bowling
Water polo (FT)	Table tennis (I)	Cricket	Lawn bowls
Soccer (FT)	Pickle ball (I)	Kickball	Pool
Hockey (FT)	Volleyball (H)		Billiards
Lacrosse (FT)			Snooker
	Wall		
Speedball (FT/OET)	Racquetball (I)		
	Squash (I)		
Rugby (OET)	Fives (H)		
Football (OET)			
Ultimate			
Frisbee (OET)			

FT = focused target; OET = open-end target; I = implement; H = hand

Adapted from Almond, 1986.

ing. For example, one sixth grade teacher began a series of invasion games units by focusing eight lessons on the tactical problems of maintaining ball possession and attacking the goal in soccer. She then took the same tactical problems and applied them consecutively to ultimate Frisbee and floor hockey during instructional units of similar length. Students developed the ability to transfer understanding of one game to another, particularly movements of players not in possession of the ball, Frisbee, or puck and decisions of players in possession. Other teachers and student teachers report similar outcomes.

To summarize, our rationale to a tactical approach to games teaching includes the following:

- Greater interest and excitement for all students, especially those of lower ability whose needs a traditional, skill-based approach has failed to meet.
- Improvements in tactical knowledge, particularly for students whose ability prevents them from consistently executing motor skills successfully in game situations. For these students, greater knowledge of what to do will be a positive first step toward improving game performance.
- Deeper understanding of game play and the

ability to transfer this understanding more effectively from performance in one game to another. This increases the possibility of developing games players with flexibility to adapt to new activities and situations when the need arises.

Physical educators have suggested that a tactical focus to teaching games is well suited to both the elementary and secondary levels (Bunker and Thorpe 1982; Doolittle and Girard 1991; Smith 1991). However, no one has proposed methods to identify, sequence, and teach the tactical problems of specific games at successive stages of development. In this book we address how practitioners can use this approach to enhance students' game performance at different development levels. We do this by offering games frameworks, providing a broader definition of game performance, and identifying levels of tactical complexity for each game.

GAMES FRAMEWORKS

An initial concern for those of you who wish to teach tactically in games and sport is developing frameworks to identify and break down relevant tactical problems, a process initially begun by Spackman (1983). By selecting teaching materials from such a framework, you ensure that students become familiar with the *game* and that skills, when taught, relate to game context. An example of how you can do this is in table 2.2. The example uses soccer, which is taught at all developmental levels, and provides a framework that identifies tactical problems, off-the-ball movements, and on-the-ball skills necessary to solve these problems.

Table 2.2 identifies the major tactical problems that teams must solve to score, prevent scoring, and restart play effectively. To score, a team must solve the progressively complex problems of how to maintain possession of the ball, attack the goal, create space while attacking, and use that space effectively. Each tactical problem includes relevant off-the-ball movements and on-the-ball skills. For example, to maintain possession of the ball, players must support teammates with the ball and be able to pass and control the ball over

Table 2.2
Tactical Problems, Movements, and Skills in Soccer

Tactical problems	Off-the-ball movements	On-the-ball skills
Scoring		
Maintaining possession of the ball	Supporting the ball carrier	Passing—short and long Control—feet, thigh, chest
Attacking the goal	Using a target player	Shooting, shielding, turning
Creating space in attack	Crossover play Overlapping run	First-time passing—give and go Crossover play Overlapping run
Using space in attack	Timing runs to goal, shielding	Width—dribbling, 1 v 1, crossing, heading Depth—shielding
Preventing scoring		
Defending space	Marking, pressure, preventing the turn, delay, covering, recovery runs	Clearing the ball
Defending the goal	Goalkeeping—positioning	Goalkeeping— receiving the ball, shot stopping, distribution
Winning the ball		Tackling—block, poke, slide
Restarting play		
Throw-in—attacking and defending		
Corner kick—attacking and defending		
Free kick—attacking and defending		

various distances. You can develop similar frameworks for any game by asking yourself the following two questions:

1. What problems does this game present for scoring, preventing scoring, and restarting play?
2. What off-the-ball movements and on-the-ball skills are necessary to solve these problems?

BROADER DEFINITION OF GAME PERFORMANCE

The two questions suggest that a tactical approach defines game performance as more than simply executing motor skills. In table 2.2 we recognize that movements made by players who do not have the ball are important, and you should consider them in games teaching. For example, a player who can pass the ball accurately is of limited value unless she has potential receivers who have moved to provide support. Off-the-ball movements are often ignored in favor of teaching on-the-ball skills, but you should teach these movements to maximize students' game performance. We believe in this strongly because, in any game, players possess the ball, Frisbee, or puck for only a brief time during play. For example, in a 30-minute, six-a-side game of soccer, if you divide 30 minutes by 10 outfield players (each team has a goalkeeper), then each outfield player is only in contact with the ball for an average of three minutes! What is he doing the remainder of the time? The answer is moving to appropriate positions to attack or defend and making decisions about how to contribute to the game. Yet, we rarely teach these aspects of game performance in physical education.

This adds up to a broader definition of game performance. Not only does game play involve the execution of motor skills but also components such as the following:

- Decision making
- Supporting
- Marking or guarding
- Covering teammates
- Adjusting position as game play unfolds
- Ensuring adequate court or field coverage by a base position

This expanded definition of game performance has implications for your goals, the content you select, and the assessment procedures you choose. Expanded goals and content will be evident in each of the subsequent sport-specific chapters, with new ideas for assessment presented in chapter 10.

LEVELS OF TACTICAL COMPLEXITY

Having identified important tactical problems and associated skills for a particular game, you face the task of ensuring that the tactical complexity of the game matches student development. This relates to the developmental appropriateness of your teaching. Some tactical problems are too complex for novice players to understand. For example, in table 2.2 we might anticipate that novice players would understand the need to maintain possession of the ball and attack the goal because this is how they score goals. On the other hand, it would be unrealistic to expect these players to understand more advanced attacking concepts, such as using width and depth in attack, because this understanding comes from experience playing the game in larger-sided forms.

You might present a tactical problem at successive stages of development, and the problem of *defending space* in soccer serves to illustrate this point. We can reasonably expect that novice players would appreciate the need for defense to prevent opponents from scoring. Defense in its simplest form involves marking, or guarding, an opponent to deny access to the ball. However, it is only as tactical awareness develops that students will appreciate the need for players to defend as a team by delaying the opponent's attacks and providing cover for teammates who challenge for the ball. From this perspective it becomes appropriate to add to the complexity of game understanding as tactical awareness develops. That is, as students improve their tactical understanding, then games should involve tactical problems of increasing complexity. If you can identify *levels of tactical complexity*, the process becomes one of developing versions of the game for students at varying stages of awareness. The key question you are addressing here is, "How tactically complex do I want the game to be in my unit?" This is in contrast to a technical approach in which the question is, "What skills should I teach in my unit?" Table 2.3 identifies possible levels of tactical complexity for soccer.

As indicated in table 2.3, you can increase each tactical problem in complexity as students develop their understanding and skills. To play the game in its simplest form, students need only to understand maintaining possession of the ball, attacking the goal, and restarting play in a simple fashion. Therefore, in teaching soccer to novice players (level I) you first might ensure that students appreciate these activities and, second, pro-

vide students with solutions to these tactical problems. Level I skills include basic short passing, receiving, shooting, throw-in, and short corner. Teaching longer passing techniques to young students would not be appropriate because they don't need this in small-sided games and few would possess the necessary strength for these skills. For this reason you might revisit maintaining possession by addressing long passing when your students can see its value and can perform these advanced skills, perhaps at level IV.

Having introduced soccer in its most basic tac-

Table 2.3
Levels of Tactical Complexity for Soccer

| Tactical problems | Levels of tactical complexity | | | | |
	I	II	III	IV	V
Scoring					
Maintaining possession of the ball	Pass and control—feet	Support		Pass—long Control—thigh, chest	
Attacking the goal	Shooting	Shooting Turning	Target player		
Creating space in attack			First-time passing	Overlap	Crossover
Using space in attack				Width—dribbling, crossing, heading	Depth—timing of runs
Preventing scoring					
Defending space		Marking, pressuring the ball	Preventing the turn	Clearing the ball	Delay, cover, recover
Defending the goal		Goalkeeper position, receiving, throwing			Making saves, kicking/punting
Winning the ball			Tackling—block, poke	Tackling—slide	
Restarting					
Throw-in	Throw-in				
Corner kick	Short kick		Near post		Far post
Free kick			Attacking		Defending

tical form, at level II you can further develop student understanding and skill. You can show students that by supporting the player with the ball they increase the probability that their team will retain possession. Developing an awareness of the need to defend space and the goal also becomes appropriate for level II students, because these players will begin to think about effective ways of preventing opponents from scoring. Simple tactical problems at level II include denying space to opponents when they are close to the ball or the goal and positioning the goalkeeper to make the goal as small as possible, decreasing the size of the target. When students understand the need for these tactics they can practice relevant movements such as marking (or guarding) and skills such as basic goalkeeping. Finally, revisiting basic starts and restarts will allow the game to take a complete, but modified form, making it easier for further development at the next level.

As indicated in table 2.3, you might teach more advanced tactical problems, such as creating and using space in attack, at a later stage. At level III students can progress, dealing with problems of creating space as they attack the goal. At this time you might revisit the problem of defending space by introducing the concept of putting pressure on the player with the ball. You could also introduce the problem of winning the ball and teach some simple tackling skills. Confront the problem of winning the ball again at level IV with work on slide tackling. Level IV students might address more advanced solutions to the tactical problems of creating and using space. At level V students should understand problems presented by the game, and the tactics and skills they employ should be more advanced. The exact level at which students should explore a tactical problem and its associated skills will depend on task complexity and levels of students' understanding and skill. We recommend that, when working with novice players, you begin with essential tactical problems related to scoring and preventing scoring. As you address more complex solutions to tactical problems, both offensively and defensively, the game will increasingly resemble the mature form.

Individualizing Instruction

As you know, within any class students vary in their levels of game understanding and performance. To individualize instruction, you can present advanced performers with more complex solutions to a specific tactical problem. For example, in a class of novice soccer players focusing on maintaining possession of the ball by accurate short passing and receiving, some students will progress faster than others. It might be appropriate to introduce more skillful students to the concept of support or even longer passing techniques to maintain a challenge. Similarly, novice softball players learning to defend space by fielding the ball and making an accurate throw to first base will progress at different rates. You could introduce higher ability students to the concept of defending the base or footwork involved in covering first base. In other words, you can increase the level of tactical complexity *within* the specific tactical problem being addressed. This is sound developmental teaching practice.

TEACHING FOR TACTICAL AWARENESS AND SKILL ACQUISITION

In this section we outline the process of teaching an individual games lesson using a tactical approach. Notice the use of small-sided games to expose students to specific tactical problems and the importance of the teacher's questions to provoke critical thinking and problem solving.

Tactical Model

A critical question that we now address is, "How do I teach for tactical awareness within the individual physical education lesson?" Bunker and Thorpe (1982), have suggested a six-stage model for games teaching. It is variably termed Teaching for Understanding or Game-Centered Games (i.e., games teaching centered on the game rather than its skill components, Waring and Almond 1995), and has provided useful guidance for physical educators. To illustrate the processes of this approach, we have consolidated the model into three stages, which we present in figure 2.1.

The model outlined in figure 2.1 suggests that teaching for tactical awareness should start with a game or, more precisely, a *game form* modified to represent the advanced form and exaggerated to present students with tactical problems (Thorpe, Bunker, and Almond 1986). For example, a tactical problem in badminton is to set up the attack by creating space on the opponent's side of the net. You might use a half-court singles game because it is similar to the full-court game (representative) but the court is narrower. This exaggerates the need to play shots to the back and front of the court to create space.

Young or novice students will be unable to play most games in the advanced form because of tactical understanding and skill limitations. The game form should clearly relate to levels of student development. Consider dimensions of playing areas, the numbers participating, and the equipment they will use. If you establish a developmentally appropriate game form, patterns of students' play can represent the advanced form. For example, small-sided volleyball games in reduced playing areas with lighter balls and lower nets use the same principles, problems, and skills as the full game.

Critical Conditions and Questions

Students will gradually learn the rules of games through the conditions you apply. An essential aspect of any game form when teaching for tactical awareness is that it should be modified, or conditioned, to encourage students to think tactically. By changing the rules of a game, you will exaggerate playing conditions to ensure that players address the question, "What must I do to succeed in this situation?" This is a question that you can directly ask students. At this stage of the lesson your questions are necessary, and the quality of questions is the key to fostering students' critical thinking and problem solving. First, ask questions related to the goal of the activity; then ask students *what* they must do to achieve that goal (i.e., what skills or movements must they use to be successful). Questions related to *why* certain skills or movements are required might also be appropriate. Once students have become aware of what they need to do and why, you can question them about *how* to perform the necessary skills. These questions help students identify what they ought to practice, thus leading to

the practice phase of the lesson. The following example illustrates the process.

Establish an appropriate game form, such as 2 versus 2 (2 v 2) soccer in a restricted (20-by-20-yard) playing area with an objective of making a specific number of consecutive passes (say four) to score. This forces students to confront what they must do to maintain possession. An appropriate teacher-student questioning sequence might be as follows:

Teacher: What was the goal of that game?

Students: For your team to keep the ball for four passes.

Teacher: What does your team have to do to keep the ball for four consecutive passes?

Students: Pass the ball.

Teacher: Yes, and what else?

Students: You have to be able to receive a pass as well.

Teacher: OK. You have to be able to pass and receive the ball. How many teams managed to make four consecutive passes? (It is likely that only a few pairs will have managed this target because it is difficult in a 2 v 2 game.)

Teacher: Well, perhaps some passing and receiving practice would be a good idea.

Through a developmentally appropriate game form and skillful teacher questioning, students realize that accurate passing and swift ball control are essential skills. At this point formal teaching of passing and control skills becomes appropriate before returning to a game. During this practice, you can describe *how* to perform the necessary skills and movements by using teaching cues related to the critical elements of each technique. Note that although passing and receiving have become the focus of the lesson, you didn't inform students of this at the beginning. Rather you led them to identify the lesson focus through a well-designed modified game and skillful questioning. Many teachers who are new to a tactical approach find it difficult to withhold this infor-

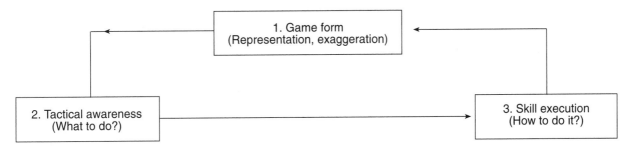

Figure 2.1 A tactical approach to games teaching.

mation at the start of a lesson. Try to avoid providing too much information early in the lesson because this will detract from the problem-solving process.

The process continues lesson by lesson with additional modifications to the game so students can explore new aspects of tactical awareness. For example, you could introduce a 3 v 3 game so students must provide effective support for the player with the ball. When they understand the need for good support, you can teach appropriate off-the-ball supporting movements before returning to a game situation. Thus you progressively develop game performance. You can extend the problem of maintaining possession by providing direction to the game with either small goals or a target player at each end of a rectangular playing area. Pose the question, "How can we get the ball past the defense?" At this point students must think in terms of passing the ball between defenders, or *splitting* the defense, an essential tactic for penetrating in attack.

To conclude this chapter, we reemphasize four essential points of a tactical approach to games teaching.

1. *Consider the tactical problems to address during your unit and decide on the complexity of solutions to these problems.* These decisions will depend on the experience and ability of your students. Though we provide tactical frameworks and levels of tactical complexity throughout this book, you can develop these easily for other games within the same category by using our examples.

2. *Within each lesson students practice skill development after they have experienced a game form that presents a tactical problem requiring the use of that skill.* In this way they appreciate the need for the skill and develop a broader view of skill development that includes both off-the-ball movements and on-the-ball skills. The timing of this practice is a critical component of a tactical approach. As the teacher, you should modify initial game forms so students can confront tactical problems.

3. *Make the link between the initial modified game and skill practice through your questions; the quality of these questions is critical.* Questions must first draw students' attention to the tactical problem (in simple terms, as in the previous example),

then to potential solutions to the problem. Of course we cannot assume that you will always get the answer you are expecting (these are students after all), but experience in this approach will enable you to think on your feet, probe further, and guide students to appropriate responses. Don't assume that students will be versed in terminology such as *overhead clear* or *drop shot.* Rather you might expect students to talk about *long* and *short* shots, at which point you can introduce correct terminology before skill practice.

4. *Having engaged in skill practice, students have the opportunity to apply their improved skills and tactical understanding in a game.* By providing your students with this opportunity, you increase the probability that they will understand the value of skills in the relevant game context. Chapter 11 provides more detailed suggestions on how to implement a tactical approach.

The sport-specific chapters that follow provide suggestions for teaching tactically in a variety of games and sports. You will notice that the chapters vary in length and levels of tactical complexity vary from game to game. This reflects differences in the tactical complexity of the games. For example, invasion games tend to be more tactically complex than net and wall games, so we have identified five levels of tactical complexity for soccer but only three for badminton.

Each chapter contains a framework of tactical problems, movements, and skills to assist you in breaking down the game tactically. We also provide suggested levels of tactical complexity to give you an idea of how to developmentally sequence your teaching based on the complexity of the game form. We suggest several lessons for each level of tactical complexity, but these are only outlines with little attention to detail of equipment and management procedures. For the sake of space we have restricted each outline to the tactical problem being addressed, the lesson focus, the objective for the lesson, an initial game form, teacher questions with likely student responses, practice ideas with teaching cues, and a closing game form. This abbreviated format provides you with a greater breadth of material to get you started. Read on and develop confidence in your ability to teach tactically!

Part II

A TACTICAL APPROACH TO TEACHING SPECIFIC GAMES AND SPORTS

CHAPTER 3

Soccer

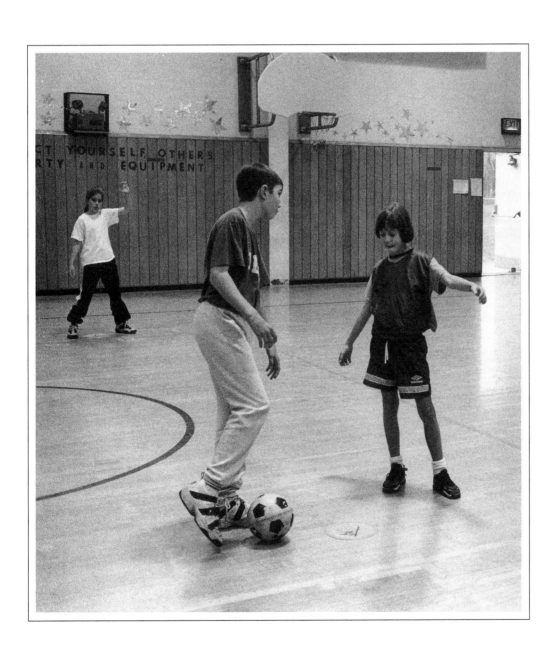

This chapter illustrates the application of a tactical approach to teaching soccer, an invasion game. Before starting it is worth reemphasizing two critical points that form the basis for lesson format. First, students practice for skill development *after* they have played a game form that presents a tactical problem requiring that skill. As the teacher you can modify game forms so students confront these problems. You can also ask appropriate questions that will encourage students to think of solutions. Second, having engaged in skill practice, students have the opportunity to apply their improved skills and tactical awareness in a game. By providing this opportunity you increase the probability that students will understand the value of skills in the relevant game context.

We make the following assumptions about facilities and equipment:

1. Soccer will be taught outdoors, though you can teach some lessons indoors.

2. There is one soccer ball for every two students. Where this is not the case, you can make adjustments for most activities.

3. Cones are available to mark the playing areas suggested (all distances are in yards), though it would be advantageous to have a series of 10-by-10 grids permanently marked (10 by 10 is ideal, but you could vary this according to available space). Ten-yard markings on a football field (American) can be useful in this regard.

4. Balls will be appropriate in size and weight to student development (i.e., smaller and lighter balls for younger students). It may also be necessary to use playing areas smaller than those recommended, depending on student development.

All lessons in this chapter begin with a game form. In determining the size of teams for these game forms, consider appropriate group size for skill practice. Keep students in their teams for skill practice to facilitate smooth transitions from one stage of the lesson to the next.

For ease of reference, we present the tactical framework and levels of tactical complexity for soccer again in tables 3.1 and 3.2. We present a brief description of activities before the specific lesson at each level.

LEVEL I

At level I, we suggest that students focus on maintaining possession of the ball and attacking the goal, because these are the fundamental tactical problems for invasion games. At this level we answer what to do and how to do it by focusing on players' actions when they possess the ball. This primarily concerns passing, ball control, and shooting skills as solutions to the tactical problems of maintaining possession and attacking goal. Adding simple restarts when the ball goes out-of-bounds at the side or goal line enables a small-sided game to evolve during instruction at this level.

We have not recommended that you pay attention to tactical problems of defense at level I, though you could easily do this by using some level II lessons. Our rationale for focusing only on tactical problems of scoring is threefold. First, beyond making students aware that each team should try to prevent the other from scoring, time on defensive aspects is not necessary for a modified game of soccer. Players need only to focus on the essential tactical problems for a game to take place, these being maintaining possession and attacking the goal. Unless teams seek solutions to these problems, a modified game will not be representative of the mature form. Second, from a motivational viewpoint we believe in the importance of early success. At level I we feel it would be counterproductive to focus on preventing offensive success. Third, the issue of time is ever present, and it is not possible to focus on all aspects of the game during an initial instructional unit.

Table 3.1
Tactical Problems, Movements, and Skills in Soccer

Tactical problems	Off-the-ball movements	On-the-ball skills
Scoring		
Maintaining possession of the ball	Supporting the ball carrier	Passing—short and long Control—feet, thigh, chest
Attacking the goal	Using a target player	Shooting, shielding, turning
Creating space in attack	Crossover play Overlapping run	First-time passing—give and go Crossover play Overlapping run
Using space in attack	Timing runs to goal, shielding	Width—dribbling, 1 v 1, crossing, heading Depth—shielding
Preventing scoring		
Defending space	Marking, pressure, preventing the turn, delay, covering, recovery runs	Clearing the ball
Defending the goal	Goalkeeping—positioning	Goalkeeping— receiving the ball, shot stopping, distribution
Winning the ball		Tackling—block, poke, slide
Restarting play		
Throw-in—attacking and defending		
Corner kick—attacking and defending		
Free kick—attacking and defending		

Table 3.2
Levels of Tactical Complexity for Soccer

Tactical problems	Levels of tactical complexity				
	I	II	III	IV	V
Scoring					
Maintaining possession of the ball	Pass and control—feet	Support		Pass—long Control—thigh, chest	
Attacking the goal	Shooting	Shooting Turning	Target player		
Creating space in attack			First-time passing	Overlap	Crossover
Using space in attack				Width— dribbling, crossing, heading	Depth—timing of runs
Preventing scoring					
Defending space		Marking, pressuring the ball	Preventing the turn	Clearing the ball	Delay, cover, recover
Defending the goal		Goalkeeper position, receiving, throwing			Making saves, kicking/punting
Winning the ball			Tackling— block, poke	Tackling— slide	
Restarting					
Throw-in	Throw-in				
Corner kick	Short kick		Near post		Far post
Free kick			Attacking		Defending

Level I Lessons

LESSON 1

TACTICAL PROBLEM: Maintaining possession of the ball.

LESSON FOCUS: Passing and receiving balls on the ground with inside of foot.

OBJECTIVES: Accurate and firm short passes.

Use one touch to control and set up for next move.

A. GAME: 3 v 3 in 30 by 20, possession game (see figure 3.1).

Goal: Five consecutive passes.

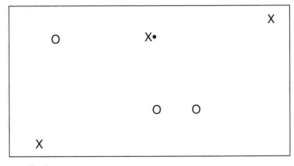

Figure 3.1

• = Ball

Questions

Q: What must you do in this game?

A: Keep the ball.

Q: How can your team keep the ball?

A: Pass.

B. PRACTICE TASK: Partner (or triad) practice approximately 10 yards apart, pass and control.

Goals: One touch to control and set up for the next pass.

Firm and accurate passing with inside of both feet.

Cues: Passing

Face the direction you are passing.

Nonkicking foot next to the ball.

Use inside of foot and turn foot square to ball.

Strike the ball through its center.

Receiving

Get in line with the ball as it comes.

One touch with inside of foot to set yourself up for next pass.

C. GAME: 3 v 3 in 30 by 20, narrow goal, no goalkeeper (see figure 3.2).

  Goals: Quick control and setup.

             Firm and accurate passing.

             Keep heads up for vision.

             Score in the small goal.

  Conditions: Three touch (maximum) before passing (depending on abilities of students).

                 Ball must stay below head height.

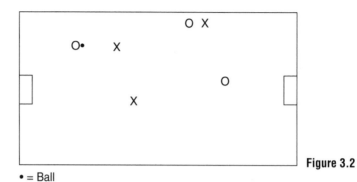

Figure 3.2

• = Ball

LESSON 2

TACTICAL PROBLEM: Maintaining possession of the ball.

LESSON FOCUS: Passing and receiving balls on the ground with outside of foot.

OBJECTIVES: Accurate and firm short passes.

                Use one touch to control and set up for next move.

A. GAME: 3 v 3 in 30 by 20, possession game (see figure 3.3).

  Goal: Five consecutive passes.

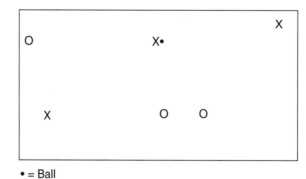

Figure 3.3

• = Ball

Questions

Q: What must you do in this game?

A: Keep the ball.

Q: How can your team keep the ball?

A: Pass.

B. PRACTICE TASK: Partner practice, pass and control or set up (5 to 10 yards apart).

Goals: One touch to control and set up.

Firm and accurate passing with outside of both feet.

Cues: Passing

Nonkicking foot next to the ball.

Use outside of foot and point toe inward.

Strike the ball through its center.

Receiving

Get in line with the ball as it comes.

One touch with outside of foot to set yourself up for next pass.

C. GAME: 3 v 3 in 30 by 20, narrow goal, no goalkeeper (see figure 3.4).

Goals: Quick control and setup.

Firm and accurate passing. } with inside or outside of foot as appropriate

Keep heads up for vision.

Score in small goal.

Conditions: Three touch (maximum) before passing (depending on abilities of students).

Keep ball below head height.

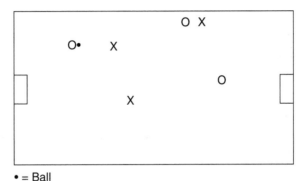

Figure 3.4

• = Ball

LESSON 3

TACTICAL PROBLEM: Attacking the goal.

LESSON FOCUS: Shooting.

OBJECTIVES: Three principles of good shooting.

a. Shoot on sight.

b. Hit the target.

c. Keep the shot low.

A. GAME: 6 v 6 on small field (30 by 30), large goals (8 yards) (see figure 3.5).

Goals: Shoot when possible.

Hit the target (i.e., the whole goal).

Questions

Q: What should you do this close to the goal?

A: Shoot.

Q: Why should you shoot?

A: Because if you don't shoot you won't score!

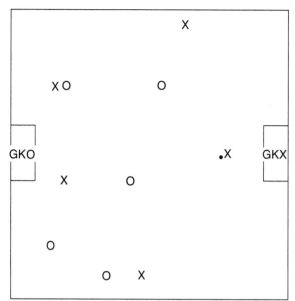

Figure 3.5

GK = Goalkeeper

Q: Where should you aim when you shoot?

A: At the whole goal; force the goalkeeper to make a save.

Q: Should you aim high or low?

A: Low.

Q: Why should you shoot low?

A: It's harder for the goalkeeper to go down to make a save than up.

B. PRACTICE TASK: Partner practice (see figure 3.6), static and moving ball (with goalkeepers if groups of three needed).

Goals: Shoot ball between two posts or cones.

Keep all shots below waist height.

Cues: Take a long step to the ball.

Nonkicking foot next to the ball.

Use the instep (or laces).

Head and toe down.

C. GAME: Repeat game A.

Goals: Specific number of shots.

Specific number of on-target shots. } depending on ability

X   X   X   X   X

Cone   Cone   Cone   Cone   Cone   Cone

•X   •X   •X   •X   •X   **Figure 3.6**

LESSON 4

TACTICAL PROBLEM: Attacking the goal.

LESSON FOCUS: Use of target player to create shooting opportunities.

OBJECTIVE: Target player to *lay (pass) the ball off* for a shot by supporting player.

A. GAME: 6 v 6 in 50 by 40, full-size goals (see figure 3.7).

    Goal: Get an early pass to target player, then support.

    Conditions: One target player per team (OT, XT); one defender marking target player.

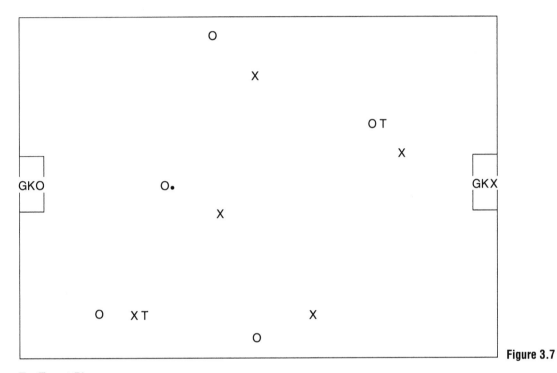

Figure 3.7

T = Target Player

Questions

Q: What should other players do when their own target player has the ball?

A: Support.

Q: Where is a good place to support?

A: In a position to receive a pass and shoot.

B. PRACTICE TASK : Shooting from target player lay off (see figure 3.8); one goalkeeper, one collector, one target player, three to four shooters.

    Goals: Accurate pass to target.

        Firm lay off (pass) by target player (to the side).

        Clean strike of moving ball by shooter.

        Specific number of shots on target.

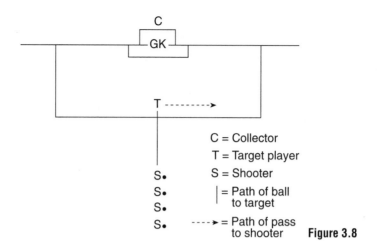

Figure 3.8

Cues: Shooter

 Firm pass to target.

 Run to side of target to receive return pass.

 Shoot the moving ball immediately.

 Target player

 Firm pass to side.

C. GAME: 6 v 6 in 50 by 40, full-size goals (see figure 3.9).

 Goals: Hit the target with shots.

 Shield or lay off by target player.

 Support for target player.

 Specific number of shots per team on goal.

 Conditions: One target player (rotate); target player cannot turn with ball. Goals scored from a lay off (pass) by the target player count double.

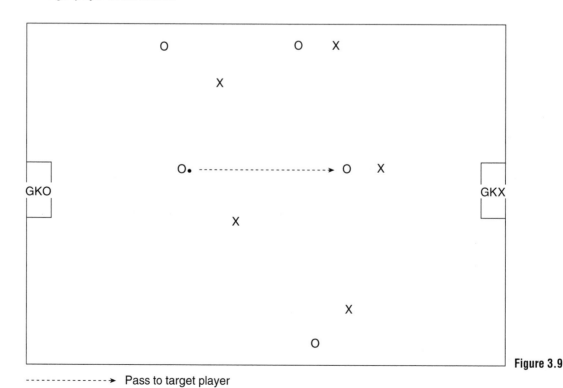

Figure 3.9

- - - - - - - - - - -> Pass to target player

LESSON 5

TACTICAL PROBLEM: Restarting play.

LESSON FOCUS: Throw-in.

OBJECTIVE: Quick use of *correctly taken* throw-in to get attack moving forward.

A. GAME: 6 v 6 in 60 by 30, full goal (see figure 3.10); narrow field so ball goes out of play often and players take many throw-ins.

    Goal: Take quick throw-ins.

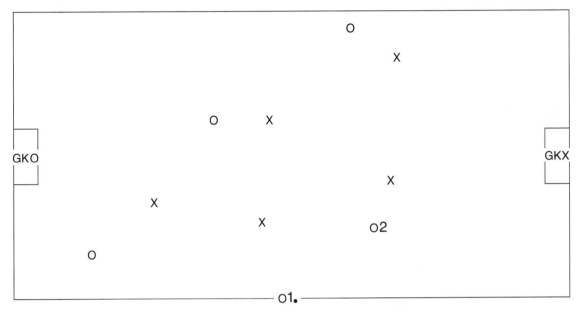

Figure 3.10

Question

Q: How can you get the ball into play quickly on a throw-in?

A: Player O1 throws to nearest player (O2) who passes it back to O1.

B. PRACTICE TASK 1: Partner practice, throw, control, return.

    Cues: Thrower

            Use two hands.

            Take ball behind head.

            Keep two feet on ground *all the time.*

            Throw to receiver's feet and move onto field.

         Receiver

            Control and return ball to thrower.

PRACTICE TASK 2: 2 v 1 (defender O) in 30 by 10 (see figure 3.11).

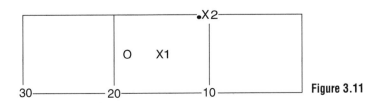

Figure 3.11

Conditions: Attack starts with throw-in at 10-yard line. Support player (X2) must get free to receive return pass.

Goals: Receiver (X1) of throw-in turns with ball or passes ball back to teammate (X2).

　　　X1 and X2 to get ball to 30-yard line under control by 2 v 1.

Cues: Thrower (X2)

　　　Use two hands.

　　　Take ball behind head.

　　　Keep two feet on ground *all the time.*

　　　Throw to receiver's feet and move onto field.

　　Receiver (X1)

　　　Control and return ball to thrower.

C. GAME: Repeat game A.

LESSON 6

TACTICAL PROBLEM: Restarting play.

LESSON FOCUS: Attacking at corner kicks, the short corner.

OBJECTIVE: Using corners to create scoring opportunities.

A. GAME: 6 v 6 in 40 by 50, full goal, referee calls many corners (see figure 3.12).

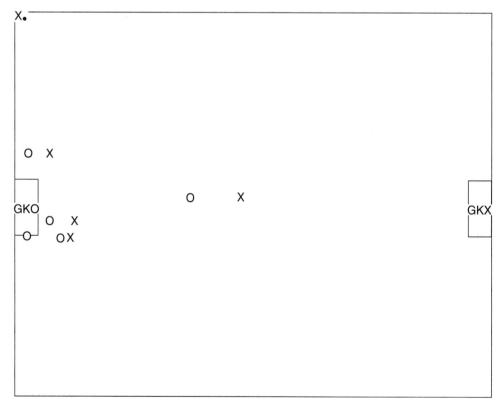

Figure 3.12

Goal: Awareness of the corner kick as a scoring chance.

Question

Q: How can you use a corner to score?

A: Get the ball into the center.

B. PRACTICE TASK: Team practice, unopposed (no goalkeeper), short corners (see figure 3.13).

Goal: Use short corners to attack goal.

Cues: Short corner.

Two (X5, X6) attackers go to corner.

X5 passes to X6.

X6 dribbles closer to goal before passing or shooting.

C. GAME: Repeat game A.

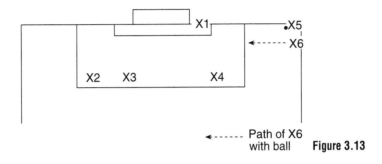

Path of X6 with ball **Figure 3.13**

LEVEL II

At level II students will again focus on tactical problems of maintaining possession of the ball and attacking the goal, but will progress to defending the goal and defending space. The focus of maintaining possession now shifts from solutions applied by players when they have the ball to the contributions of teammates without the ball. This early focus on off-the-ball movement is critical because soccer players spend much more time without the ball than in possession, and they should spend this time in productive movement. Offensively players need to learn when and where they should move to help their team keep possession of the ball. This is true in all invasion games.

After additional attention to attacking the goal, students focus on defending space and the goal. It is appropriate to shift the focus to defense at this point because it will be clear to students that they must solve these defensive problems for their team to succeed. Modified games at level II will enable students to see the value in marking or guarding opponents and for the goalkeeper to be properly positioned to receive the ball when it comes. Brief attention to the goalkeeper's distribution of the ball enables the game to develop its complexity by the end of level II instruction. Distribution at this level is rolling or throwing the ball, because these are more appropriate methods than kicking in small-sided games.

Level II Lessons

LESSON 1

TACTICAL PROBLEM: Maintaining possession of the ball.

LESSON FOCUS: Supporting the ball carrier.

OBJECTIVE: Students being in position to receive a pass.

A. GAME: 3 v 3 in 30 by 20, narrow goal (see figure 3.14).

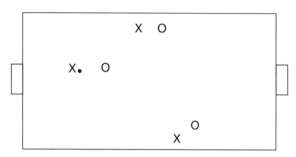

Figure 3.14

Goals: Accurate passing with inside and outside of feet.

Players move into position to receive a pass.

Player with the ball looks for support.

Conditions: Three touch (each player has two touches to receive the ball and one to pass or shoot); keep ball below head height.

Questions

Q: How can players without the ball help a player who has the ball?

A: Be in a position to receive a pass.

Q: Where should supporting players go?

A: Away from defenders into an open space.

Q: Any open space?

A: Where you can receive a pass—a passing lane.

B. PRACTICE TASK: 2 v 1 in 20 by 10, pass and support (see figure 3.15); two attackers (X and S). On whistle defender (O) attacks ball; supporter (S) moves to either side; attacker (X) draws defender and passes. Play 2 v 1 for six passes or until O wins ball.

Goals: Supporting player to move to a good position.

Attacker (X) waits for defender (O) to close in before passing.

Three repetitions and rotate.

Cues: Supporter moves quickly to side on whistle.

Defender attacks the ball on whistle.

Attacker passes as defender advances.

C. GAME: Repeat game A.

O = Defender
S = Supporter
X = Attacker
• = Ball

Figure 3.15

Griffin/E1193/Fig3.15/MA-Craig R. R2

LESSON 2

TACTICAL PROBLEM: Maintaining possession of the ball.

LESSON FOCUS: Supporting the ball carrier.

OBJECTIVE: Constant support for player with the ball.

A. GAME: 6 v 6 in 50 by 30, full or narrow goal (see figure 3.16).

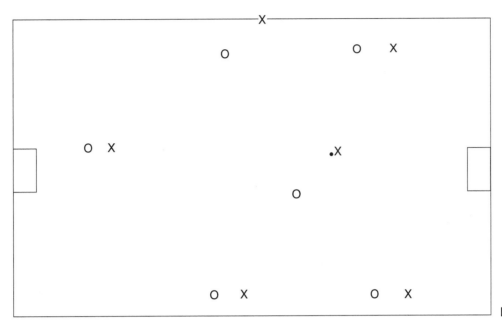

Figure 3.16

Goals: Be in a position to receive a pass.

Be aware that ball carrier needs support to be able to pass.

Conditions: Three touch (depending on abilities); keep ball below head height.

Questions

Q: How can players without the ball help a player who has the ball?

A: Be in position to receive a pass.

Q: Where should supporting players go?

A: Away from defenders and into a passing lane.

B. PRACTICE TASK 1: 3 v 1 (passive defender) in 10 by 10, unopposed possession (see figure 3.17).

Goals: Be aware of best place to be for support.

Provide two options for ball carrier.

Cues: As the ball is passed, X2 moves to support the player who will give the next pass (X1).

Move quickly and call for the ball.

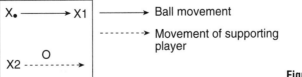

Figure 3.17

PRACTICE TASK 2: 3 v 1 (active defender) in 10 by 10, possession (see figure 3.18); rotate defender at 10 passes or when ball goes out of grid.

Goals: Ten consecutive passes with ball in grid.

Provide two options for ball carrier.

Maximum possible *angle of support*.

Condition: Defender must attack the ball.

Cues: Move to support the passer (don't get stuck with defender between you and the ball).

Move quickly and call.

Passer wait for the defender to come to you before passing.

Firm passes.

C. GAME: Repeat game A.

Goals: Ball carrier should always have two open receivers.

Support quickly and call for the ball.

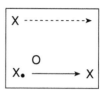

Figure 3.18

LESSON 3

TACTICAL PROBLEM: Attacking the goal.

LESSON FOCUS: Turning with the ball.

OBJECTIVE: Quick turns while in possession of the ball.

A. GAME: 1 v 1 in 20 by 10, two feeders (F) (see figure 3.19); if O wins the ball from X, she becomes the attacker.

Goal: Receive pass from feeder and turn to give a pass to other feeder.

Questions

Q: What does the attacker need to do in this situation?

A: Turn quickly.

Q: How can attacker turn past defender?

A: Flick with outside of foot and move forward onto ball.

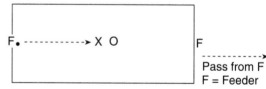

Figure 3.19

B. TASK PRACTICE: In partners, receive pass and turn, 10 yards apart.

Cues: Receive and turn in one move.

Push the ball with outside of foot.

Clock analogy (receive from 12:00; push ball to 4:00 or 8:00).

C. GAME: Repeat game A.

GAME: 3 v 3 in 20 by 20, two feeders (see figure 3.20).

Goals: Receive pass from feeder.

Work as a team to give a pass to other feeder.

Each pass to feeder earns one point.

Condition: Cannot return a pass to feeder who gave the pass.

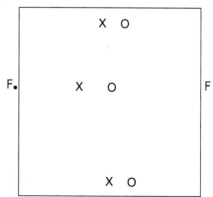

Figure 3.20

LESSON 4

TACTICAL PROBLEM: Attacking the goal.

LESSON FOCUS: Shooting.

OBJECTIVES: Receive ball and execute quick shot on target.

Follow the shot for rebound.

A. GAME: Shooting derby, 2 v 2 in 30 by 20 (see figure 3.21); two feeders, one goalkeeper, one collector, full goal (eight players total). Switch every eight trials.

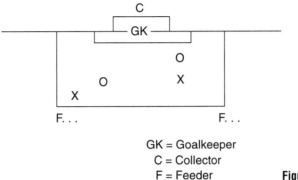

GK = Goalkeeper
C = Collector
F = Feeder **Figure 3.21**

Goal: One touch to control, then shoot on target.

Question

Q: If you receive the ball this close to goal, what should you try to do?

A: Turn and shoot.

B. PRACTICE TASK: Pressure shooting in penalty area (see figure 3.22); three shooters (alternating every three shots), two feeders, one goalkeeper, two collectors. Switch every eight trials.

Goal: Specific number of shots on target.

Cue: Set up for shot with one touch to right or left (left if you receive pass from left feeder, right if pass comes from right feeder).

C. GAME: 4 v 4 in 30 by 20, full-size goals.

Goals: Even number of shots from 10 and 20 yards.

Specific number of shots on target.

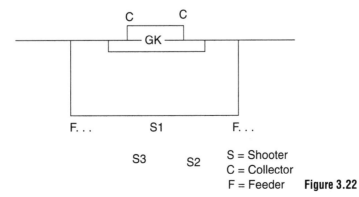

S = Shooter
C = Collector
F = Feeder **Figure 3.22**

LESSON 5

TACTICAL PROBLEM: Defending space.

LESSON FOCUS: Marking (guarding) and pressuring the ball.

OBJECTIVE: Understanding need to mark players and pressure the ball to defend space.

A. GAME: 4 v 4 in 40 by 30, full goal.

    Goals: Defenders to position between opponent and own goal.

        Defenders to position so can see opponent *and* ball.

    Condition: Mark (or guard) an opposing player.

    Questions

    Q: How can you make it hard for opponents to receive the ball?

    A: Mark (or guard) them.

    Q: Where should you stand to mark them?

    A: Between your opponent and your goal.

    Q: As the ball gets closer to your opponent, what should you do?

    A: Get closer to your opponent.

    Q: As your opponent gets closer to your goal, what should you do?

    A: Again, get closer to your opponent.

B. PRACTICE TASK: 1 v 1 plus two feeders in 20 by 10 (see figure 3.23).

    Goals: Prevent opponent turning.

        Keep appropriate distance.

        Use appropriate stance.

    Condition: Feeders at 0 and 20 (alternate feeds).

    Cues: *Close down* opponent quickly.

        Stop one arm's-length away.

        Get low.

        Use staggered stance.

        Wait for opponent to try and turn.

        Don't dive into the tackle.

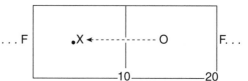

Figure 3.23

C. GAME: Repeat game A.

    Goals: Close down space between you and opponent as ball is played.

        Prevent opponent from turning.

LESSON 6

TACTICAL PROBLEM: Defending the goal.

LESSON FOCUS: Goalkeeping, positioning.

OBJECTIVE: Appropriate positioning of goalkeeper to narrow the angle.

A. GAME: 2 v 2 in 20 by 20, full goal with one goalkeeper per team (see figure 3.24).

Goal: Give attacker as little to shoot at as possible.

Condition: Goalkeeper cannot come past 10-yard line.

Question

Q: How can goalkeeper give attacker less to shoot at?

A: Move out or sideways to narrow the angle.

B. **PRACTICE TASK:** Goalkeeper versus goalkeeper (1 v 1) in 20 by 20, full goal (see figure 3.25).

    Goals: Goalkeeper moves to narrow angle.

        Move side to side and off line.

    Conditions: Start dribble from 0 each time.

        Shoot from different point outside 10 each time.

    Cues: Goalkeeper comes off goal line toward the ball.

        Stay low.

C. **GAME:** 4 v 4 in 40 by 30, full goal, rotate goalkeepers.

    Goals: Goalkeeper moves to narrow the angle.

        Move side to side and off line.

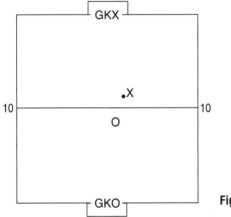

Figure 3.24

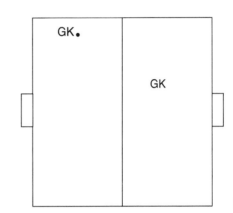

Figure 3.25

LESSON 7

TACTICAL PROBLEM: Defending the goal.

LESSON FOCUS: Goalkeeping, gathering the ball.

OBJECTIVES: Get body behind the ball.

        Bring ball into chest.

A. **GAME:** Goalkeeper versus goalkeeper (1 v 1) in 20 by 10.

    Goal: Get into line with the oncoming shot.

    Condition: Cooperative shots at half pace.

Questions

Q: Where should goalkeeper be positioned to stop the ball?

A: Get body in line with the ball.

Q: What is the best way to hold the ball securely?

A: Cradled into the chest.

B. PRACTICE TASK: Partner practice (hand feeds at low, medium, and high levels).

Goals: Get the body behind the ball (in line with the shot).

Take ball into chest.

Condition: Make partner move as he improves.

Cues: Get into line with the oncoming shot.

Take ball into the chest.

Cradle the ball.

Protect it.

C. GAME: 2 v 2 in 20 by 20, full goal plus goalkeepers.

Goals: Goalkeepers narrow the angle.

Put body behind ball.

Take ball into chest.

LEVEL III

Level III builds directly onto level II, further investigating the tactical problems of attacking the goal and defending space. We increase tactical complexity by introducing problems of creating space in attack and winning the ball. We investigate additional methods of restarting play, specifically using restarts as scoring opportunities.

The introduction of an offensive target player at level III allows students to see how to create shooting opportunities as a team. An emphasis on one-touch passing will also enable them to more effectively create space for shooting chances. Having introduced the target player, we can now investigate solutions preventing this target player from turning with the ball and attacking the space between her and the goal. Both offensively and defensively, the game will look tactically more developed at level III.

Level III Lessons

LESSON 1

TACTICAL PROBLEM: Maintaining possession of the ball.

LESSON FOCUS: Supporting the ball carrier.

OBJECTIVE: Provide support so passer can split the defense (i.e., pass ball between two defenders).

A. GAME: 2 v 2 to target player in 30 by 20, two target players (OT and XT) along end line (total 3 v 3) (see figure 3.26).

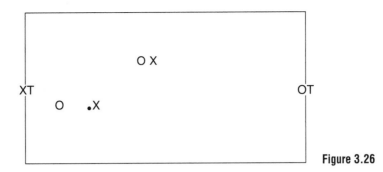

Figure 3.26

Goal: Get ball to target player (who can move along the end line).

Conditions: Three touch; keep ball below head height.

Question

Q: How can target player help teammates find him?

A: Move sideways along end line constantly to support.

B. PRACTICE TASK: 4 v 2 (defenders) in 20 by 20, possession game (see figure 3.27).

Goals: Ten consecutive passes (splitting defenders with a pass counts as two passes).

Give angle of support so passer can split defense.

Condition: Defenders must attack the ball.

Cues: Passer split the defenders.

Supporters position so passer can split defenders.

C. GAME: 6 v 6 in 50 by 40, full goal.

Goal: Split defenders with pass to put teammate in scoring position.

Condition: Keep ball below head height.

```
X3 --------->          X4


       O               O


X2                   .X1
```

------> Movement of supporting player (X3) so passer (X1) can split defenders

Figure 3.27

LESSON 2

TACTICAL PROBLEM: Attacking the goal.

LESSON FOCUS: Penetration using a target player.

OBJECTIVE: Use target player for early penetration.

A. GAME: 4 v 4 in 30 by 20, full-size goals (see figure 3.28).

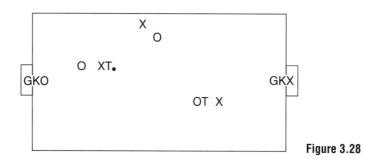

Figure 3.28

Goals: Get ball to target player quickly with accurate pass.

Target player to hold ball and threaten goal.

Condition: Each team must leave a target player in opponent's half and a central defender in own half.

Question

Q: What can target player do when she receives ball?

A: Hold (keep possession of the ball), turn, or lay ball off.

B. PRACTICE TASK: 2 v 1 to goal (plus one goalkeeper) in 20 by 10 (see figure 3.29). Start with feed to target player by support player; switch every four trials.

Goal: Target player to hold, shield and turn, or lay the ball off (short sideways pass) to a teammate.

Cues: Target player

Hold.

Turn and shoot.

Look for support.

Follow shot for rebound.

Support player

Support target player.

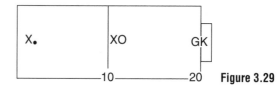

Figure 3.29

C. GAME: Repeat game A.

Goal: Target player to hold and turn, or hold and lay the ball off to supporting players.

LESSON 3

TACTICAL PROBLEM: Creating space in attack.

LESSON FOCUS: One touch (or first-time) passing.

OBJECTIVE: Using a first-time pass to create space (a first-time pass is given immediately without any touches to control the ball).

A. GAME: 2 v 2 plus two outside corner players per team in 20 by 20 (total 4 v 4) (see figure 3.30).

Goals: Possession.

Ten passes.

Conditions: Four players in grid can only use first-time pass. Outside players can move 10 yards along each line. Inside players cannot tackle outside players.

Question

Q: What does the first-time pass enable you to do?

A: Move the ball quickly.

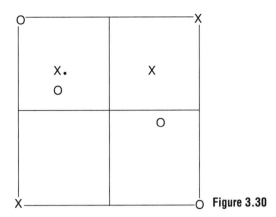

Figure 3.30

B. **PRACTICE TASK:** 3 v 1 pressure pass (two balls) (see figure 3.31); first-time passes (alternate balls).

   Goal: Accurate redirection of ball by a first-time pass to the player without a ball.

   Cues: Decide early where the ball has to go.

   Redirect ball firmly with inside or outside of foot.

C. **GAME:** 4 v 4 in 40 by 30, small goals, no goalkeeper.

   Condition: Two players per team must play one touch (designate one of these players as target player), rotate.

   Goals: Speed of ball movement.

   Speed of support.

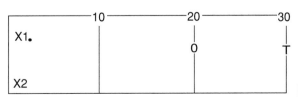

Figure 3.31

LESSON 4

TACTICAL PROBLEM: Creating space in attack.

LESSON FOCUS: One-touch passing.

OBJECTIVE: Using a first-time pass to beat a defender (give and go).

A. **GAME:** 2 v 1 to target player (T) in 30 by 10 (see figure 3.32). Start with feed to defender (O) on 20; defender gives first-time pass back and moves forward.

   Goal: X1 and X2 must get ball to target player as a team.

   Condition: Defender must go to the ball.

   Question

   Q: How can two players help each other beat one defender?

   A: Use *give-and-go.*

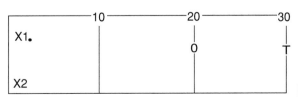

Figure 3.32

B. PRACTICE TASK: 2 v 2 (passive defenders on 10 and 30) in 40 by 10 (see figure 3.33).

    Conditions: Defenders must go to ball. Each defender can only advance 10 yards maximum. Attackers must beat each defender with a give-and-go.

    Cues: Supporter

            Position yourself ahead of ball.

            Return pass (first time) behind defender.

        Ball carrier

            Draw defender (toward you).

            Give (pass) and go (for return).

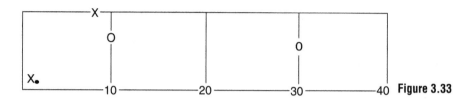

Figure 3.33

C. GAME 1: Repeat game A.

    Goal: Appropriate timing of give-and-go.

    GAME 2: 4 v 4 in 40 by 30, small goals, no goalkeeper.

    Goal: Use give-and-go at appropriate times to beat opponents.

    Conditions: Two players per team play one touch, rotate. Award extra goal for successful give-and-go that beats an opponent.

LESSON 5

TACTICAL PROBLEM: Winning the ball.

LESSON FOCUS: Containment and tackle.

OBJECTIVES: Stay on feet.

           Make a solid tackle.

A. GAME: 3 v 3 in 30 by 20, no goal (see figure 3.34).

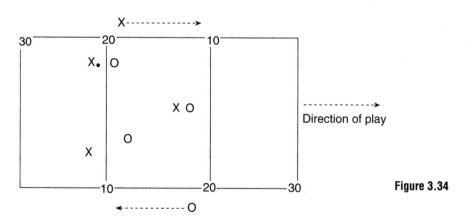

Figure 3.34

Goal: Get ball to 30-yard line under control.

Condition: Take on your opponent (try to dribble around) before passing.

Question

Q: How can you slow attacker down and win the ball?

A: Channel (i.e., push opponent in a particular direction) and tackle.

B. PRACTICE TASK 1: 1 v 1 in 20 by 10; defender (O) passes ball to attacker (X) and advances to close him down. X tries to dribble around O to the 20 (see figure 3.35).

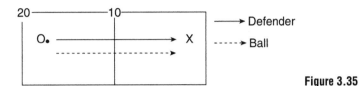

Figure 3.35

Goal: Channel and tackle.

Condition: Defender feeds from 20, can move to close down attacker when ball crosses 10.

Cues: Channel attacker to weak side (i.e., to left if player is right-footed).

Stay on your feet and wait for attacker to move (to go around you).

Get your foot in for solid tackle (or poke ball out of play).

PRACTICE TASK 2: 1 v 1 block tackle practice (standing). With a partner, on a count of three both players make a solid inside-of-foot tackle on the ball.

Goal: Firm tackle.

C. GAME: Repeat game A.

LESSON 6

TACTICAL PROBLEM: Restarting play.

LESSON FOCUS: Near post corner.

OBJECTIVE: Use near post corner to create scoring opportunities.

A. GAME: 6 v 6 in 40 by 50, full goal, referee calls many corners.

Condition: Place a player on near (front) post for each corner.

Goal: Awareness of corner as a scoring chance.

Question

Q: How can near post corner be effective?

A: Near post player can redirect ball for incoming attackers.

B. PRACTICE TASK: Team practice, unopposed, near post corner (see figure 3.36).

    Goal: Use near post corner to score.

    Cues: Corner taker (X1) aim for head of near post player (X2).

        Near post player (X2) redirect ball back and out with head or foot (a flick).

        Attackers (X3, X4, and X5) run to meet the flick.

C. GAME: Repeat game A.

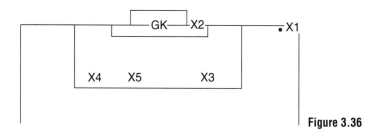

Figure 3.36

LESSON 7

TACTICAL PROBLEM: Restarting play.

LESSON FOCUS: Attacking at free kicks.

OBJECTIVE: Use free kicks as scoring opportunities.

A. GAME: 6 v 6 in 60 by 40, full goal, referee calls many free kicks in a variety of positions on the field.

    Goal: Awareness of free kicks as scoring opportunities.

    Question

    Q: How can you use a free kick to threaten goal?

    A: Shoot, pass, cross, or overlap depending on position of free kick.

B. PRACTICE TASK: Team practice, opposed, direct or indirect free kicks from variety of angles, three teams working at each goal. All free kicks are from outside the penalty area (see figure 3.37).

    Goal: Use different strategies to attack from free kick, depending on angle and type of kick (strategies include shot, chip, and overlap or cross).

    Cues: Shooting, hit the target.

        Pass to shoot, pass ball into shooter's path.

        Cross to center of goal area.

C. GAME: Repeat game A.

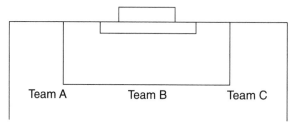

Figure 3.37

LEVEL IV

At the beginning of level IV students revisit the problem of maintaining possession of the ball, because they will now be able to investigate this tactical problem in a larger playing area. Solutions to the problem will include long passing and ball control with the thigh and chest. A focus on the overlapping run to create space in attack will provide additional width in attack, which students must now use effectively. Solutions to the problem of using this space will include effective dribbling, crossing the ball, and heading toward goal.

The offensive focus on crossing and heading will require further attention to the defensive problems this creates. These problems are defending space in the penalty area and winning the ball from offensive opponents in wide positions. Solutions to these problems will include clearing the ball and making sliding tackles.

Level IV Lessons

LESSON 1

TACTICAL PROBLEM: Maintaining possession of the ball.

LESSON FOCUS: Long passing.

OBJECTIVE: Use long pass to keep possession and switch play.

A. GAME: 6 v 6 in 60 by 40, full goal.

 Goal: Use long pass to switch defense to attack quickly.

 Condition: One target player per team (rotate).

 Questions

 Q: How can you use the space on the field?

 A: Stay spread out.

 Q: How can a long pass help you?

 A: Reach teammates who are away from the ball; get from defense to attack quickly.

B. PRACTICE TASK: Long pass, partner practice, static and rolling ball.

 Goal: Distance and accuracy of pass *above head height.*

 Cues: Long step to the ball.

 Nonkicking foot next to ball.

 Kicking foot under ball.

 Contact ball with top of the foot (laces of the shoe).

 Lean back as you follow through.

C. GAME: Repeat game A.

LESSON 2

TACTICAL PROBLEM: Maintaining possession of the ball.

LESSON FOCUS: Receiving the long pass.

OBJECTIVE: Control and setup of the ball with feet, thigh, chest.

A. GAME: 4 v 4 in 50 by 40, no goals, throw and control game.

> **Condition:** Throw and control (player 1 throws to player 2, who controls the ball with any part of the body then picks it up and throws it to player 3—progress is made down the field in this way).

> **Goal:** Stop ball under control on goal line at end of playing area.

> **Question**

> *Q: What must you do to succeed in receiving a long pass?*

> A: Receive and control the ball from the air.

B. PRACTICE TASK: Partner practice, hand feeding to feet, thigh, chest.

> **Goals:** Bring ball down to feet quickly.

>> *Kill the bounce* and set up for next move to right, left, front.

> **Cues:** Chest—Chest out to ball.

>> Withdraw chest on impact.

>> Kill the bounce when ball falls.

>> Thigh—Thigh up to ball.

>> Withdraw thigh on impact.

>> Kill the bounce when ball falls.

>> Foot—Kill the bounce with inside or outside of foot.

>> Drag foot across the ball to kill the bounce.

C. GAME: 4 v 4 in 60 by 40, no goals.

> **Goal:** Stop ball under control on goal line.

> **Conditions:** Target players (rotate); maximum of 10-yard dribble.

LESSON 3

TACTICAL PROBLEM: Maintaining possession of the ball.

LESSON FOCUS: Combining short and long passing.

OBJECTIVE: Use combination of short and long passes to maintain possession.

A. GAME: 6 v 6 in 60 by 40, no goal, possession game (see figure 3.38).

> **Goal:** Stop ball under control on goal (end) line.

> **Conditions:** Three touch, restricted areas, two forwards, two midfield, two defenders.

> **Questions**

> *Q: Is it best to use long or short passes or a combination?*

> A: Combination.

> *Q: Why is a combination of short and long passes best?*

> A: To make your opponents move around and keep them guessing.

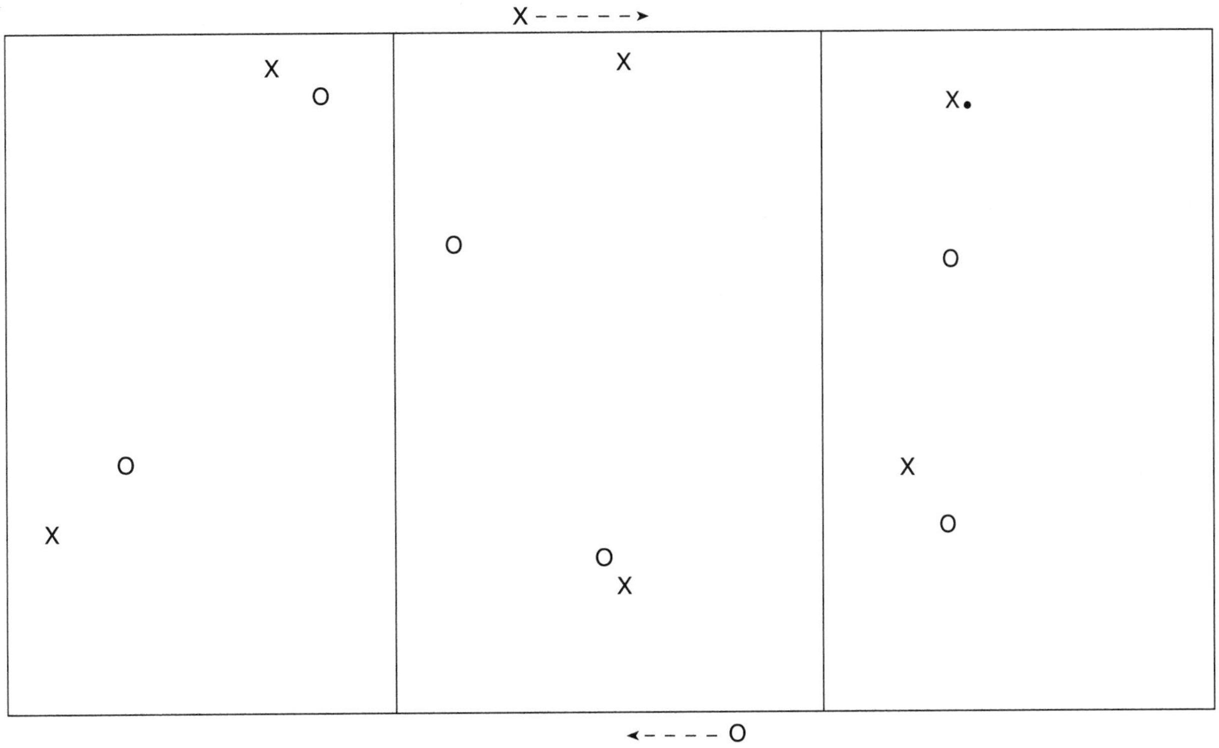

X - - - - - ➤

X   O

X   O

X   O

X•

O

O

O

O

X

O

X

O

X

◄ - - - - O

Figure 3.38

B. PRACTICE TASK: 4 v 4 plus two outside corner players per team in 30 by 20, possession (total 6 v 6) (see figure 3.39).

Goals: Combine short and long passes to keep ball.

Use short passes to draw opponents in.

Follow with long pass to open game up.

Conditions: Corner players can move 10 yards along each sideline. Inside players cannot tackle outside corner players.

Cue: Short, short, short (passes to draw in opponents), long (pass to the space that has been created).

C. GAME: 6 v 6 in 60 by 40, full goals, no restrictions.

Goal: Combine short and long passes to maintain possession and move the ball into a scoring position.

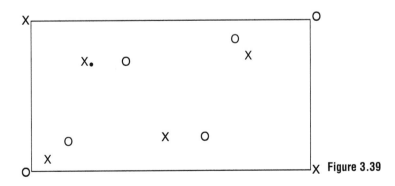

Figure 3.39

LESSON 4

TACTICAL PROBLEM: Creating space in attack.

LESSON FOCUS: Overlapping run.

OBJECTIVE: Use overlapping runs to create space at the flanks (an overlapping is made by a supporting player around the side of a teammate with the ball, usually at the side of the field).

A. GAME: 6 v 6 in 30 by 50, short and wide, full goal.

Goal: Awareness of need to use width to best advantage in attack.

Questions

Q: Where is the most space on this field?

A: In wide areas.

Q: How can you use this space?

A: Get players into wide areas to receive a pass.

Q: What can wide players do when they get the ball?

A: Cross the ball into the center.

B. PRACTICE TASK: Overlap and cross drill (see figure 3.40). Passer (X) passes to target player (T); X overlaps, receives return pass from T, and crosses the ball. Nonpasser (Y) and target player (T) run to center of goal to meet the cross.

Variation: X passes to T; Y overlaps, receives pass from T, and crosses. X and T run to center of goal.

Goals: Speed of overlap run.

Timing of pass to runner.

Condition: Static defenders (O) at first, change to active defenders (O).

Cues: X pass to T and run wide around T (overlapping run down the sideline).

T receive and pass the ball back into X's path.

Y sprint to center of goal area.

C. GAME: Repeat game A.

Goal: Use overlapping run in game situation.

Condition: If you pass to the wing you must follow the pass to overlap the receiver.

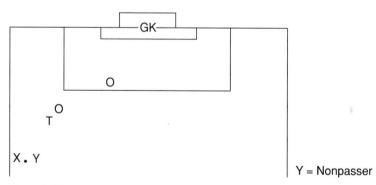

Figure 3.40

LESSON 5

TACTICAL PROBLEM: Using space in attack.

LESSON FOCUS: Using width in attack.

OBJECTIVES: Awareness of field areas best suited to dribbling.
Acquisition of dribbling skills.

A. GAME: 6 v 6 in 50 by 50, short and wide, full goal.

Goal: Awareness of the field areas that contain most space in attack (i.e., the flanks or wings).

Question

Q: Other than a cross, what else do wide players have space to do?

A: Run at and around defenders, *dribble*.

B. PRACTICE TASK 1: Threes, continuous dribbling relay.

Goals: Control with inside and outside of both feet.
Pace and change of pace.

Cues: Push or stroke the ball.
Keep the ball close.

PRACTICE TASK 2: Repeat task 1 with cone for defender.

Goals: Beat the defender (i.e., the cone) with ball.
Push and run, fake shot and push, step over and push.

Cues: Push and run.
Fake the shot and push (the ball around the cone with the outside of the foot).
Accelerate.

C. GAME: Repeat game A.

Condition: Mark or guard 1 v 1.

Goal: Attack the space behind your opponent whenever possible.

LESSON 6

TACTICAL PROBLEM: Using space in attack.

LESSON FOCUS: Using width in attack.

OBJECTIVE: Beating a defender with the dribble.

A. GAME: 2 v 2 in 30 by 20, to opposite goal line.

Goal: Awareness of need to progress forward when teammates are marked and necessity of beating opponent.

Condition: Mark or guard 1 v 1.

Questions

Q: If there is space behind your opponent, what can you try to do?

A: Go around her.

Q: How?

A: Dribble, push the ball past, and accelerate.

B. PRACTICE TASK 1: 1 v 3 in 30 by 10, static defenders on 10, 20, 30 (see figure 3.41).

    Goals: Beat each defender in turn and cross the 30 with ball under control.

          If tackled, retrieve ball and continue to next defender.

          Use push and run, feint shot and push, step over and push.

    Condition: Defenders cannot move.

    Cues: Push and run.

          Feint and push.

          Accelerate.

    PRACTICE TASK 2: Extend practice task 1.

    Condition: Defenders can only move along their lines.

C. GAME: 4 v 4 in 40 by 30, small goals (no goalkeeper).

    Goal: Beat opponents 1 v 1 in game situation.

    Conditions: Mark 1 v 1.

          Attempt to beat an opponent before passing.

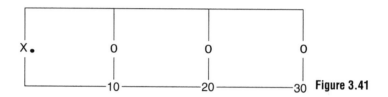

Figure 3.41

LESSON 7

TACTICAL PROBLEM: Using space in attack.

LESSON FOCUS: Using width in attack.

OBJECTIVE: Deliver an accurate cross following the dribble.

A. GAME: 4 v 3 (including goalkeeper) in 20 by 40 (short and wide), one feeder (F) feeds to any X (see figure 3.42).

    Goals: Attack to score from a cross.

          Awareness of necessity of a good cross.

          Defense to bring the ball under control to the 20.

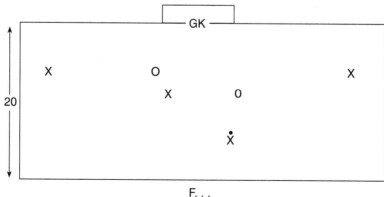

Figure 3.42

Question

Q: If you have a chance to deliver a cross, where should you aim?

A: Center of goal, but *away from goalkeeper.*

B. PRACTICE TASK: Continuous crossing drill in 60 by 50, two full goals (see figure 3.43). Crossers (X) dribble and cross away from goalkeeper. Goalkeeper collects and feeds X waiting at side of goal; X proceeds down the side of the field to cross the ball. After making a cross, X moves to side of goal and waits for next feed from goalkeeper. Numbers in this practice can vary; figure 3.43 shows eight-player drill going counterclockwise. Crosses come from right.

Goals: Flighted ball from the wings.

Ball crossed *away* from goalkeeper.

Cues: Move down the field quickly.

Cross the ball away from the goalkeeper.

C. GAME: 6 v 6 in 60 by 50 (plus one coach and one feeder per team); alternate feeds for each team. Feeder must feed to either right or left winger.

Goal: Use width of field to its maximum.

Conditions: Each team has two permanent wingers. Feeders give alternate feeds to each team; must feed to winger.

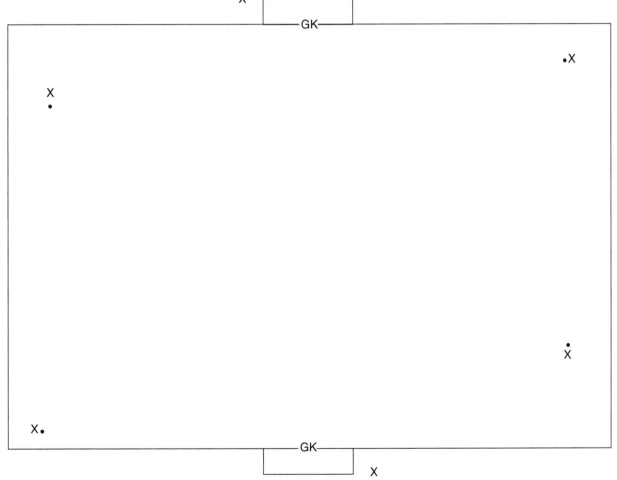

Figure 3.43

LESSON 8

TACTICAL PROBLEM: Using space in attack.

LESSON FOCUS: Using width in attack.

OBJECTIVE: Enable students to score with the head.

A. GAME: Heading game, 3 v 3 in 30 by 20, small goal.

> **Goals:** To score with head.
>
> > Awareness of need to change direction of ball with head.
>
> **Conditions:** Throw, head, throw, head (thrown ball must be headed to another teammate and caught). The game is only by throwing, heading, and catching (progress is made up the field this way). Must head ball *down* into goal to score.

Questions

Q: When might you be able to score with your head?

A: From a cross.

Q: Where should you head the ball to?

A: At the goal and *down.*

Q: Why head it down?

A: To make it harder for the goalkeeper.

B. PRACTICE TASK 1: Threes static practice (see figure 3.44), one header (X), two feeders (O). Alternate feeds; head back to feeder.

O•   X   •O **Figure 3.44**

> **Goals:** Correct contact point (hairline).
>
> > Use body for momentum.
> >
> > Heading down to a receiver.
>
> **Cues:** Get behind the ball.
>
> > Contact the ball on the hairline.
> >
> > Use the trunk for momentum.
> >
> > Head the ball down.

PRACTICE TASK 2: Threes right angle practice (see figure 3.45), one header (X), two feeders (O).

Goals: Change direction with header.

> Head down to receiver.

X   •O

O   **Figure 3.45**

Cues: Get behind the ball.

Contact the ball on the hairline.

Use the trunk for momentum.

Head the ball down.

Head across the ball's line of flight to change its direction.

C. GAME: 6 v 6 in 60 by 40, full goals.

Goals: Score with head.

Understand value of using full width of field.

Conditions: Two permanent wingers per team; can only score with head. Can pick up and hand feed inside 10 yards (if necessary due to low-quality crosses).

LESSON 9

TACTICAL PROBLEM: Defending space.

LESSON FOCUS: Clearing the ball.

OBJECTIVE: Clearing the ball from danger with height, width, length.

A. GAME: 4 v 4 (three defenders plus goalkeeper), attack versus defense in 30 by 50 (see figure 3.46).

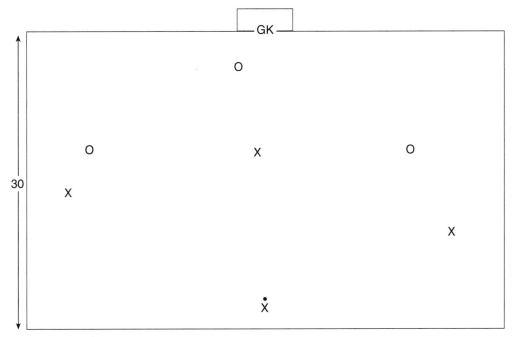

Figure 3.46

Goals: Attack and score.

Defense keep ball away from goal.

Conditions: Attack ends with goal or ball out of play at end. Restart with attack at 30; throw-in as normal for ball out at sideline.

Questions

Q: If cross comes in what should you do?

A: Clear it.

Q: Where should you clear to?

A: High, wide, or long, in that order.

Q: Why is the order important?

A: High gives time to get under the ball again. Wide moves away from the goal to the side. Long gives distance away from the goal.

B. PRACTICE TASK: Clearances practice (see figure 3.47), high-thrown (for accuracy) feeds to feet or head for each defender, one feeder (F from wing). Defender (O) clears ball and goes to back of defender line to wait for next feed.

Goals: Each defender (O) to clear with height, width, length.

Clear ball out of play at nearest point if necessary (back over feeder's head is ideal).

Cues: Accelerate to meet the ball.

As high, wide, and long as possible.

Clear away from, not across goal.

C. GAME: Repeat game A.

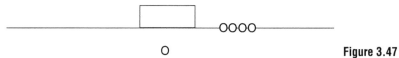

Figure 3.47

LESSON 10

TACTICAL PROBLEM: Winning the ball.

LESSON FOCUS: Slide tackle.

OBJECTIVE: Ability to tackle at a stretch using poke and slide tackle.

A. GAME: All-in tackling in 20 by 20.

Goal: Players will tackle at a stretch with poke or block.

Conditions: Knock out other balls but keep your own. Once your ball is out, go to adjoining 20 by 20 grid and start again.

Questions

Q: If you cannot stay on your feet to tackle what must you do?

A: Go down on the ground to tackle, but make sure you win the ball.

Q: How should you go down?

A: Slide.

B. PRACTICE TASK: 1 v 1 slide tackle practice in 20 by 10 (see figure 3.48).

Figure 3.48

Goals: Correct position and technique for slide tackle.

Defender to make slide tackle inside 20.

Conditions: Both start at 0. Defender (O) can only move to tackle after attacker (X) starts to run with ball, medium speed.

Cues: Get close to ball carrier.

Fold leg nearest opponent under as you slide.

Knock ball out with other leg (left leg in figure 3.48).

C. GAME: 5 v 5 in 60 by 40, full goal with goalkeeper.

Condition: Head height rule (ball must stay below head height).

Goal: Mark, channel the opponent, and tackle using whichever technique is most appropriate; slide tackle is a last resort.

LEVEL V

By the time students reach level V, the game will be tactically complex and approaching the mature form. There will be more large-field play, and solutions to tactical problems will require more advanced movements and teamwork. For example, additional solutions for creating space will include the crossover play for either a shot or a cross. Additional use of space will include adding depth to the attack by making appropriately timed supporting runs toward goal.

The defense of space will also become more complex, with students learning how to cover each other and recover to provide depth in defense. Because attacking players will be shooting more effectively at this point, goalkeeping will require additional development. This will include diving to make saves and distributing the ball over greater distances. Level V culminates with a further investigation of offensive and defensive aspects of restarting play.

Level V Lessons

LESSON 1

TACTICAL PROBLEM: Using space in attack.

LESSON FOCUS: Using depth in attack.

OBJECTIVE: Understanding value and use of support from behind.

A. GAME: 4 v 4 in 40 by 30, full goal.

Goal: See value of supporting from a defensive position.

Conditions: Target player on each team; cannot turn with the ball.

Question

Q: What options are available to the target player when he receives the ball?

A: Turn, pass to the side, *pass back.*

B. PRACTICE TASK 1: Fours, 3 v 1 in 30 by 20 (see figure 3.49).

> **Goals:** Get ball to 30 under control.
>
>> Target player to control and shield the ball, give a pass to either teammate (X), and make a run forward or diagonal for the return pass.
>
> **Conditions:** Start with feed to feet of target player (T) at 15 yards; three touch (two touches to control the ball, one to pass; this speeds up the game). Defender (O) must go to the ball.
>
> **Cues:** Target player look for support to side *and* behind.
>
>> Supporters, one to side and one behind.

PRACTICE TASK 2: 4 v 2 in 40 by 30, extension of practice task 1.

> **Goals:** Get ball to 40 under control.
>
>> Target player to control and shield the ball, give a pass to a teammate, and make a run forward or diagonal for the return pass.
>
> **Conditions:** Start with feed to feet of target player (T) at 20 yards; three touch. Defenders must go to the ball.

C. GAME: Repeat game A.

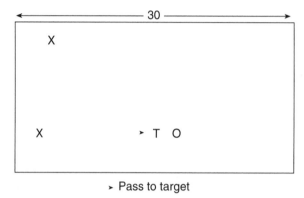

> Pass to target

Figure 3.49

LESSON 2

TACTICAL PROBLEM: Using space in attack.

LESSON FOCUS: Using depth in attack.

OBJECTIVE: Making well-timed attacking runs to the penalty area.

A. GAME: Eights, 2 v 2 plus two crossers (CO and CX) and two goalkeepers in 30 by 50 (short and wide) (see figure 3.50).

> **Goal:** Understanding that a static attacker is easier to mark than a moving one.
>
> **Conditions:** Goalkeeper must feed a crosser (who is unopposed); crosser serves ball toward opposing goal.
>
> **Questions**
>
> *Q: Where should you (X1 and X2) be as the ball is crossed—level, behind, or in front of the ball?*
>
> A: Behind the ball.
>
> *Q: Why is this positioning important?*
>
> A: So you can move forward onto the cross.

B. PRACTICE TASK: In pairs (see figure 3.51). Striker feeds winger, winger crosses, striker finishes. Switch roles.

> **Goals:** Time the run so attacker is moving onto the cross.
>
>> Score with head or foot.

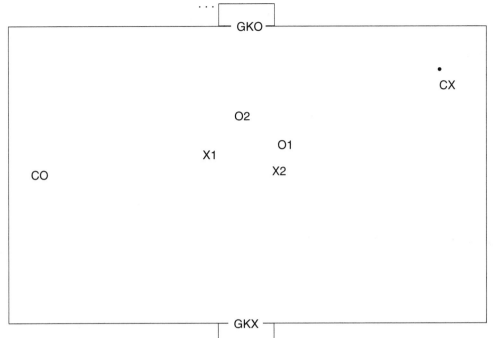

Figure 3.50

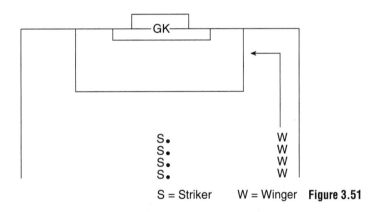

S = Striker   W = Winger   **Figure 3.51**

Cues: Striker hold the run so you stay behind the ball.
Wait for the cross and move onto it.
Winger cross away from the goalkeeper.

C. GAME 1: Repeat game A.

GAME 2: 4 v 4 in 40 by 50, full goal.

Goal: Well-timed runs to meet crosses.

Condition: Three touch in central 20 (middle of field).

LESSON 3

TACTICAL PROBLEM: Creating space in attack.

LESSON FOCUS: The crossover play.

OBJECTIVE: Use crossover play to create space.

A. GAME: 3 v 3 in 20 by 20, possession game.

    Goal: Awareness of need to create space in a confined area.

    Condition: No pass over 10 yards.

    Question

    Q: How can you create space in a confined area?

    A: Short passes, crossover.

B. PRACTICE TASK 1: Free dribbling in 30 by 20 with crossovers, one ball per two players.

    Goal: Introduce crossover play by allowing players to exchange possession using crossover with any player.

    Cues: Passer leaves ball for receiver.

        Communicate "leave it" or "mine."

    PRACTICE TASK 2: Situation drill, crossovers leading to shot and cross (see figure 3.52).

    Goal: Awareness of situations in which crossover play is most useful or appropriate.

    Cues: Receive and shoot

        Passer (X1) leaves ball for receiver (X2).

        Communicate "leave it" or "mine."

        X2 receives and shoots.

    Receive and cross

        Passer (X2) leaves ball for receiver (X1).

        Drill begins with ball in a wide position.

        Communicate "leave it" or "mine."

        X1 receives and crosses.

        X2 continues toward goal to meet the cross.

C. GAME: 6 v 6 in 50 by 40, full-size goal.

    Goal: Use crossover play in appropriate places and at appropriate times to create space and scoring chances.

    Condition: Must do one crossover play in attacking half before approaching goal in each attack.

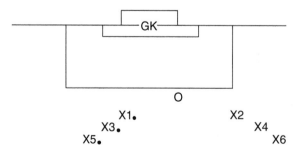

O = Static defender

Figure 3.52

LESSON 4

TACTICAL PROBLEM: Defending space.

LESSON FOCUS: Delaying the attack.

OBJECTIVE: Understanding that first role of individual defender is to delay the attack, keeping ball in front, to give time for teammates to recover; delay and channel.

A. GAME: 3 v 3 (including goalkeeper) in 30 by 20 (see figure 3.53); one full goal, attack versus defense.

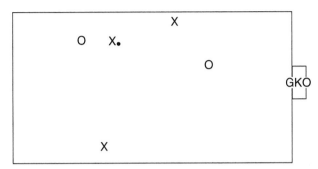

Figure 3.53

Goal: Creation of uneven numbers situations.

Condition: Head height rule.

Questions

Q: What should you do if you have fewer defenders than your opponents have attackers?

A: Delay the attack to give teammates time to recover.

Q: How can you delay your opponents?

A: Use channeling to make opponent go where *you* decide.

B. PRACTICE TASK: 2 v 1 in 30 by 10, no goal (see figure 3.54).

Goals: Defender close space quickly.

　　　Don't dive in for a tackle; stay on feet.

　　　Channel path of ball between your opponents to delay the attack (also known as *jockeying*).

　　　Challenge for ball at appropriate moment.

Condition: Attackers must get ball to end line under control.

Cues: Defender close the space.

　　　Position to force the sideways pass.

　　　Move across and back; slide and drop back.

C. GAME: 3 v 3 in 30 by 20, two small goals (no goalkeeper).

Goals: When defending close space quickly.

　　　Don't dive in; stay on feet.

　　　Channel path of ball.

　　　Challenge for ball at appropriate moment.

Condition: Head height rule.

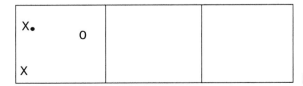

Figure 3.54

LESSON 5

TACTICAL PROBLEM: Defending space.

LESSON FOCUS: Making recovery runs.

OBJECTIVE: Make appropriate recovery runs to get goalside of the ball and cover first defender.

A. GAME: 2 v 2 in 30 by 10.

    Goals: Ball to end line.

        Understanding need to cover teammate.

    Condition: Head height rule.

    Questions

    Q: What should forward players do if one teammate is trying to delay an attack?

    A: Recover to help defensively.

    Q: Where should the recovering defenders recover to?

    A: Behind the first defender.

B. PRACTICE TASK: 2 v 1 plus one retreating defender in 30 by 10 (see figure 3.55).

    Goals: Defenders to work as a pair to stop attackers reaching end line, tandem defense.

        One goes to ball, other covers and stays with opponent.

    Conditions: Retreating defender cannot move until attackers start. Retreating defender must get goalside of first defender before challenging for the ball.

    Cues: First defender delay the attack.

        Recovering defender recover quickly to behind teammate.

        Take your own opponent.

        Cover your teammate.

        Communicate.

C. GAME: 4 v 4 in 40 by 30, full goal with goalkeeper.

    Goals: Defending in numbers.

        Players goalside.

        Cover for first defender.

        Communicate.

    Condition: Keep ball below head height.

Figure 3.55

LESSON 6

TACTICAL PROBLEM: Defending the goal.

LESSON FOCUS: Goalkeeping, diving to save.

OBJECTIVES: When and how to dive to tip a ball round, over.

Saving in 1 v 1 situation.

A. GAME: 2 v 2 in 20 by 10, full goal plus goalkeeper (see figure 3.56).

Goals: Shoot on sight.

Hit target to force save.

Question

Q: What are goalkeeper's priorities in saving a shot?

A: Hold it if possible; tip ball out of play if necessary. *Do not give up rebounds.*

B. PRACTICE TASK: Goalkeeper versus goalkeeper (1 v 1) in 20 by 10, two full goals.

Goals: Goalkeeper tip ball round if cannot hold.

If diving, take off from foot nearest ball.

In 1 v 1 go down to smother ball at attacker's feet.

Condition: If you take ball across the 10, you must go around goalkeeper; otherwise shoot from outside 10.

Cues: Hold or tip the ball out of play.

Take off on nearest foot to ball when diving.

C. GAME: Repeat game A.

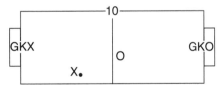

Figure 3.56

LESSON 7

TACTICAL PROBLEM: Defending the goal.

LESSON FOCUS: Goalkeeping, distributing the ball.

OBJECTIVE: Quick, accurate, efficient distribution.

A. GAME: 4 (three defenders plus one goalkeeper) v 2 (attackers) in penalty area (approximately 20 by 40) (see figure 3.57).

Goals: Defenders move away from goalkeeper to support.

Bring ball outside penalty area under control.

Goalkeeper aware of value of effective distribution.

Attackers win ball and shoot.

Conditions: Attacker starts with feed to goalkeeper from 20; goalkeeper cannot kick.

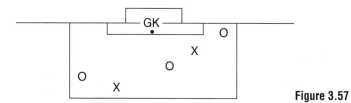

Figure 3.57

Questions

Q: Who should goalkeeper give ball to?

A: First available player.

Q: How should ball be given?

A: Rolled if possible.

Q: Why is rolling best?

A: It gets the ball to the ground quickly. It is easier to receive and control a rolled ball than a bouncing ball.

B. PRACTICE TASK: Partner practice, rolling, overarm throws.

Goal: Quick, accurate distribution so receiver can easily control ball.

Cues: Roll firm and flat.

Overarm—keep a straight arm for increased distance.

Bent arm throw for speed.

C. GAME: Repeat game A.

LESSON 8

TACTICAL PROBLEM: Restarting play.

LESSON FOCUS: Attacking at corner kicks, the far post corner.

OBJECTIVE: Use far post corners to create scoring opportunities.

A. GAME: 6 v 6 in 40 by 50, full goal, referee calls many corners at random.

Goal: Awareness of corner as a scoring chance.

Question

Q: What can be the advantage of a far post corner?

A: Ball is going away from defense.

B. PRACTICE TASK: Team practice, unopposed, far post corners (see figure 3.58).

Goal: Use far post corners to score.

Cues: Corner taker cross away from goalkeeper to the far post area.

All players at edge of penalty area attack far post area when kick is taken.

C. GAME: Repeat game A.

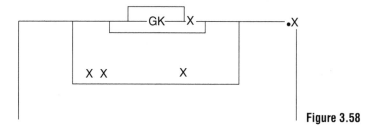

Figure 3.58

LESSON 9

TACTICAL PROBLEM: Restarting play.

LESSON FOCUS: Defending at corner kicks.

OBJECTIVE: Preventing scoring chances at corners.

A. GAME: 6 v 6 in 40 by 50, full goal, referee calls many corners at random.

Goal: Awareness of need to defend effectively against corners.

Question

Q: How can you defend corners effectively?

A: Mark opponents and clear the ball.

B. PRACTICE TASK: Team practice, opposed (see figure 3.59).

Goal: Appropriate marking and positioning of defenders for near post, far post, short corners.

Cues: Mark an opponent.

Be first to meet the ball when it is crossed.

Clear the ball high, wide, and long.

C. GAME: Repeat game A.

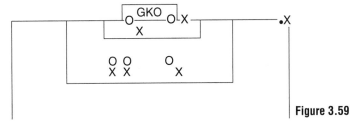

Figure 3.59

LESSON 10

TACTICAL PROBLEM: Restarting play.

LESSON FOCUS: Defending at free kicks.

OBJECTIVES: Efficient defense at free kicks.

Setting a wall.

A. GAME: 6 v 6 in 60 by 50, full goal, referee calls many free kicks.

Goal: Quick, efficient defensive setup.

Question

Q: How can you defend a free kick successfully?

A: Mark opponents or set a wall.

B. PRACTICE TASK: Team practice, opposed, direct or indirect free kicks from variety of angles; attacking team decides where to take each free kick from and whether it is direct or indirect.

Goals: Correct marking.

Setting of two-, three-, four-, five-player walls; five players if free kick is central, two if wide, three or four in between.

Cues: Set the wall quickly.

Tallest players to outside of wall.

Mark opponents if you are not in wall.

Line up outside of wall with the near post so wall covers half the goal (see figure 3.60).

C. GAME: Repeat game A.

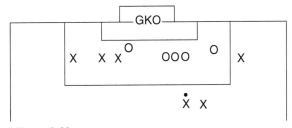

Figure 3.60

SUMMARY

This chapter has provided you with five levels of tactical complexity for teaching soccer. In using these levels you may choose to base an instructional unit on one particular level. For example, with novice players you would probably focus on level I lessons. We recommend focusing the unit on one level of tactical complexity because this enables your students to develop their performance both offensively and defensively as they progress in their understanding of the game.

Nevertheless, you may choose to develop your students' understanding of solutions to one specific tactical problem during a unit. In this case you could select material related to this tactical problem from across the five levels of tactical complexity. Whichever approach you choose, the important point is that you base your instruction on developing tactical awareness and an understanding of the game of soccer, not simply performing isolated kicking, trapping, and heading skills.

You can use many, if not most, of the lessons in this chapter with other invasion games, such as floor or field hockey, team handball, and ultimate Frisbee. Although we have not included specific chapters for these games, they are similar to soccer in tactical complexity. The tactical problems of these other invasion games are the same as those in soccer, even though some solutions may use different on-the-ball skills. You will see this in the next chapter on basketball.

By following levels of tactical complexity you provide your students with an opportunity to progressively increase their understanding and performance. The levels we present in this chapter are comprehensive, and though games might break down because of inadequate skill execution, student performance will improve with increased understanding of what to do in game situations.

CHAPTER 4

Basketball

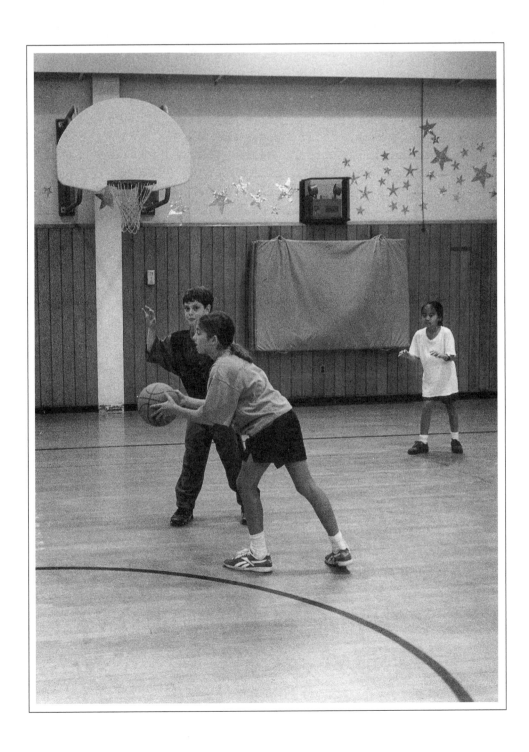

As an invasion game, basketball shares many tactics found in soccer. In this chapter we will apply several tactics from chapter 3 to conditioned games and practices specific to basketball. Once you've had an opportunity to apply similar tactics to soccer and basketball, it should be easy for you to apply them to other invasion games, such as ultimate Frisbee, floor hockey, or lacrosse.

The recommended lesson format follows the game-practice-game sequence outlined in chapter 2. If you're thinking, "I don't have enough baskets," you're not alone. Some practitioners we have worked with have created some solutions, for example (a) bolting extra hoops on the wall; (b) rotating teams onto a court; (c) rotating players into a game; (d) assigning four teams (of two or three students) to one basket, two teams to each side of the basket; (e) using stations that alternate game play and practice situations; (f) using half-court games; and (g) assigning extra students responsibilities, such as coaching, scoring, officiating, and serving as team trainer. As in the previous chapter, we assume that teachers will use appropriate size and weight basketballs to facilitate game play and skill development and foster success. The size of teams for the conditioned game will depend on what tactics and skills you want to emphasize. For example, a 1 v 1 game forces students to dribble and make cuts to get away from their defender, and a 3 v 3 game allows players more opportunities to pass, set screens, and use a give-and-go. You can assign players or teams a court or basket at the beginning of a unit and they can remain there for most game and practice activities. This will eliminate the need for organizing and reorganizing students and allow your lessons to run smoothly.

We present the tactical framework and levels of tactical complexity for basketball in tables 4.1 and 4.2. A brief description of each level appears before lesson outlines.

LEVEL I

At level I, we suggest that students focus on skills related to offense. We recognize that defensive skills are important, but if introduced too soon may prohibit the development of offensive skills, especially if peers play defense aggressively. Introduce defensive skills after students have developed some proficiency with off- and on-the-ball skills. Rather than eliminating the defense, we recommend controlling defensive play by instituting three levels of involvement:

1. Cooperative Defense—Player assumes defensive posture two arm lengths from opponent, is relatively passive, and at times even coaches the opponent.
2. Active Defense—Player assumes defensive posture about one and a half arm lengths from opponent, has active hands and feet, but makes no attempt to intercept the ball.
3. Competitive Defense—Player assumes defensive posture, is positioned appropriately, depending on whether the opponent has the ball, and attempts to intercept the ball.

One of our local practitioners refers to these levels as *cold*, *warm*, and *hot*. She assigns defensive levels according to each student's game-play ability. This has helped her challenge the more highly skilled players, and at the same time provide successful and equally challenging experiences for novice players.

Table 4.1
Tactical Problems, Movements, and Skills in Basketball

Tactical problems	Off-the-ball movements	On-the-ball skills
Scoring		
Maintaining possession of the ball	Supporting the ball carrier Fake and replace	Triple threat Passing—chest, bounce, overhead Catching—target hand, jump stop Pivot, jab step, drop step, dribble, ball fake, offensive rebound
Attacking the basket	Post play	Jump shot, set shot Layup, power layup Follow the shot
Creating space in attack	Clear out Pick away Fast break V-cut, L-cut	Skip pass Baseball pass
Using space in attack	Setting a screen Pick-and-roll Give-and-go	
Preventing scoring		
Defending space	Jump ball alignment, free throw alignment, full court press	
Defending the basket area (key)	Boxing out Zone defenses Match-up defense Player to player	Rebound, outlet pass
Winning the ball	Defense off the ball	Defense on the ball
Restarting play		
Jump ball—offensive and defensive		
Sideline throw-in—offensive and defensive		
End line throw-in—offensive and defensive		
End line throw-in following a score off a press		

Table 4.2
Levels of Tactical Complexity for Basketball

Tactical problems	Levels of tactical complexity			
	I	II	III	IV
Scoring				
Maintaining possession of the ball	Triple threat Ball fake	Support		
Attacking the basket	Shooting Dribbling	Give-and-go	Post play	Offensive plays against zone
Creating space in attack	Dribbling to reposition V-cut, L-cut	Screen on ball	Skip pass Pick off the ball and roll	Clear out Fast break
Using space in attack		Outlet pass		Transition from defense to offense
Preventing scoring				
Defending space		Defending against screen		Offensive and defensive free throws
Defending the basket (key)				Zone defense
Winning the ball		Defense on ball and off Boxing out	Defense on post player	Zone defense on and off ball
Restarting play				
Jump ball			Offensive Defensive	
Inbound pass from sideline				Inbound plays
Inbound pass from end line		Long pass Pick away		
Inbound pass from end line after score		Baseline movement		Inbound plays off press

Level I Lessons

LESSON 1

TACTICAL PROBLEM: Maintaining possession of the ball.

LESSON FOCUS: Triple threat, ball fake, passing, and receiving a pass.

OBJECTIVES: Present target to passer.

Protect the ball using triple threat and ball fake.

Use quick, accurate passes.

A. GAME: 2 v 2, half court, possession game.

Goal: Shoot as often as possible.

Conditions: Complete three or more consecutive passes before shooting.

No dribbling; all restarts at half court.

Questions

Q: What was the goal of your game?

A: Shoot as often as possible following three consecutive passes.

Q: What did you and your teammates do to be successful?

A: Make quick and accurate passes. Catch the ball under control. Move to an open space.

Q: What did you or your teammates do to keep the defense from stealing the ball or blocking your shot?

A: Protect the ball by keeping your body between the defender and the ball. Hold the ball firmly with two hands; use body to protect it. Use a ball fake or jab step. Use quick passes.

Q: Did you use any signals to let your teammate know you wanted to receive the pass?

A: Held hand up or out to let passer know where to pass ball.

Q: When you were catching the ball, how did you stop to keep from traveling?

A: Landed on both feet simultaneously after catching ball—jump stop.

Q: Once you received the ball, what was the best way to hold it so the defense didn't know whether you were going to shoot or pass?

A: Hold the ball as if you're going to shoot (triple threat position), with one hand behind ball and other at its side.

Q: Do we have any teams that were able to get a shot off every time they had possession of the ball?

A: If not, we should practice maintaining possession so our team will have more opportunities to shoot and score.

B. PRACTICE TASK: With a partner (or in threes or fours) practice passing from point to wing, to baseline, to a high and low post (pass cannot be made between post positions). Mark positions with tape, polyspots, and so forth (see figure 4.1). Player passes, then moves to another position. Player receiving ball must (1) present a target for the passer, (2) receive ball in a triple threat position and jump stop, (3) give a ball fake with a jab step before passing, and (4) perform a quick, accurate pass to her partner.

Goals: Present target to passer.

Receive ball in triple threat position and with a jump stop.

Perform jab step and ball fake.

Use quick, accurate passes.

Cues: Target hand.

Triple threat.

Fake a pass, make a pass.

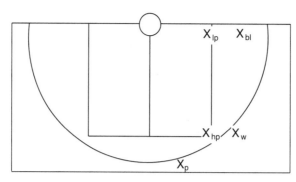

bl = Baseline
w = Wing
p = Point
lp = Low post
hp = High post

Figure 4.1

C. GAME: 2 v 2, half court, possession game.

Goal: Shoot as often as possible.

Conditions: Complete three or more consecutive passes before shooting; no dribbling.

Maintain possession of the ball by providing a target for the passer, receiving ball in triple threat and using a jump stop, using a ball fake and jab step, and making quick, accurate passes.

LESSON 2

TACTICAL PROBLEM: Attacking the basket.

LESSON FOCUS: Shooting within five to eight feet of the basket.

OBJECTIVE: Receive pass, square to basket, and shoot accurately.

A. GAME: 3 v 3, half court, five-minute scoring game.

Goal: Score as often as possible.

Conditions: Complete three or more consecutive passes before attempting shot (use triple threat, fake and jab, quick passes, and target hand to call for ball). One point for each shot attempted, two points for each basket scored; all restarts begin at half court. No dribbling.

Questions

Q: What was the goal of your game?

A: Score following three consecutive passes.

Q: From where on the court did you score most of your points?

A: Close to the basket.

Q: Why is it better to shoot from a position close to the basket, rather than far from the basket?

A: More likely to score when closer—higher percentage shot.

Q: Besides shooting from a close range, what else did you do to successfully perform a shot?

A: Square shoulders to basket, elbow under ball and close to body, one hand behind the ball and the other at side of the ball, staggered stance with knees slightly bent, follow through, aim.

B. PRACTICE TASK: All players shoot three shots from each of the five spots marked around the basket (approximately six to eight feet away). Partner rebounds ball and passes accurately to peer. Peer provides target, receives ball in triple threat, squares up, and shoots.

Goal: Score on two out of three shots at each spot.

Cues: Shooting, square up, B.E.E.F.

Base firm.

Elbow under ball.

Extend arm.

Follow through or flip wrist.

C. GAME: 3 v 3, half court, five-minute scoring game.

Goal: Score as many field goals as possible.

Conditions: Same as initial game.

LESSON 3

TACTICAL PROBLEM: Maintaining possession of the ball to support teammate.

LESSON FOCUS: Create passing lanes.

OBJECTIVES: Use ball fakes, jab steps, and quick movements.

Off-the-ball player uses quick *fake and replace* movements to create passing lanes.

A. GAME: 2 v 2, half court, possession game.

Goal: Support or help your teammate when he has the ball.

Conditions: Complete at least three passes before shooting; one point for three consecutive passes, two points for every field goal.

Questions

Q: What was the goal of the game?

A: Support player with the ball.

Q: What did you have to do to provide support?

A: Move to an open space; get away from the defense.

Q: How were you able to get away from your defender?

A: Use cuts and fakes.

Q: Was it easier to get away from defenders when you were moving quickly or at just a normal speed?

A: Quickly.

Q: Was it easier to get away from defenders when you were close to them or far from them?

A: Close.

Q: When you were trying to get away from defenders, was your first quick step or jab step toward them or away from them?

A: Toward them.

B. PRACTICE TASK 1: Moving to the open space, 3 v 1 passive defender. Use offensive positions on one or both sides (3 v 2 passive defenders) of the basket. Players pass, then move to an offensive position (point, wing, baseline, or high or low post) adjacent to the ball (see figure 4.2). Players must still provide a target for receiving ball, receive ball in triple threat, and use ball fake before passing.

Goal: Use quick jab steps and fake and replace movements to create a passing lane and receive a pass.

PRACTICE TASK 2: 2 v 2 with passive defenders, ball starts at point. As point player fakes, wing player uses fake and replace to get away from defender; then wing player ball fakes while point player cuts. Encourage players to cut when possible so they are closer to basket.

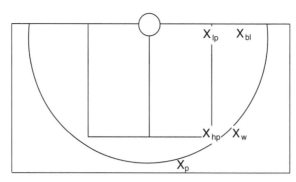

bl = Baseline
w = Wing
p = Point
lp = Low post
hp = High post

Figure 4.2

Goal: Use quick jab steps and fake and replace movements to create a passing lane and receive a pass.

Cues: Quick cuts.

Fake a pass, make a pass.

C. **GAME:** 2 v 2, half court, possession.

Goal: Support player with the ball.

Conditions: Complete at least three passes before shooting; one point for three consecutive passes, two points for every field goal.

LESSON 4

TACTICAL PROBLEM: Creating space in the attack.

LESSON FOCUS: Create passing lanes.

OBJECTIVE: Use an L-cut or V-cut to elude a defender.

A. **GAME:** 2 v 2, half court, possession game.

Goal: Support player with the ball.

Conditions: Complete at least three passes before shooting; one point for three consecutive passes, two points for every field goal.

Questions

Q: What was the goal of the game?

A: Support the player with the ball.

Q: How were you able to support the player with the ball?

A: Use fake and replace, jab step; move quickly.

Q: Is a zigzag or curved pathway better when performing a cut?

A: Zigzag.

Q: Can you describe the angle of these cuts using letters of the alphabet?

A: *V* and *L*.

Q: Why would V- or L-cuts be better than curved cuts or pathways?

A: It's harder for defender to stay with you.

Q: What did you do if your defender was closely guarding you?

A: Use a cut to get away.

Q: When would a V-cut be most effective, close to the lane or away from the lane?

A: Away from the lane 10 to 12 feet.

Q: When would the L-cut be most effective?

A: Close to the lane near the baseline.

Note: The only difference between V- and L-cuts is the angle from which the offense moves into the defense, then toward the pass.

B. PRACTICE TASK : Cutting, receiving a pass with a jump stop and triple threat position, 2 v 2 with one person coaching and evaluating drill work (see figure 4.3). O1 will *ball fake, jab step,* and pass to O2, who will use the *V-cut* as O1 is ball faking. O2 will catch the ball in a *triple threat position using a jump stop.* Repeat three times and rotate; defense will play passive, being cooperative with the offensive players. O3 will *ball fake, jab step,* and pass to O4 who will use the L-cut as O3 is using ball fake. O4 will catch ball in a *triple threat position using a jump stop.* Repeat three times and rotate. After performing *V-cut* and *L-cut* on one side of basket, have players rotate and perform cuts on other side of the basket. The coach will make sure the *V-cut or L-cut* and *triple threat positioning,* and so forth is done correctly.

Goals: Catch ball using a jump stop and hold in triple threat position.

Ball fake and jab step before passing.

Off-the-ball player should V-cut while teammate is using ball fake and jab step.

C. GAME: 2 v 2, half court, possession game.

Goal: Support the player with the ball using V-cuts and L-cuts to get open.

Conditions: Complete at least three passes before shooting; one point for three consecutive passes, two points for every field goal.

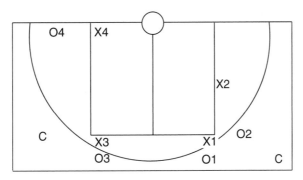

C = Coach

X = Defense

O = Offense

Figure 4.3

LESSON 5

TACTICAL PROBLEM: Attacking the goal.

LESSON FOCUS: Identify when there is an open lane to the basket; then dribble to drive and shoot.

OBJECTIVE: Use a power dribble to score.

A. GAME: 3 v 3, half court, possession game.

Goal: Shoot as often as possible using a drop step and dribble to drive to the basket.

Condition: No dribbling, except to drive to the basket.

Questions

Q: What are the three options in the triple threat?

A: Shoot, pass, dribble.

Q: When should you use the dribble option?

A: When you do not have a shot or someone to pass to and when you have an open lane to the basket.

Q: When should you use a dribble?

A: Drive to the basket or reposition to make a pass.

Q: Why should you limit dribbling?

A: Easy for defense to follow, slower than passing.

Q: When closely guarded, what kind of footwork should you use to divert or move your defender?

A: Jab step to move defender away.

Q: What kind of footwork should you use to get past your defender?

A: Drop step and crossover to get past defender and into position to pass or shoot.

Q: Which direction would it be best to drive, toward or away from the basket?

A: Toward.

Q: Why?

A: Closer player is to the basket, easier it is to score.

Q: Once you've decided to drive quickly to the basket, how can you keep from running too far under the basket and hitting the underside of the backboard with your shot?

A: Jump stop–two-foot stop, then jump straight up.

Q: What else do you need to do to make the shot?

A: Aim, using the square, elbow under ball, follow through.

B. PRACTICE TASK 1: Partners, use passive defender. Using one ball for pair, the player with the ball must use a ball fake, jab step, and drive to the basket; jump stop and shoot as partner is a passive defender.

Goals: Demonstrate good form while performing jump stop and shot.

Use square on backboard to shoot.

Cues: Arm should look like a yo-yo.

Ball down, eyes up.

Two-foot jump stop.

Eyes on target.

In the square, in the basket.

Question

Q: How do you think the dribble would change when someone is guarding you?

A: Keep ball closer to body and keep ball between yourself and the defender.

PRACTICE TASK 2: 1 v 1, one ball per pair; start at foul line. Check ball and get in a triple threat position.

Goal: To score in 15 seconds or less.

C. GAME: 3 v 3, half court, possession game.

Goal: Shoot as often as possible using a dribble and drive.

Condition: No dribbling, except to drive to the basket.

LESSON 6

TACTICAL PROBLEM: Using space in the attack.

LESSON FOCUS: Use the dribble for repositioning to make a pass.

OBJECTIVES: Use proper dribbling technique.

Use proper positioning with body between defensive player and the ball.

Identify the need for repositioning to create passing lanes.

A. GAME: 3 v 3, half court, possession game.

Goal: Score without dribbling.

Conditions: Three consecutive passes before shooting; players allowed to dribble when needed.

Questions

Q: What was the goal of the game?

A: Score without dribbling.

Q: When did you need to dribble?

A: When no one was open to pass to.

Q: Players off the ball, what was happening when you weren't able to create a passing lane to support the ball carrier?

A: Couldn't get away from defense; couldn't get a good angle to cut; ball carrier too far away; too many players in one place.

Q: What should the players on the ball do under these circumstances?

A: Dribble to reposition themselves to create an open passing lane or move closer to basket.

Q: Should you dribble toward or away from the defense?

A: Away.

Q: Should you dribble toward your teammates or away from your teammates?

A: Away.

Q: Why should you dribble away and not toward?

A: Opens up more space for teammates to move.

Q: What other ways are there to distract or get away from your defender long enough to open up a passing lane?

A: Use a jab step to distract the defense; use a drop step to dribble and drive past the defender.

Q: What should players off the ball do to create open passing lanes?

A: Move to open space using fake and replace, V-cut, L-cut.

B. PRACTICE TASK: 2 v 2 dribble reposition drill with passive defender, one ball for team. Player with ball must use a ball fake, jab step, then drop step and drive to the basket; passive defender will attempt to shut down lane. Offense off the ball will use various cuts to create a passing lane. Extra two players will be coaches. One will watch the passive defenders and make sure they close down the lane; other coach will watch offense to see if they reposition themselves to create open passing lanes. Switch roles after three attempts.

Goal: Dribble to reposition and create a passing lane.

Cues: Quick cuts.

Drop and drive.

Watch belly button of offensive player attempting fake.

Anticipate.

C. GAME: 3 v 3, half court, possession game.

Goal: Use a dribble only when there are no open passing lanes and off-the-ball players need to create a passing lane.

Condition: No dribbling, except to drive to the basket or reposition to make a pass.

LEVEL II

We recommend a review of level I tactical problems before introducing level II tactics. Continue to reinforce the triple threat, ball fake, attacking the goal, and so forth, allowing students to refine and integrate these skills as they practice and play the game. There may be one or two specific lessons you will need to repeat or extend to improve your students' skill or tactical understanding.

Level II lessons focus on prevention of scoring, specifically winning the ball and defending space. If games break down because the defense is too active, you may want to restrain the defensive players by assigning degrees of intensity (passive, active, or competitive). Focus on form and positioning relative to the ball, the basket, and other defensive players.

Two lessons in this section focus on attacking the goal. Unlike the individual skills covered in level I, the offensive skills here involve other team members and require teamwork and cooperation. You may find that this is a good place to talk about the meaning of being a member of a team and the importance of working together.

Level II Lessons

LESSON 1

TACTICAL PROBLEM: Winning the ball.

LESSON FOCUS: Defensive positioning on and off the ball.

OBJECTIVES: Proper defensive position.

Active hands and active feet.

Use eyes to *see the ball*.

A. GAME: 3 v 3, half court.

Goal: Keep opposing team from scoring.

Conditions: Use competitive defense to guard opposing player. *No* dribbling; complete at least three passes before shooting. Defensive team scores one point if offensive team does not complete three passes. *No* violations or fouls.

Questions

Q: What did you do to keep the opposing team from scoring?

A: Closely guard, rebound so they wouldn't get a second shot.

Q: What defensive position or actions interfered most and kept your opponent from scoring?

A: Keep your body between opponent and goal. Be sure you can always see the ball. Guard opponent closely. Keep hands and feet moving; active defense.

B. PRACTICE TASK 1: With a partner, players practice on-the-ball and off-the-ball defensive positioning (partners can also coach each other). Players can dribble, but as soon as they pick up dribble, defensive player moves closer and has active hands and feet.

Goal: Steal ball without fouling, or cause a turnover.

PRACTICE TASK 2: 1 v 1, active to competitive defense; player with ball dribbles forward in zigzag pathway. Defensive player maintains defensive posture and attempts to block the offensive player's forward progress.

Goal: Keep offensive player out of key without fouling.

Cues: Medium body posture.

Active hands and active feet.

See the ball.

C. GAME: Repeat game A.

LESSON 2

TACTICAL PROBLEM: Winning the ball.

LESSON FOCUS: Preventing offensive team from passing, receiving passes, and scoring.

OBJECTIVES: Close defensive positioning on player *with* the ball.

Active hands.

Use ball-side hand to deny a passing lane to off-the-ball players.

A. GAME: 3 v 3, half court, possession game.

Goal: Prevent offensive team from passing, receiving passes, and scoring.

Conditions: *No* dribbling; at least three consecutive passes before shooting. Defensive team receives one point for turnovers and two points for steal (without fouling).

Questions

Q: How did you position yourself to prevent the offensive team from passing?

A: Overplay toward potential passing lanes; closely guard player with the ball.

Q: How did you position yourself to deny a pass?

A: Overplay toward ball; keep hand in passing lane.

B. PRACTICE TASK 1: With a partner, players practice on-the-ball and off-the-ball defensive positioning (partners can also coach each other).

Goal: Steal ball without fouling, or cause a turnover.

PRACTICE TASK 2: 2 v 2, competitive defense, two other players serve as coaches, one ball. Offensive player at point, other at wing position. Ball starts at point. From triple threat, offensive player uses ball fake to give teammate opportunity to get open or dribbles to open a passing lane if necessary. Rotate after turnover or six consecutive passes. Coach 1 gives feedback for on-the-ball defense; coach 2 gives feedback for off-the-ball defense.

Goal: Offensive pair attempts to make six consecutive passes.

Cues: Medium body posture.

Active feet and active hands.

See the ball.

Anticipate.

C. GAME: Repeat game A.

LESSON 3

TACTICAL PROBLEM: Winning the ball.

LESSON FOCUS: Defensive positioning following a shot to regain possession of the ball.

OBJECTIVES: Box out opposing player at release of shot.

Rebound, then outlet the ball.

A. GAME: 3 v 3, half court, possession game.

Goals: Prevent offensive team from scoring.

If they do shoot do not allow a second shot.

Conditions: *No* dribbling; at least three consecutive passes before shooting. Defensive team receives one point for winning or rebounding the ball after only *one* shot.

Questions

Q: What was the goal of the game?

A: Prevent scoring and prevent second shot.

Q: What did you do to prevent second shot?

A: Get the rebound after the first shot.

Q: How did you position yourself to get the rebound?

A: Move between defensive player and basket.

B. PRACTICE TASK: 2 v 2, with one shooter and one outlet; O4 shoots ball (see figure 4.4). On the release, X1 and X2 turn and box out offensive players. X3 moves right or left, depending on side of basket rebound occurs. Player rebounding ball turns and passes to outlet, X3. Repeat three times, then rotate.

Goal: Successfully rebound and outlet three times in a row.

C. GAME: Repeat game A.

Goal: Same

Condition: Defensive team gets one point for successful rebound *and* outlet pass.

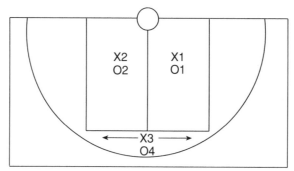

Figure 4.4

LESSON 4

TACTICAL PROBLEM: Attacking the basket.

LESSON FOCUS: Use the give-and-go to score.

OBJECTIVES: Pass and cut to basket.

Shoot after receiving pass off.

A. GAME: 3 v 3, half court.

Goals: Pass and cut to basket.

Present *target* if open.

Shoot if ball is returned.

Conditions: Must have at least two passes before taking a shot; all shots must be within five feet of the basket.

Questions

Q: What was the goal of the game?

A: Pass and cut; present target if open.

Q: What happened when you were able to get open?

A: Ball was returned and shot was attempted.

Q: How did you get open?

A: Used a ball fake, ran ahead of defender, kept body between defender and ball on way to basket.

Q: What did the other offensive player do to create an open lane for you to attack the basket?

A: Moved out of the key.

B. PRACTICE TASK: 2 v 2 with active defenders, one ball. Other two players serve as coaches. Each offensive player practices give-and-go three times, then rotates. Move to other side of basket and repeat; practice give-and-go three times with competitive defense (use either side of basket).

Goal: Successfully perform give-and-go three times in a row.

Cues: Pass and cut.

Target hand.

Keep defender behind you.

Question

Q: What did you do to complete the give-and-go when there was competitive defense?

A: Use more fakes. Dribble to create passing lanes. Get open to support player with the ball.

Cues: Firm passes.

Present a target hand.

Get and stay between defender and ball.

C. GAME: Repeat game A.

Goal: Same.

Condition: Score one extra point if give-and-go is used to score.

LESSON 5

TACTICAL PROBLEM: Creating space in the attack.

LESSON FOCUS: Using pick and screen to create space.

OBJECTIVES: Set an on-the-ball pick.

Shoot or drive off a pick.

A. GAME: 3 v 3, half court.

Goal: Offense attempts to screen or block the on-the-ball defender so the player with the ball can attack the goal.

Conditions: Different team member restarts play on each possession; one extra point for a basket scored off a screen. Players call their own fouls.

Questions

Q: What were you trying to do in the game?

A: Perform a screen.

Q: Why use a screen?

A: To create an open shot for the player with the ball.

Q: What is a screen?

A: An offensive technique to take the defensive player guarding a teammate out of the play or to delay that player long enough to open a teammate for a pass or shot.

Q: What would be a good body position for the player setting a screen?

A: Wide base, bent knees, arms across body to protect self.

Q: What would be the best way for the player with the ball to use the screen?

A: Fake, then move toward screen; stay close to screen as you pass to keep defender from following.

B. PRACTICE TASK: 2 v 1, two coaches, active defense, one ball. Offensive players execute a screen. Defensive player plays active defense, supportive yet challenging opponent. One coach will watch to see if the screen is set correctly; other coach will watch to see if offensive player uses screen correctly.

Goal: Successfully execute a screen three times in a row.

Cues: Stand firm, straddle feet.

Hands across chest ready to take a charge.

Roll toward basket or roll to a passing lane.

C. GAME: Repeat game A.

LESSON 6

TACTICAL PROBLEM: Defending space.

LESSON FOCUS: Defending against a screen.

OBJECTIVES: Demonstrate three ways to fight through a screen.

        a. Fight over top of screen.

        b. Slide between screen and defender.

        c. Duck behind screen and screen's defense.

A. GAME: 3 v 3, half court.

Goals: Offense attempts to screen or block the on-the-ball defender so the player with the ball can attack the goal.

Defense attempts to get around the screen and stay with the ball.

Conditions: Different team member restarts play on each possession; one extra point for a basket scored off a screen. Players call their own fouls.

Questions

Q: What is an on-the-ball screen?

A: It allows the player with the ball to drive past the screener and lose the defender to set up a shot or a drive.

Q: How can the screen be defended?

A: Fight through the screen or switch player to guard.

Q: How can you keep from being screened?

A: Teammate calls, "screen."

Q: How can you get around the screen once it is set?

A: Fight over the top of the screen; slide between the screen and the defender; duck behind the screener and the screener's defense.

B. PRACTICE TASK: 2 v 2, two coaches, one ball, competitive defense. Offensive players execute a screen. Defensive players being screened must fight through screen and stay with their opponents; must play competitive defense. Coaches evaluate passive defender's ability to get around the screen.

Goal: Fight over or through screen and keep offensive player from shooting.

Cues: Work hard to stay with opponent.

Talk, let teammate know screen is there.

Stand away from the person setting screen to allow teammate to easily move around pick.

C. GAME: Repeat game A.

LEVEL III

Lessons at level III continue to increase in tactical complexity. Game forms involve 4 v 4 situations emphasizing player-to-player defensive and offensive play. Tactics such as creating space and using space in the attack require higher levels of skill and tactical understanding. We introduce jump balls to start and restart play. Level III lessons may require more space than levels I and II lessons.

As with level II, you may want to review content from previous levels. You may find that some students are not ready for level III. If this is a problem, consider ability grouping so advanced players have an opportunity to improve and lower ability players can continue to refine basic skills and tactical knowledge. With the tactical approach, ability grouping is easy because you can assign groups or teams to individual courts or half courts. Therefore, each team can work on independent tasks or tactical problems.

Our experiences with ability grouping have been mostly positive. Discretion is key when ability grouping students. A teacher at a local high school assigns levels to each court: high school court, college court, and pro court. Then, she directs the students to assign themselves accordingly. In many cases, we have found self selection by students better than having the teacher assign students to ability groups. Of course, there are always certain classes and certain students that will need your guidance to attain effective groupings.

Level III Lessons

LESSON 1

TACTICAL PROBLEM: Winning the ball.

LESSON FOCUS: Positioning to gain possession of the ball from a jump ball.

OBJECTIVES: Matching up with a player on the circle.

Positioning for offensive jump balls.

Positioning for defensive jump balls.

A. GAME: 4 v 4, half court.

Goal: Gain possession of the ball off the jump ball.

Conditions: After every basket use a jump ball to restart play. Players rotate, allowing each to participate in the jump ball. Team gaining possession of the jump ball continues offensive play until they score or the other team wins the ball.

Questions

Q: What did you and your teammates do to gain possession of the ball off the jump ball?

A: Match up with opponent on the jump ball circle.

Q: If you knew your team would win the jump ball, how did you line up on the circle?

A: Close to the basket so we could turn and score.

Q: If you knew your team would lose the jump ball, how did you line up on the circle?

A: Between offense and basket so we could defend the goal.

B. PRACTICE TASK 1: Practice jump ball technique. Players match up according to height. Four players per group, one ball, one circle; two players jump. One player tosses; one player coaches. Do three jumps, then rotate. Rotate through twice, allowing six jumps each.

Goal: Each team tries to gain possession on three of six jump balls.

Cues: Match up.

Position for offensive jump ball.

Look for quick shot.

Anticipate.

PRACTICE TASK 2: Practice defensive jump balls, 3 v 3, one tosser, one coach, one ball, one circle, one basket. Play jump ball out until team scores or other team wins ball. Rotate after each jump ball.

Goal: Force opponent to make at least five passes before shooting.

Cues: Match up.

Position for defensive jump ball.

Drop back quickly.

Protect the basket.

Anticipate.

PRACTICE TASK 3: Practice offensive jump balls, 3 v 3, one tosser, one coach, one ball, one circle, one basket. Teams of 3 v 3 practice offensive jump ball; attempt to score off the jump ball. One player tosses jump ball; one player coaches. Rotate after a basket is scored.

Goal: After gaining possession of the jump ball, score within three passes.

Cues: Match up.

Anticipate offensive or defensive jump balls.

React.

Transition quickly.

C. GAME: Repeat game A.

LESSON 2

TACTICAL PROBLEM: Defending space.

LESSON FOCUS: Player-to-player team defense.

OBJECTIVES: Calling picks and screens.

Moving around picks and screens.

Stay with player.

A. GAME: 4 v 4, half court.

Goals: Defense uses player-to-player competitive defense to keep opponent from scoring.

Offense uses picks to score and create passing lanes in the attack.

Conditions: Call your own fouls. Use dribble only to drive to basket.

Questions

Q: How did you defend the offensive team?

A: Player-to-player defense.

Q: What are the advantages of player-to-player defense?

A: All players are closely guarded, which increases chance to win the ball; all defensive members know their responsibility.

Q: What are the disadvantages of player-to-player defense?

A: Defense can get spread out too far away from basket; difficult to match players of equal ability.

Q: How can you help your teammates while in player-to-player defense?

A: Let them know when pick is being set; pick up the player when scoring threat.

Q: What should you do when you're picked or screened?

A: Move around pick so you can stay with your player.

B. PRACTICE TASK 1: Players review and practice on- and off-the-ball defensive positions.

PRACTICE TASK 2: 3 v 3, two coaches, one ball, competitive defense. Offensive players execute on-the-ball screens. Defensive players being screened must fight through screen and stay with their opponents; must play competitive defense. Coaches evaluate passive defender's ability to get around the screen.

Goal: Keep opponent from getting an open shot.

PRACTICE TASK 3: 3 v 3, two coaches, one ball, competitive defense. Offensive players execute off-the-ball screens. Defensive players being screened must fight through screen and stay with their opponents. Coaches evaluate passive defender's ability to get around the screen.

Goal: Keep opponent from getting an open shot.

Cues: Call screens "screen left" or "screen right."

Quick movements, jab steps and fakes.

Stay between your player and the basket.

C. GAME: Combine practice tasks 2 and 3.

Goals: Keep offensive team from scoring for 30 seconds.

Rotate coaches into game after two minutes (four 30-second periods).

LESSON 3

TACTICAL PROBLEM: Creating space in the attack.

LESSON FOCUS: Use pick or screen to create space in the attack.

OBJECTIVE: Set a pick or screen off-the-ball to allow another off-the-ball player to support or attack.

A. GAME: 4 v 4, half court.

Goals: Offense attempts to screen or block an off-the-ball defender so offensive player can move to support ball carrier.

Defense attempts to get around the screen and stay with the offensive player.

Conditions: Different team member restarts play on each possession; one extra point for a basket scored off a screen. Players call their own fouls.

Questions

Q: How did you use the off-the-ball screen to free up your teammate?

A: Set a pick or screen on the defender same as on the ball.

Q: How did you know where to set the screen?

A: Set screen so teammate can get open to receive a pass, depending on where a passing lane can be opened; face away from direction teammate needs to run.

Q: How should you move to best use the screen?

A: Cut toward the screen, brushing or nearly brushing shoulders as you pass the pick or screen.

B. PRACTICE TASK: Practice pick off-the-ball, 3 v 3, two coaches, one ball, one court or half court.

Goal: Use pick or screen to detain defensive player.

Cues: Anticipate ball movement.

Screen so the player can move *to* the ball or *to* the basket.

Brush shoulders so defender can't get through or past screen.

C. GAME: Repeat game A.

LESSON 4

TACTICAL PROBLEM: Using space in the attack.

LESSON FOCUS: Rolling off a screen to create a scoring opportunity.

OBJECTIVE: Use a pick or screen and roll toward basket.

A. GAME: 4 v 4, half court.

Goals: Offense after setting a screen (on or off ball) cuts toward the basket.

Defense attempts to get around the screen and stay with the offensive player.

Conditions: Different team member restarts play on each possession; one extra point for a basket scored off a screen. Players call their own fouls.

Questions

Q: After you set the screen, what did you do?

A: Moved toward the basket.

Q: How did this movement create space in your attack?

A: Created a passing lane, set up a potential high percentage shot (i.e., layup).

Q: Which picks, high or low, provided more opportunities to shoot?

A: High, because they allowed player to roll away from defense and kept defensive player from getting between offense and the basket.

B. PRACTICE TASK: Practice pick and roll to basket, 3 v 3, two coaches, one ball, full or half court.

Goal: Score three times in a row off a pick and roll.

Cues: *Open up to the ball* when rolling to the basket.

Watch for ball.

Attack basket quickly.

C. GAME: Repeat game A.

LESSON 5

TACTICAL PROBLEM: Using space in the attack.

LESSON FOCUS: Offense against player-to-player defense.

OBJECTIVE: Use picks or screens to free on-the-ball and off-the-ball players to create support and scoring opportunities.

A. GAME: 4 v 4, half court.

Goals: Defense plays competitive player-to-player defense.

Offense scores as many points possible.

Conditions: Different team member restarts play on each possession. Players call their own fouls; 30-second offensive clock. Defensive team gets three points if offensive team does not get a shot off within 30 seconds.

Question

Q: What did you do to score against the player-to-player defense?

A: Set picks or screens to free teammates. Use cuts to get away from defenders; move ball quickly and accurately.

B. PRACTICE TASK 1: Practice a teacher-designed offensive. Play against a player-to-player defense, 4 v 4, active defense, one ball, full or half court.

Goal: Score three times in a row using offensive play.

PRACTICE TASK 2: Teams create and practice their own offensive plays against player-to-player defense. Each team of four creates an offensive play, then practices it against opponent (other four players); active defense.

Goal: Score three times in a row using offensive play.

Cues: Anticipate ball and player movement.

Identify opportunities to get player open.

C. GAME: Repeat game A.

Condition: Team scores extra point when they execute play successfully.

LESSON 6

TACTICAL PROBLEM: Winning the ball and using space in the attack.

LESSON FOCUS: Transition from offense to defense.

OBJECTIVES: Rebound and outlet.

Set up offense as quickly as possible.

A. GAME: 4 v 4, half court.

Goals: Defense uses outlet pass after rebounding ball.

Offense scores as many points as possible.

Conditions: Remember to box out and use outlet pass on a defensive rebound. Players call their own fouls; 30-second offensive clock. Defensive team gets one point for successful rebound *and* outlet pass.

Questions

Q: Why should you make an outlet pass after rebounding the ball?

A: Get ball out of key and away from opponents; get ball down the floor faster.

Q: Which player should get the outlet pass?

A: Player not involved in rebound, but on same side of key where ball rebounds.

Q: Where should the outlet player go to receive the outlet pass?

A: To the sideline nearest the player rebounding the ball; move quickly to create a passing lane.

B. PRACTICE TASK 1: 4 v 4, with one shooter and one outlet; O4 shoots ball (see figure 4.5). On the release X1, X2, and X3 turn and box out offensive players. X4 moves right or left, depending on side of basket rebound occurs. Player rebounding ball turns and passes to outlet, X4. Repeat three times, then rotate.

Goal: Successfully complete three outlet passes in a row.

Cues: Rebound.

Protect ball.

Pivot away from basket.

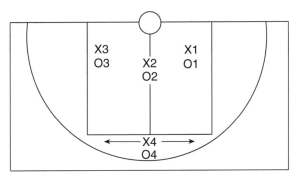

Figure 4.5

PRACTICE TASK 2: Extend practice task 1. After outlet, point guard or off guard moves upcourt and toward center court to create a passing lane. Next available player fills outside lane, opposite the rebound. Trailing players move downcourt as quickly as possible and assume offensive positions.

Goal: After rebounding the ball, use no more than five passes to score.

Cues: Get and go.

Quick movement down court.

Stay wide and spread out to maintain passing lanes.

C. GAME: Repeat game A.

LEVEL IV

Level IV lessons require 5 v 5 game play. One primary tactic at this level involves defending the basket, specifically 2-1-2 and 3-2 zone defense, and defensive alignment during a free throw. On the flip side, we introduce team scoring tactics that involve using space in the attack, for example, offensive plays used against 2-1-2 and 3-2 zone defenses, offensive alignments used during a free throw, and setting up a fast break.

The tactical focus, using space in the attack, requires full-court play. Therefore, you may need special consideration to provide full-court play experiences. We recommend using Siedentop's (1994) *Sport Education Curriculum*, which advocates using students to coach, officiate, record statistics, keep score, act as trainers, and fulfill other team management responsibilities. This will help you maintain high levels of student involvement, while exposing your students to other aspects of sport participation.

Level IV Lessons

LESSON 1

TACTICAL PROBLEM: Using space in the attack and attacking the goal.

LESSON FOCUS: Outlet pass and fast break.

OBJECTIVES: Execute pivot and outlet pass from rebound.

Move ball down floor using wide formation, and score from break.

A. GAME: 5 v 5, full court.

Goal: Defense uses outlet pass after rebounding ball and attempts to score before opponent sets up.

Conditions: Remember to box out and use outlet pass on a defensive rebound. Players call their own fouls; 30-second offensive clock. Defensive team gets one point for successful rebound *and* outlet pass and three points for scoring off the break (within eight seconds of the rebound).

Questions

Q: After the rebound, what did you do to get the ball down the floor quickly?

A: Quick, accurate passes, quickly create open passing lanes down court.

Q: What was the best way to create these passing lanes?

A: Move down the court, spread out, and use the whole court.

B. PRACTICE TASK: 5 v 5, with one shooter and one outlet; X5 shoots ball (see figure 4.6). On the release X1, X2, and X3 turn and box out offensive players. O5 moves right or left, depending on side of basket rebound occurs. Player rebounding ball turns and passes to outlet, O5. After outlet, point guard or off guard moves upcourt and toward center court to create a passing lane; next available player fills outside lane, opposite the rebound. Trailing players move downcourt as quickly as possible and assume offensive positions. Repeat three times, then rotate.

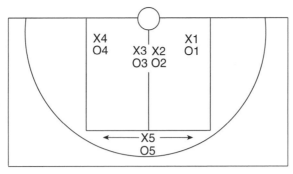

Figure 4.6

Goal: Score off the fast break three times in a row.

Cues: Anticipate.

Move quickly to support.

Support downcourt toward the basket.

Stay wide.

C. GAME: Repeat game A.

LESSON 2

TACTICAL PROBLEM: Winning the ball.

LESSON FOCUS: Rebounding from foul lane.

OBJECTIVE: Offensive and defensive positioning for free throws.

A. GAME: 5 v 5, full court.

Goal: One free throw awarded on all fouls.

Conditions: If free throw made, opposing team gets ball out of bounds at end line; *no* dribbling in the front court.

Questions

Q: How should offensive team line up on a jump ball?

A: Between defensive players on sidelines of key, one player at half court to defend against a potential fast break attempt.

Q: How should the defensive team line up on a jump ball?

A: On the *block* next to basket, then one player on other side of offensive player, one player close to shooter ready to block out.

B. PRACTICE TASK: Offensive and defensive teams alternate free throws. Practice defensive positioning after release of ball and practice making outlet passes, as in a fast break. If offensive team gets rebound, continue play until they score or defense wins the ball.

Goals: Defensive team gets all rebounds off the free throw.

Offensive team regains possession of missed free throw.

Cues: Step in at release.

Step in quickly and firmly hold position.

Keep body against opponent.

C. GAME: Repeat game A.

LESSON 3

TACTICAL PROBLEM: Defending space.

LESSON FOCUS: 2-1-2 zone defense.

OBJECTIVES: Execute a 2-1-2 zone defense as a team.

Execute proper defensive positioning of individual player when on the ball and when off the ball.

A. GAME: 5 v 5, full court.

Goal: Use a 2-1-2 defense to keep opponent from scoring.

Conditions: *No* dribbling in the front court; must complete at least three passes to different players before attempting a shot.

Questions

Q: Where did the offensive team take most of its shots?

A: Outside the key area.

Q: Was the zone defense easier or harder to play than the player-to-player defense?

A: Easier, because you didn't have to move as much, easier to keep offense away from basket, easier to get rebounds because you're closer to basket.

Q: What were some disadvantages of the zone defense compared with the one-on-one defense?

A: Couldn't always get to the ball, hard to defend long-range shooters, hard to play when two players are in your zone, can't see all offensive players at once.

B. PRACTICE TASK 1: Practice 2-1-2 zone shift with one team playing defense and other team around perimeter. Offensive team passes ball quickly around perimeter, allowing defensive team to practice positioning and covering players inside their area of the zone. Practice talking to each other to communicate position of offensive players.

Goal: Give the offensive team *no* open shots within 15 feet of the basket.

PRACTICE TASK 2: Same as previous task but focus on on-the-ball and off-the-ball defensive positions, picking up or escorting players as they pass through your area of the zone, and when not to pick up an offensive player (e.g., guarding players too far from basket to be a shooting threat).

Goal: Know positions of off-the-ball players at all times.

Cues: Talk.

Anticipate.

Play aggressive on-the-ball defense.

Cover players in your zone.

C. GAME: Repeat game A.

LESSON 4

TACTICAL PROBLEM: Creating and using space in the attack.

LESSON FOCUS: Offense against a 2-1-2 defense.

OBJECTIVES: Run offensive plays off a 2-1-2 defense.

Identify strengths and weaknesses of a 2-1-2 defense.

A. GAME: 5 v 5, full court.

Goals: Use a 2-1-2 defense to defend space around the basket.

Offense work to score off the 2-1-2 defense.

Conditions: *No* dribbling in the front court; complete at least three passes to different players before attempting a shot.

Question

Q: What did you do to score off the 2-1-2 zone defense?

A: Move ball quickly; draw one or more defenders to create passing lanes. Use screens to create shooting opportunities.

B. PRACTICE TASK 1: Practice a teacher-designed offensive play against a 2-1-2 defense, 5 v 5, active defense, half or full court.

Goal: Score three times in a row against a 2-1-2 defense.

Cues: Move ball quickly.

Lots of off-ball-movement.

Pick or screen away.

PRACTICE TASK 2: Teams create and practice their own offensive plays against 2-1-2 defense. Each team of five creates an offensive play, then practices it against opponent (other five players); active defense.

Goal: Score three times in a row against a 2-1-2 defense.

Cues: Quick passes.

Quick cuts.

Support.

Screen.

C. GAME: Repeat game A.

Condition: Team scores extra point when they execute a play as planned and score a basket off the play.

LESSON 5

TACTICAL PROBLEM: Defending space.

LESSON FOCUS: 3-2 defense.

OBJECTIVES: Execute a 3-2 zone defense as a team.

Execute proper defensive positioning of individual player when on the ball and when off the ball.

A. GAME: 5 v 5, full court.

Goal: Use a 3-2 defense to defend space around the basket.

Conditions: *No* dribbling in the front court; complete at least three passes to different players before attempting a shot.

Questions

Q: What did you do defensively to get the offense to shoot outside the key?

A: Guard them closely when inside the key area.

Q: Was the zone defense easier or harder to play than the player-to-player defense?

A: Easier because you didn't have to move as much, easier to keep offense away from basket, easier to get rebounds because you're closer to basket.

Q: What were some disadvantages of the 3-2 zone defense compared with the 2-1-2 defense?

A: Top of key not always covered, baseline open.

B. PRACTICE TASK 1: Practice 3-2 zone shift with one team playing defense and other team around perimeter. Offensive team passes ball quickly around perimeter, allowing defensive team to practice positioning and covering players inside their area of the zone. Practice talking to each other to communicate position of offensive players.

Goal: Using a 3-2 zone, regain possession of the ball three times in a row.

PRACTICE TASK 2: Same as previous task but focus on on-the-ball and off-the-ball defensive positions, picking up players as they pass through your area of the zone, and when not to pick up or escort an offensive player (when playing too far from basket to be a shooting threat).

Goal: Know positions of off-ball-players at all times.

Cues: Talk.

Anticipate.

Play aggressive on-the-ball defense.

Cover off-ball-players moving into or through your area.

C. GAME: Repeat game A.

LESSON 6

TACTICAL PROBLEM: Creating and using space in the attack.

LESSON FOCUS: Offense against a 3-2 defense.

OBJECTIVES: Run offensive plays off a 3-2 defense.

Identify strengths and weaknesses of a 3-2 defense.

A. GAME: 5 v 5, full court.

Goals: Use a 3-2 defense to defend space around the basket.

Offense works to score off the 3-2 defense.

Conditions: *No* dribbling in the front court; complete at least three passes to different players before attempting a shot.

Question

Q: What did you do to score off the 3-2 zone defense?

A: Move ball quickly; draw one or more defenders to create passing lanes. Use screens to create shooting opportunities.

B. PRACTICE TASK 1: Practice an offensive play against a 3-2 defense; 5 v 5, active defense, half or full court.

Goal: Score three times in a row off a 3-2 defense.

PRACTICE TASK 2: Teams create and practice their own offensive plays against 3-2 defense. Each team of five creates an offensive play, then practices it against opponent (other five players); active defense.

Goal: Score three times in a row off a 3-2 defense.

Cues: Quick passes.

Quick cuts.

Support.

Screen.

C. GAME: Repeat game A.

Condition: Team scores extra point when they execute play successfully.

LESSON 7

TACTICAL PROBLEM: Restarting play.

LESSON FOCUS: Inbound pass from offensive end line.

OBJECTIVE: Run a set play to allow inbound pass to occur.

A. GAME: 5 v 5, full court.

Goal: Score within 10 seconds of inbounding the ball from the end line.

Conditions: *No* dribbling except to drive to the basket; use a 2-1-2 defense to defend space around the basket. Restart play from end line.

Question

Q: What did your team do to score within 10 seconds of the inbound pass?

A: Pass quickly, move quickly, set up screens and picks to create open passing lanes.

B. PRACTICE TASK 1: Practice a teacher-designed end line play against a 2-1-2 defense, 5 v 5, active defense, half court.

Goal: Score three times in a row against a 2-1-2 defense.

PRACTICE TASK 2: Teams create and practice their own end line plays against 2-1-2 defense. Each team of five creates an offensive play, then practices it against opponent; active defense.

Goal: Score three times in a row against a 2-1-2 defense.

Cues: Know your role.

Execute your role.

Timing is everything.

C. GAME: Repeat game A.

Condition: Team scores extra point when they execute play successfully.

SUMMARY

In this chapter, we have provided four levels of lessons. They do not encompass the full range of possibilities, and you can develop many other lessons and sequences. We hope we have given you a starting point to develop your own sequence of lessons at four or *even more* levels, depending on the time available and abilities of your students or players.

The important thing is to let students play at a level in which they are comfortable. Impose only those conditions that they are ready to handle. If they or you are frustrated, stand back and assess the situation. Talk to your students. They need to understand how to modify games so everyone can play and be successful. Remember, it is not participation, but *success* that increases the likelihood of your students' future involvement in basketball. So, sound the buzzer and let the games begin!

CHAPTER 5

Volleyball

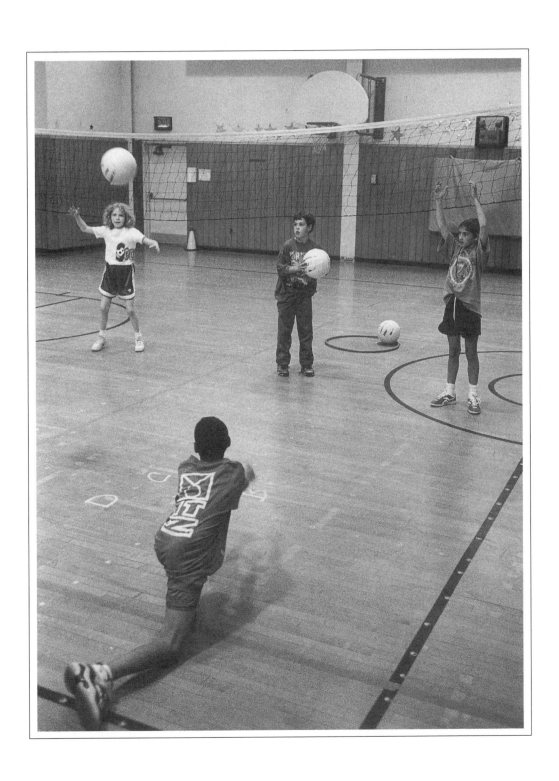

Imagine the following scenario. The volleyball nets are set up, lines are marked for court boundaries, and students enter the gymnasium dressed and ready for a unit in volleyball. After a brief warm-up, the teacher introduces the forearm pass and students practice this skill with partners in two lines, not involving the volleyball court or net in any way. As they practice from a partner toss, the students begin asking, "When are we going to play a *game*?" At this point we would suggest teachers consider that these drills are not fun (i.e., interesting or challenging) and have little to do with the game of volleyball. Drills, such as practicing a volleyball skill against the wall, passing back and forth with a partner, practicing passing or digging in a circle, or using a shuttle formation for drill passing, simply are out of context; they do not relate to the game of volleyball. Perhaps what is happening here is that the *skills* of the game are being taught appropriately; the drills, however, have no carryover to the game.

Now consider an alternative. A tactical approach is problem solving that places students at the center of the decision-making process about *what* to do (tactical awareness) and *how* to do it (skill execution). For students to think tactically, they must face the question, "What should I do *in this situation*?" Instead of simply providing a "do this" message, you, as the teacher, arrange playing conditions to address this question. For example, you could begin the class with a game such as 3 v 3 in a minivolleyball court. The goal is to use a minimum of two contacts on a side. After initiating the game from a free ball toss, students must solve the problem of setting up to attack. These conditions identify the focus of skill and movement practice: the need for accurate passing and supportive movement.

Table 5.1 presents an example of a framework of the tactical problems in volleyball that relate to scoring and preventing scoring. The framework also presents specific off-the-ball movements and on-the-ball skills necessary to address tactical problems. In other words, instead of *drilling* on-the-ball skills to achieve isolated skill development, the focus shifts to *solving* tactical problems to achieve improved game performance.

Let us now look at an example of the most basic tactical problem in volleyball, the three-contact concept (pass-set-hit). Setting up to attack in volleyball involves on-the-ball skills of forearm and overhead passing and hitting. The relevant off-the-ball movements, which are often over-looked, involve opening up (establish an unobstructed space), transition (establish a new position), support (back up teammates), and pursuit (follow and save to continue play). A player who does *not* receive the serve needs to support teammates, be ready to pursue a bad pass, and transition for the next play. All this should be done by players who do *not* have anything to do with the initial pass of the ball. If taught, these off-the-ball movements could optimize student awareness and performance. As a teacher you would teach tactical concepts such as *free ball* and *serve receive* from the beginning to the end of the unit.

As in chapters 3 and 4, lessons reflect a game-practice-game cycle and begin with a game form (i.e., 2 v 2, 3 v 3, 4 v 4, etc.) as described previously. Game forms that guide your lessons allow modifications (i.e., lower net, smaller court) to represent the advanced form and exaggerations (i.e., two-contact rule) to present students with tactical problems (Thorpe, Bunker, and Almond 1986).

BASIC TRIAD FORMATION

In this chapter we suggest a basic triad formation. For example, figure 5.1 shows the triad for practicing setting. Implementing the triad involves a minimum of three players fulfilling three roles described as (a) initiator, (b) performer, and (c) follow-through player within each drill (Griffin 1994). The initiator starts the drill with a skill or simulated skill from the game, such as a toss or serve. The drill initiator provides game tempo for the practice to assist the performer's trial intensity. The performer is the primary player and focus of the drill. The follow-through player could either act as the target and stop and retrieve the ball, or execute the next logical skill or tactic. In figure 5.1 the initiator is T (tosser), performer is S (setter), and the follow-through person is H (hitter).

The power of the triad formation is that it is gamelike. You can conduct it on a volleyball court using the net and simulating the tempo and flow of volleyball games. It has sequences such as toss-pass to target, toss-set to target, serve-serve-receive to target, pass-set-hit, or other skill combinations of the game. Practicing forearm passing in this format, for example, provides students with an awareness of *how do I* set up to attack. You can modify the triad formation and adapt it to meet the contextual needs of your students,

Table 5.1
Tactical Problems, Movements, and Skills in Volleyball

Tactical problems	Off-the-ball movements	On-the-ball skills
Scoring (offense)		
Setting up to attack	Base Open up Support Pursuit Transition	Forearm pass • free ball • serve receive Overhead pass • set
Winning the point	Transition • to attack • to base	Attack • hit/spike • down ball • dink/tip • roll shot Serve • underhand • overhand
Attacking as a team	Serve receive Free ball Cover Transition Communication	Pass-set-attack combinations
Preventing scoring (defense)		
Defending space on own court	Base Open up Pursuit	
Defending against an attack	Base • read • adjust Transition	Dig Solo block
Defending as a team	Base Floor defense • up defense • back defense Communication	Counterattack Double block

facilities, and equipment. The following are suggestions for working in the triad formation.

1. *Use more than three students.* The triad does not mean three students practicing. Adding roles such as another performer, a retriever (collector), and a feeder can help the flow of practice with limited space (e.g., number of courts) and limited equipment (e.g., balls and nets). This is especially useful when students are novice players because the ball does not always go where they want it to go.

2. You can *organize the triad* by teams or by volleyball court, depending on the type of drill and the size of the class.

3. Have a *two-ball minimum.* This formation only requires a minimum of two balls to run the drill smoothly. The target person who bounce passes the ball to the tosser can hold the second

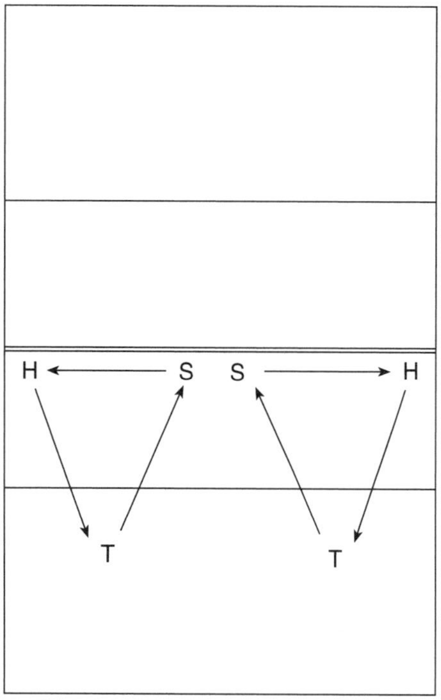

T = Tosser
S = Setter
H = Hitter

Figure 5.1

ball. Using a bounce pass is a built-in safety feature because it allows sufficient time for the tosser to react and successfully catch the ball.

4. *Modify the formation.* If students are unable to toss the ball over the net, you can modify the drill by having the tosser duck under the net and toss at the net. This is still a gamelike triad but a modification that may be more developmentally appropriate for your students.

When structuring game forms in net games pay attention to court dimensions and number of students involved as well as the equipment you will use. Modifications simplify and slow down the flow of the game, providing students the opportunity to think tactically. For example, small-sided volleyball games in reduced playing areas with a lower net and a larger, softer ball use the same regulations, solutions, and skills as the full game.

SUMMARY TIPS FOR TEACHING VOLLEYBALL

We have had great success with the following tips.

1. *Initiate games from a free ball.* Teaching the serve to young (novice) students is *not* necessary in small-sided games to create maximum game play. For novice players or in the beginning of a unit, free ball (i.e., an easy, rainbow toss over the net) games allow for *real* game play for your students. Remember that receiving serve is one of the most difficult skills of the game. Beginning games with a free ball toss will structure your students for success and enable them to focus on solving the tactical problems of volleyball.

2. *Encourage a no ace rule or cooperative serve rule.* After you introduce the serve into the game you should establish a *no ace* rule, which makes serve receive easier for a while.

3. *Add volleyball courts by using badminton courts.* Use badminton courts (nets and lines) to make better use of facilities and equipment. This allows more game play and practice.

4. *Practice variations.* Here is a list of ways you can vary practice tasks:

a. Vary number of passers.
b. Vary initial starting point for serve or receive.
c. Vary flight of ball.
d. Vary speed of ball.
e. Use one or two sides of the court.
f. Vary types of serve.
g. Vary areas of the court to serve to or receive in.
h. Add hitters, blockers, and diggers.

LEVELS OF TACTICAL COMPLEXITY

Tactics you teach should never exceed the technical or skill abilities of students. Table 5.2 provides an example of levels of tactical complexity that you can apply to students at different levels of tactical awareness.

Table 5.2
Levels of Tactical Complexity for Volleyball

Tactical problems	Levels of tactical complexity				
	I	II	III	IV	V
Scoring					
Setting up to attack	Pass • forearm • set Open up Pursue and save Base	Transition			Play sets
Winning the point	Spike Transition	Spike	Serve	Spike • cross court • line • roll • tip	
Attacking as a team			Serve receive (3 v 3)	Serve receive (6 v 6)	Attack coverage
Preventing scoring					
Defending space on your own court		Free ball Base Open up			
Defending against an attack			Dig	Block • solo	
Defending as a team					Floor position Double block

LEVEL I

Level I sets students up to play the simplest form of volleyball and encourages understanding of the principles of ball placement and court positioning. These principles lay the groundwork for solving the tactical problems of setting up for attack and winning the point. The on-the-ball skills would include basic forearm (free ball pass) and overhead pass (set), and attack (hit or spike). Off-the-ball movements include base position, opening up, pursuit, and transition.

Level I Lessons

LESSON 1

TACTICAL PROBLEM: Setting up to attack.

LESSON FOCUS: Base position and forearm pass.

OBJECTIVE: Accurate forearm free ball pass to the setter position.

A. GAME: 3 v 3.

    Goal: Setting up to attack the ball.

    Conditions: Court narrow and short; initiate game from a playable toss (*free ball*). Alternate free ball and rotate after each rally. Use up to three hits on a side (see figure 5.2).

    Notes: Playable toss is two hands soccer throw-in (rainbow toss).

        Base position is a player's "home" or "recovery" position during a game.

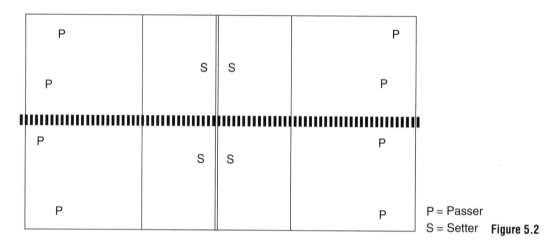

P = Passer
S = Setter   **Figure 5.2**

Questions

Q: Were you able to set up for an attack? If so, why; if not, why not?

A: No. Cannot get the ball to the setter to set up for an attack. Cannot get the ball to the hitter or spiker.

Q: What do we need to do first to have the opportunity to set up for an attack?

A: Forearm pass.

Q: Where must you pass the ball?

A: Setter or target, front line.

Q: How do you perform the forearm pass?

A: Medium body posture, feet to the ball, flat platform, and finish to target.

B. PRACTICE TASK: Forearm pass practice, triad.

    Goals: Two or three good passes before rotation.

        A good pass is within one step of the setter.

        Focus on medium body posture and belly button to target.

    Conditions: Tosser prompts by hitting the side of the ball, then gives a playable toss to the passer, who passes the ball to the setter. Setter catches the ball, then bounce passes it back to tosser (see figure 5.3).

    Variation: Move passer to other back row positions.

    Cues: Medium body posture.

        Feet to the ball.

Flat platform.
Belly button to target.
Call "mine."

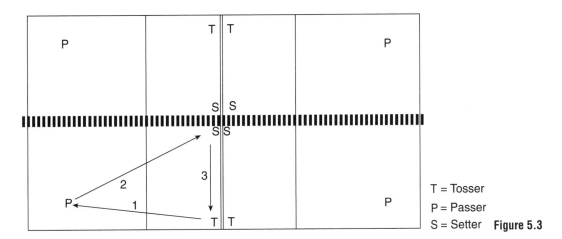

T = Tosser
P = Passer
S = Setter   **Figure 5.3**

C. GAME: 3 v 3.

Goals: Use a forearm pass as first contact on your side of the net.

Earn one point if the ball goes to the setter.

Condition: Same as initial game.

LESSON 2

TACTICAL PROBLEM: Setting up to attack.

LESSON FOCUS: Forearm pass and setter open up.

OBJECTIVES: Accurate forearm pass to the setter in game play.

Setters open up to play on their side of the court.

A. GAME: 3 v 3.

Goals: Use a forearm pass as the first contact on your side of the net.

Earn one point if the ball goes near the setter.

Conditions: Court narrow and short; initiate game from a playable toss (free ball). Alternate free ball and rotate after each rally. Use up to three hits on a side; setter is in a ready position.

Questions

Q: What direction does the setter face when the ball is on the other side of the net?

A: Face the net.

Q: What does the setter need to do once the ball is on his side of the net?

A: Turn to see the ball.

Q: How does the setter do this?

A: Pivot and call "here."

Q: What is the role of the setter in a game?

A: Set the ball to the hitter or spiker.

B. PRACTICE TASK: Open up and forearm pass practice, triad.

    Goals: Two or three good passes before rotation and setter must open up.

        A good pass is within one step of the setter.

        Forearm pass, focus on posture, flat platform, and belly button to target.

    Conditions: Tosser prompts by hitting (slapping) the side of the ball, then gives a playable toss to the passer, who passes the ball to the setter. The setter is in ready position at the net, and when the ball is hit, setter opens up and catches the ball, then bounce passes it back to tosser (see figure 5.4).

    Cues: Ready position at the net.

        Medium to high posture.

        Hands high for block.

        Pivot (turn) to the passers.

        Call "here."

        See the passer play the ball.

        Adjust to set the ball (happy feet).

C. GAME: 3 v 3.

    Goals: Use a forearm pass as first contact on your side of the net.

        Earn one point if the ball goes near the setter and the setter opens up.

    Condition: Same as initial game.

    Note: To increase the difficulty of the game slightly, add the condition of communication such as saying "mine" or "here."

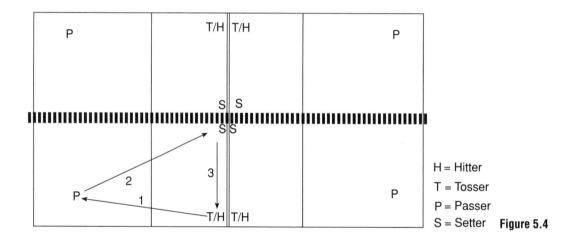

H = Hitter
T = Tosser
P = Passer
S = Setter   **Figure 5.4**

LESSON 3

TACTICAL PROBLEM: Setting up to attack.

LESSON FOCUS: Setter overhead pass (set) and open up.

OBJECTIVES: Accurate forearm pass to the setter.

        Setter opens up and sets to target (hitter).

A. GAME: 3 v 3.

    Goals: Use a forearm pass as first contact on your side of the net.

        Earn one point if the ball goes to the setter and the setter opens up.

Conditions: Court narrow and short; game initiated from a playable toss (free ball). Alternate free ball and rotate after each rally. Use up to three hits on a side; setter is in a ready position.

Questions

Q: What direction does the setter face when the ball is on the other side of the net?

A: Face the net.

Q: What does the setter need to do once the ball is on her side of the net?

A: Turn to see the ball.

Q: How does the setter do this?

A: Pivot, turn, and call "here."

Q: What is the role of the setter in a game?

A: Set the ball to the hitter or spiker.

Q: How does the setter set the ball?

A: With fingers (volleyball shaped hands), hands above head, push ball out, deflect ball.

B. **PRACTICE TASK 1:** Open up and set practice, triad.

Goals: Setter must open up.

Make three or four good sets to the hitter.

A good set is a rainbow ball (four feet high).

Conditions: Tosser prompts by hitting (slapping) the side of the ball, then gives a playable toss (simulates a good forearm pass) to the setter, who sets the ball to the hitter. Setter is in ready position at the net. When the ball is hit, setter opens up and sets the ball to the hitter, who catches it and bounce passes it back to tosser (see figure 5.5).

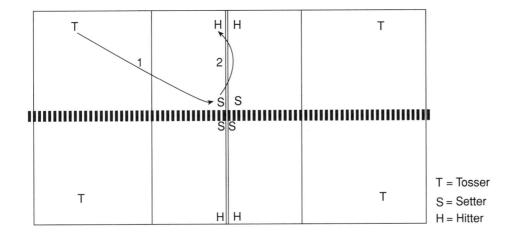

T = Tosser
S = Setter
H = Hitter

Figure 5.5

Cues: Medium posture.

Hands high (at forehead).

Volleyball shaped hands.

Square to target.

Finish like superman (extend arms and legs).

PRACTICE TASK 2: Extend previous drill (only if students are ready for the challenge).

Goals: Setter must open up.

Make three or four good sets to the hitter.

A good set is a rainbow ball (four feet high).

Conditions: Target (hitter) prompts by hitting (slapping) the side of the ball, then gives a playable toss (free ball) to the passer, who passes to setter. The setter is in ready position at the net. When the ball is hit, setter opens up and sets the ball to the hitter, who catches it and starts again (see figure 5.6).

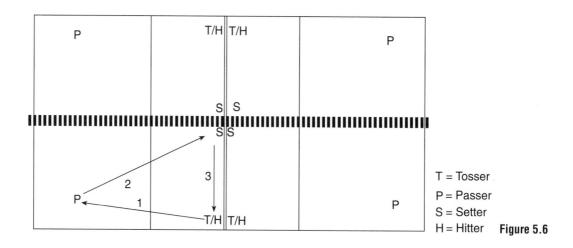

T = Tosser
P = Passer
S = Setter
H = Hitter   **Figure 5.6**

Variation: Move passer to other back row positions.

C. **GAME:** 3 v 3.

  Goals: Use a forearm pass as first contact on your side of the net.

    Earn one point if the ball goes to the setter and the setter opens up.

  Condition: Same as initial game.

LESSON 4

TACTICAL PROBLEM: Setting up to attack.

LESSON FOCUS: Pursuit and save.

OBJECTIVE: Successfully pursue and save a ball off the court and playable.

A. **GAME:** 3 v 3.

  Goal: Use a forearm pass as first contact on your side with setter opening up and setting.

  Conditions: Court narrow and short; game initiated from a playable toss (free ball). Alternate free ball and rotate after each rally. Use up to three hits on a side. Setter is in a ready position.

  Questions

  Q: Can you play a ball that is not in the court but in the air?

  A: Yes.

  Q: What do you do when your teammate passes the ball in playable territory but off the court?

  A: Chase it.

  Q: How do you do this?

  A: Quickly, running forward.

  Q: What skill do you use to make the save?

  A: Reverse forearm pass.

B. **PRACTICE TASK:** Pursuit and save practice, triad formation.

  Goals: Three to five trials to pursue and save the ball.

    Use two hits to send ball over the net to reinforce moving as a system.

  Conditions: Tosser tosses a high playable ball out-of-bounds for passers to pursue and save. After tosser tosses, return to setter base to play setter role (see figure 5.7).

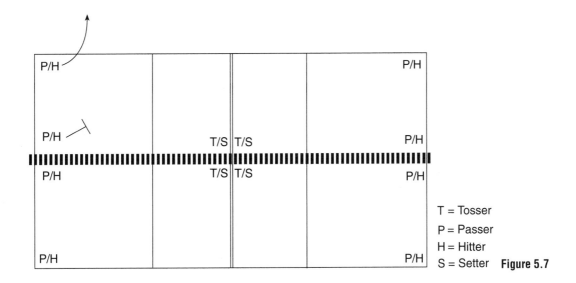

T = Tosser
P = Passer
H = Hitter
S = Setter   **Figure 5.7**

Cues: Individual

  Medium posture.

  Run toward the ball.

  Run hands apart.

  Reverse forearm pass.

  Back to the court.

  Platform parallel to the ground.

  High playable ball.

  Team

  Move as a system.

  The contact player is the point.

  All players shift.

C. GAME: 3 v 3.

  Goals: Pursue and save a ball not directly to the target setter.

  Continuous rally earns a point.

  Condition: Same as initial game.

LESSON 5

TACTICAL PROBLEM: Winning the point.

LESSON FOCUS: Transition to attack.

OBJECTIVE: Successful transition by passer to hitter.

A. GAME: 3 v 3.

  Goals: Setting up to attack.

  Earn one point when team uses two hits (contacts) on a side.

  Conditions: Court narrow and short; initiate game from a playable toss (free ball). Alternate free ball and rotate after each rally. Use up to three hits on a side. Setter is in a ready position.

Questions

Q: What was the goal of the game?

A: Two hits on a side.

Q: What do you set up to do when using two hits?

A: To attack.

Q: How do you attack?

A: Hit, spike, win the point.

B. PRACTICE TASK: Passer transitions to attack, triad.

> **Goals:** Three to five trials for the passer-hitter.
>
> > Passer-hitter passes then transitions to attack (hit).
>
> **Conditions:** Organization shows court A and B (two teams of three players). Tosser tosses a free ball to passer-hitter, and passer forearm passes the ball to setter. Setter catches the ball and tosses a rainbow set (four feet high, two feet off the net). As setter is catching, passer-hitter transitions to hitter to attack. After hitter attacks the ball he returns to the passing line (see figure 5.8).
>
> **Note:** For safety and organization during hitting practice, have two teams work together on the same side of the court.
>
> **Cues:** Hitting
>
> > Feet to the ball.
> >
> > Jump.
> >
> > Throw hands high.
> >
> > Swing fast.
>
> Transition
>
> > Establish a new position.

C. GAME: 3 v 3.

> **Goals:** Setting up to attack.
>
> > Earn one point when team executes a pass-set-hit combination.
>
> **Condition:** Same as initial game.

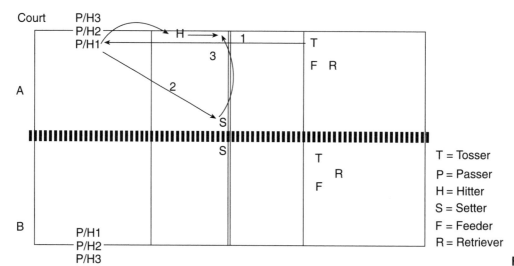

Figure 5.8

LEVEL II

Having introduced volleyball in its most basic tactical form, you can further develop students' understanding at level II. Students continue to solve the tactical problem of setting up to attack and winning the point by learning more about the on-the-ball skill of hitting (spiking) and the movement of transition (establishing a new po-sition). You can introduce the problem of defending space on your own court, involving the off-the-ball movements of base and adjust. Tactical problems at level II include defending space against a free ball to set up to attack. This involves understanding many off-the-ball movements, such as base position and transition, with students playing in conditions initiated from a free ball toss.

Level II Lessons

LESSON 1

TACTICAL PROBLEM: Setting up to attack.

LESSON FOCUS: Review setting up to attack.

OBJECTIVES: Accurate forearm pass and opening up by the setter.
Increase difficulty of practice level.

A. GAME: 3 v 3.

Goals: Setting up to attack.

Earn one point when team uses two hits (contacts) on a side.

Conditions: Court narrow and short; initiate game from a playable toss (free ball). Alternate free ball and rotate before each free ball your team gives. Use up to three hits on a side. Setter is in a ready position.

Questions

Q: What was the goal of the game?

A: Two hits on a side.

Q: What did you do to be successful?

A: Forearm pass, set, open up, communicate, transition.

Q: Why do you want set up to attack?

A: A spike or hit is harder to return.

Q: How many teams were able to earn points?

A: Two, three, and so on.

B. PRACTICE TASK: Setting up to attack, triad formation.

Goals: Two or three good passes before rotation.

A good pass must be within one step of the setter.

Focus on medium posture, feet to ball, flat platform, belly button to target.

Conditions: Tosser stands behind the 10-foot line and tosses (two hands soccer throw-in) free ball to passer. Tosser should move passer up and back and laterally. Passer forearm passes ball to setter and setter catches ball (see figure 5.9). Tosser can also do an easy overhead serve at the 10-foot line to increase difficulty level.

Cue: Review level I lessons.

C. GAME: 3 v 3.

Goal: Two hits (contacts) on a side earns one point.

Condition: Same as initial game.

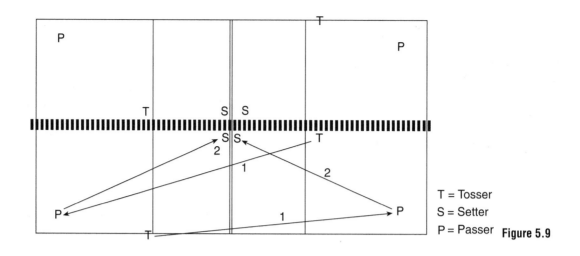

T = Tosser
S = Setter
P = Passer **Figure 5.9**

LESSON 2

TACTICAL PROBLEM: Setting up to attack.

LESSON FOCUS: Transition to attack.

OBJECTIVES: Accurate forearm pass (free ball) to setter.

Setter opens up and sets.

Successful transition of hitter to attack.

A. GAME: 3 v 3.

Goals: Accurate forearm pass to setter.

Setter opens up and earns one point.

Conditions: Court narrow and short; initiate game from a playable toss (free ball). Alternate free ball and rotate before each free ball your team gives. Use up to three hits on a side; setter is in a ready position.

Note: Arrange players in positions of passer, setter, and hitter as shown in figure 5.10.

Questions

Q: What direction does the setter face when the ball is on the other side of the set?

A: Face the net.

Q: What does the hitter do as the ball crosses the net?

A: Turn and move off the net.

Q: What is the hitter's role in the game?

A: Attack, spike the ball.

Q: Were teams able to set up their hitter? If not let's practice.

A: Not very effectively.

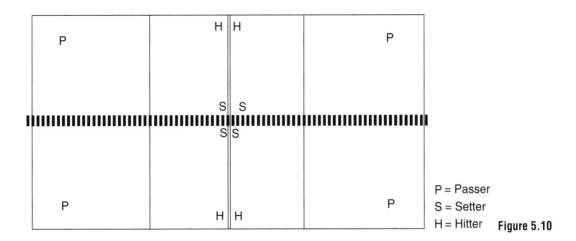

P = Passer
S = Setter
H = Hitter   **Figure 5.10**

B. PRACTICE TASK 1: Base position at the net and transition off the net.

Goal: Two or three good off-the-net transitions and forearm passes.

Conditions: Hitter is at the net in base position. Setter slaps (prompts) the ball, then hitter transitions off the net and setter *tosses* a short free ball to hitter who passes setter. Setter catches and practice is repeated (see figure 5.11). To increase difficulty setter sets the ball and hitter approaches to hit but catches the ball.

Cues: Move *when* ball is coming over.

Turn to see your court.

Run off the net to medium posture.

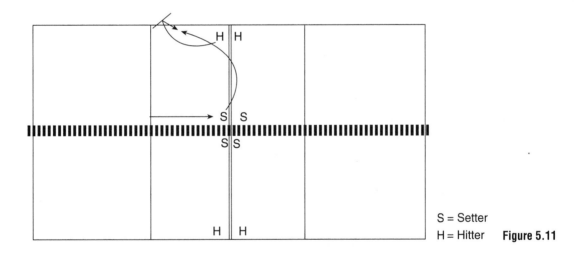

S = Setter
H = Hitter   **Figure 5.11**

PRACTICE TASK 2: Forearm pass, open up and transition off the net.

Goals: Hitter transitions off the net.

Setter opens up.

Passer forearm passes to setter.

Setter sets and hitter attacks.

Conditions: Two teams working together, three balls. Initiate game from a free ball by setter. Rotate after three trials (see figure 5.12).

Note: For safety and organization during hitting practice have two teams work together on the same side of the court.

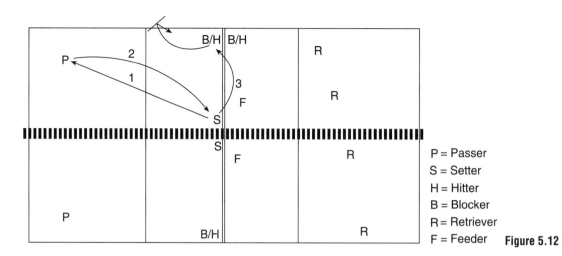

P = Passer
S = Setter
H = Hitter
B = Blocker
R = Retriever
F = Feeder

Figure 5.12

C. GAME: 3 v 3.

Goal: One point score for a pass-set-hit combination.

Condition: Same as initial game.

LESSON 3

TACTICAL PROBLEM: Winning the point.

LESSON FOCUS: Approach for attack (spike approach).

OBJECTIVE: Successful hitter transition off the net and approach.

A. GAME: 3 v 3.

Goals: Use forearm pass as first contact.

Hitter transition off the net.

Attempt to attack (hit or spike).

Conditions: Court narrow and short; initiate game from a playable toss (free ball). Alternate free ball and rotate before each free ball your team gives. Use up to three hits on a side; setter is in a ready position.

Notes: You can change the size of the court to meet students' needs.

Arrange players in positions of passer, setter, and hitter as in figure 5.10.

Questions

Q: What is the hitter's base position at the net?

A: Face the net.

Q: Why does the hitter want to face the net?

A: To see how play develops on opponent's side, to block bad pass.

Q: What should the hitter do when the ball is crossing the net?

A: Transition, move off the net.

Q: How does the hitter approach to attack?

A: Run to the ball, approach.

B. PRACTICE TASK: Approach to attack.

Goal: Three or four trials then rotate.

Conditions: Two teams will practice together (i.e., teams A and B). Setter will hit ball (prompt) to transition and toss a high outside set after hitter has transition off the net. Hitter will approach to attack (hit or spike) the ball (see figure 5.13).

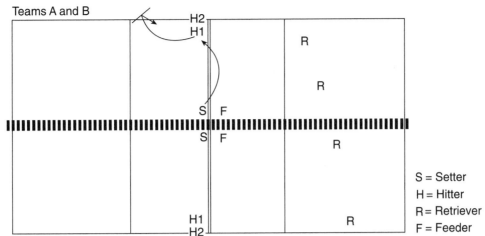

Teams A and B

H2
H1

R

R

S F

S F

S = Setter
H = Hitter
R = Retriever
F = Feeder

H1
H2

R

Teams C and D

Figure 5.13

Variations in hitting practice
1. Teams can continue hitting practice by switching sides of the courts. This allows hitting practice from both the left and right front positions.
2. Teams hit from behind the 10-foot line. Setter will then toss high set at the 10-foot line. This allows hitters to swing fast and through without hitting the net.

Cues: Feet to the ball.

Jump.

Throw hands high.

Swing fast.

Heel of open hand to strike ball.

Wrist snap.

C. GAME: 3 v 3.

Goals: Use forearm pass as first contact.

Hitter transition off the net.

Attempt to attack (hit or spike) earns one point for your team.

Conditions: Court narrow and short; initiate game from a playable toss (free ball). Alternate free ball and rotate before each free ball your team gives. Use up to three hits on a side; setter is in a ready position.

LESSON 4

TACTICAL PROBLEM: Winning the point.

LESSON FOCUS: Set to attack.

OBJECTIVE: Accurate setting and successful transition off the approach to attack (hit or spike).

A. GAME: 3 v 3.

Goals: Use forearm pass as first contact.

Hitter transition off the net.

Attempt to attack (hit or spike) earns one point.

Conditions: Court narrow and short; initiate game from a playable toss (free ball). Alternate free ball and rotate before each free ball your team gives. Use up to three hits on a side; setter is in a ready position.

Questions

Q: What was the goal of the game?

A: Get a point by attacking (hitting or spiking) the ball.

Q: What should the hitter get ready to do once the ball is on her side of the net?

A: Block.

Q: How does the hitter get ready to hit?

A: Transition off net.

B. PRACTICE TASK: Set and hit practice.

Goal: Three trials pass and hit before rotating.

Conditions: Two teams and three balls; tosser slaps ball (prompts) so the setter and hitter make off-the-ball movements (open up, transition). Tosser tosses ball using a good forearm pass to setter. Setter sets (forearm or overhead pass); hitter hits or spikes (see figure 5.14).

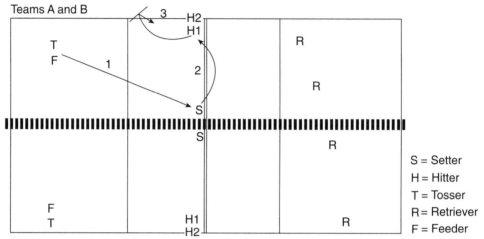

Figure 5.14

C. GAME: 3 v 3.

Goals: Use forearm pass as first contact.

Hitter transition off the net.

Attempt to attack (hit or spike) earns one point.

Condition: Same as initial game.

LESSON 5

TACTICAL PROBLEM: Defending space on your own court.

LESSON FOCUS: Free ball defense, base and open up.

OBJECTIVE: Successful defense of space on your own court.

A. GAME: 3 v 3.

Goals: Base position.

Use forearm pass as first contact.

Setter opens up.

Two hits (contacts) earns a point.

Conditions: Court narrow and short; initiate game from a playable toss (free ball). Alternate free ball and rotate before each free ball your team gives. Use up to three hits on a side; setter is in a ready position.

Questions

Q: What do you do when a free ball comes over the net?

A: Move to play the ball in your area.

Q: What does the setter do?

A: Opens up.

Q: What does the hitter do?

A: Transition off the net.

Q: What does the passer do?

A: Split the court, balance the court, play in the middle of the court.

B. PRACTICE TASK: Defending against a free ball.

Goal: Three trials then rotate.

Conditions: Two teams and three balls. Team A's passer is tosser for team B; tosser slaps ball and prompts to be ready. Setter, hitter, and passer call "free" and make appropriate off-the-ball movements. Setter opens up and calls "here." Hitter transitions off the net. Passer balances the court by playing in the middle back. Tosser tosses ball (a free ball). Passer, setter, hitter attempt a pass-set-hit (see figure 5.15).

C. GAME: 3 v 3.

Goals: Defending space in own court against a free ball.

Teams earn one point for calling "free."

Condition: Same as initial game.

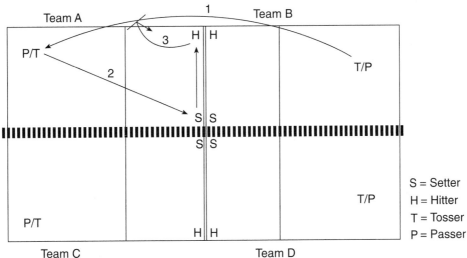

S = Setter
H = Hitter
T = Tosser
P = Passer

Figure 5.15

LEVEL III

Now it is time to introduce the serve (underhand or no-ace overhead). It is important that students practice serve reception in a basic serve receive formation. Also appropriate at this level is to introduce the dig, which is a specific type of forearm pass for receiving balls that are attacked (hit or spiked). It is critical at this level to emphasize the flow and tempo of the game by putting on-the-ball skills and off-the-ball movements in more complicated combinations. Remind your students that if they are not doing something (playing the ball, moving to base, in transition, or adjusting) they are doing something wrong. Remember volleyball is a moving game!

Level III Lessons

LESSON 1

TACTICAL PROBLEM: Attacking as a team.

LESSON FOCUS: Two player serve receive.

OBJECTIVE: Team serve receive forearm pass and support.

A. GAME: 3 v 3.

   Goal: Two hits (contacts) on a side earns one point.

   Conditions: Court narrow; initiate game from a playable toss (free ball). Alternate free ball and rotate before each free ball your team gives. Use up to three hits on a side; setter is in a ready position.

   Note: Arrange players in positions of passer, setter, and hitter as in figure 5.16.

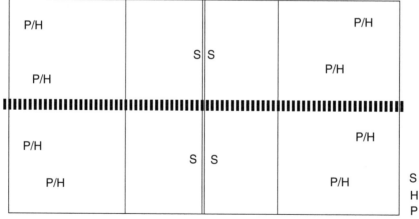

S = Setter
H = Hitter
P = Passer **Figure 5.16**

Questions

Q: What do players do to serve receive as a team?

A: Organize, play a position, set up in a formation.

Q: How do you serve receive as a team?

A: Communicate, support.

B. PRACTICE TASK: Two-player serve receive.

   Goal: Four to six trials and rotate.

Conditions: Two teams and three balls. Tosser slaps ball (prompts) and tosses free ball or easy underhand or overhead serve for passer 1 and passer 2 to receive. Setter is target setter and catches ball (see figure 5.17).

Cues: On-the-ball skill.

Block the ball with your forearms.

Off-the-ball movements.

Call ball "good" or "out."

Open up.

Support.

Note: If you can, use a full court situation; otherwise continue using minicourts.

C. GAME: 3 v 3.

Goals: Use forearm pass as first contact.

Nonpasser opens up or supports.

Nonpasser calls "good" or "out" and earns one point.

Condition: Same as initial game.

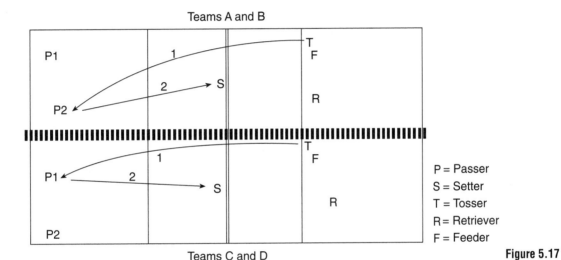

Teams A and B

Teams C and D

P = Passer
S = Setter
T = Tosser
R = Retriever
F = Feeder

Figure 5.17

LESSON 2

TACTICAL PROBLEM: Winning the point.

LESSON FOCUS: Starting the point on the attack.

OBJECTIVE: Overhead serve and transition into the court.

A. GAME: 3 v 3.

Goal: Force passers to move for serve receive.

Conditions: Court narrow; initiate game from a no-ace serve playable. Alternate serve; rotate on serve (sideout). Use up to three hits on a side; setter is in a ready position.

Note: Arrange players in positions of passer, setter, and hitter as shown in figure 5.18.

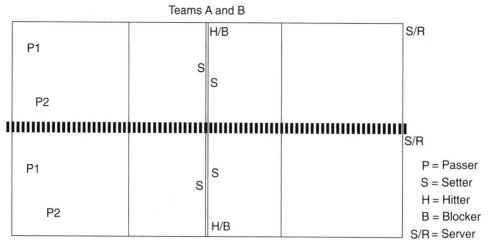

Teams A and B

Teams C and D

P = Passer
S = Setter
H = Hitter
B = Blocker
S/R = Server

Figure 5.18

Questions

Q: Where do you serve to get passers to move?

A: Open spaces.

Q: How do you do this?

A: Change your serve.

B. PRACTICE TASK: Serve and transition to the court.

Goal: Two to four trials and rotate.

Conditions: Two teams and three balls. Server serves and transitions into the court to receive a free ball from tosser. Passer passes to setter. Setter catches and server 2 begins turn (see figure 5.19).

Cues: Tee up the ball.

Lift ball.

Firm contact.

Finish to the top of the net.

Note: If you can, use a full court situation; otherwise continue using minicourts.

C. GAME: 3 v 3.

Goal: Same as initial game.

Conditions: Same as initial game.

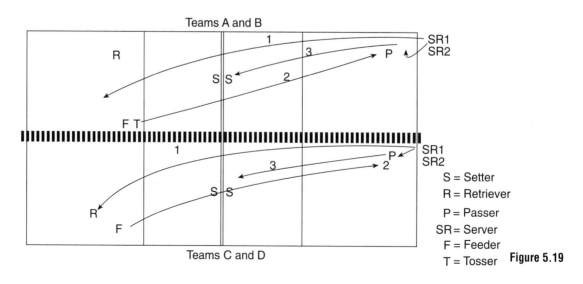

Teams A and B

Teams C and D

S = Setter
R = Retriever
P = Passer
SR = Server
F = Feeder
T = Tosser

Figure 5.19

LESSON 3

TACTICAL PROBLEMS: Setting up to attack and winning the point.

LESSON FOCUS: Combining skills and movements.

OBJECTIVE: Pass-set-hit combinations.

A. GAME: 3 v 3.

Goals: Two-player serve receive.

Pass-set and attempt to hit earns a point.

Conditions: Court narrow; initiate game from a no-ace serve. Alternate serve; rotate on serve (sideout). Use up to three hits on a side.

Questions

Q: What was the goal of the game?

A: Get a point by hitting the ball.

Q: How does a team do this?

A: Forearm pass, set, transition, open up, communicate, support.

Q: How many teams are earning points in the game?

A: None, one, or two.

B. PRACTICE TASK 1: Pass-set-hit combination.

Goal: Three trials pass and hit before rotating.

Conditions: Two teams and three balls. Tosser slaps ball (prompts) so setter and hitter make off-the-ball movements (open up, transition). Tosser tosses ball to passer who forearm passes to setter. Setter sets (forearm or overhead pass); hitter hits or spikes (see figure 5.20).

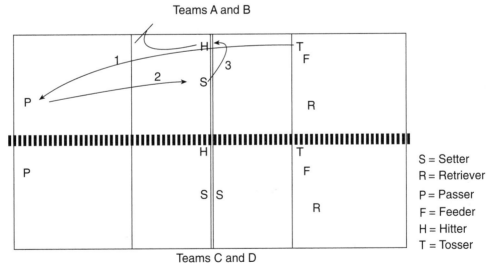

Teams A and B

Teams C and D

S = Setter
R = Retriever
P = Passer
F = Feeder
H = Hitter
T = Tosser

Figure 5.20

Note: Tosser can also do any easy underhand or overhead serve.

PRACTICE TASK 2: Serve receive-set-hit combination.

Goal: Three trials pass and hit before rotating.

Conditions: Two teams and three balls. Server slaps ball (prompts) so setter and hitter make off-the-ball movements (open up, transition). Server tosses ball to passer who forearm passes to setter. Setter sets (forearm or overhead pass); hitter hits or spikes (see figure 5.21).

Note: Server can also do any easy underhand or overhead serve.

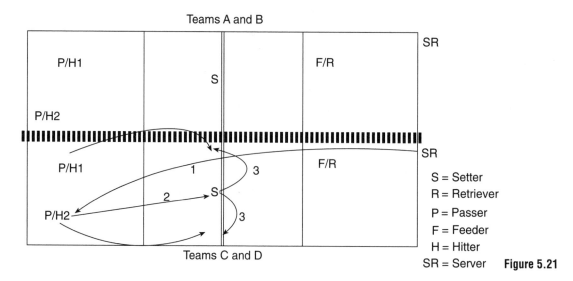

Figure 5.21

S = Setter
R = Retriever
P = Passer
F = Feeder
H = Hitter
SR = Server

C. GAME: 3 v 3.

Goals: Same as initial game.

Conditions: Same as initial game.

LESSON 4

TACTICAL PROBLEM: Defending against an attack.

LESSON FOCUS: Digging.

OBJECTIVE: Containing a dig on your own court.

A. GAME: 3 v 3.

Goals: Win a point with a hit or spike if possible.

Awareness of the need to contain the dig on your side of the court.

Conditions: Court narrow; initiate game from a no-ace serve. Rotate on serve (sideout); use up to three hits on a side.

Note: Arrange players in positions of passer, setter, and hitter as in figure 5.22.

Questions

Q: What is your job as a back row player of the team?

A: Dig the ball, keep the ball in play, save the ball.

Q: How can you dig a spike ball and contain it on your side of the court?

A: Be low, dig to self.

Q: Why should you contain the ball on your side of the court?

A: To counterattack, to set and hit.

B. PRACTICE TASK: Digging triad.

Goal: Two to four trials and rotate.

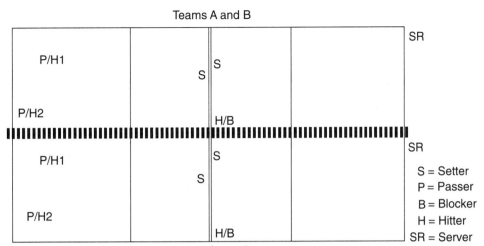

Teams A and B

S = Setter
P = Passer
B = Blocker
H = Hitter
SR = Server

Teams C and D   **Figure 5.22**

Conditions: One team and three balls. Tosser slaps ball (prompts) so digger adjusts to low posture. Tosser tosses or hits a down ball (mock spike) to digger 2 crosscourt. Digger digs ball to self (see figure 5.23).

Note: This practice task may not seem gamelike, but if players focus on digging to self it will help them learn to *contain the ball on their side of the court*. If players can dig high to self then the next progression would be to dig to the center of the court.

Cues: Low posture.

   J stroke.

   Dig to the center of the court.

Note: Repeat practice going to digger 1 down the line.

C. GAME: 3 v 3.

   Goals: Same as initial game.

   Conditions: Rally score games; regular serve.

   Note: Rally score is when all sideouts earn a point in addition to regular points scored. Think of it as a fast forward game.

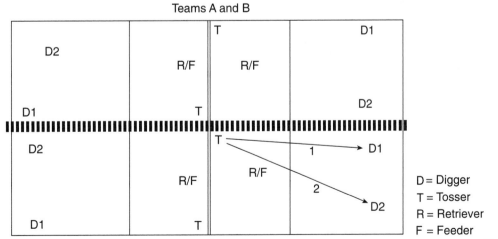

Teams A and B

D = Digger
T = Tosser
R = Retriever
F = Feeder

Teams C and D   **Figure 5.23**

LESSON 5

TACTICAL PROBLEM: Defending against an attack.

LESSON FOCUS: Containing a dig on your own court.

OBJECTIVE: Digging a spiked ball.

A. Game: 3 v 3.

 Goals: Win a point with a hit or spike if possible.

 Awareness of the need to contain the dig on your side of the court.

 Conditions: Court narrow; initiate game from a no-ace serve. Rotate on serve (sideout); use up to three hits on a side.

 Note: Arrange players in positions of passer, setter, and hitter as shown in figure 5.24.

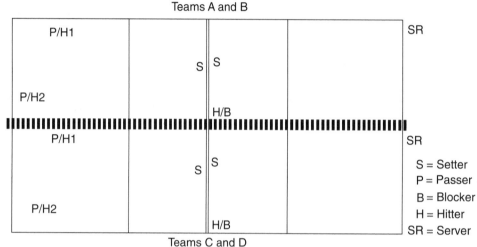

Figure 5.24

Questions

Q: What do you do to defend against a spike?

A: Watch the hitter, dig low.

Q: How do you contain a dig on your side of the court?

A: Be low, dig to center of the court.

B. PRACTICE TASK: Dig a spike.

 Goal: Two to four trials and rotate.

 Conditions: Two teams and three balls. Setter slaps ball (prompts) so hitter transitions off the net to hit. Setter tosses a high outside set. Hitter hits or spikes ball. Digger adjusts to low posture. Digger digs to self (see figure 5.25).

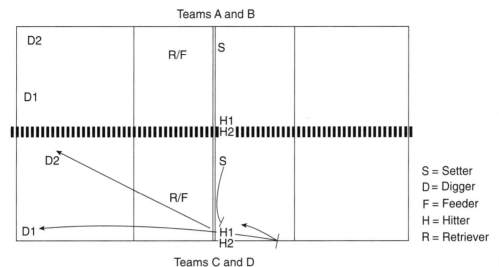

Teams A and B

Teams C and D

S = Setter
D = Digger
F = Feeder
H = Hitter
R = Retriever

Figure 5.25

C. GAME: 3 v 3.
   Goals: Same as initial game.
   Condition: Rally score games.

LEVEL IV

Level IV tactical complexity deals with problems of attacking as a team by increasing the number of players to four or six and expanding the court size. At this time, it would be appropriate to revisit the basic problems of setting up for attack and winning the point. You could also introduce an offensive serve receive pattern (i.e., W serve receive). Practicing a serve receive pattern provides students the opportunity to understand the open up, transition, support, and base position as these off-the-ball movements relate to an advanced game form. The depth and breadth of the levels of complexity allow you to introduce a specialized setter position. This position can increase the attack possibilities to include left, right, and middle attack. We encourage you to return to initiating games from a free ball to maximize game play opportunities; then move again gradually to a serve.

Level IV Lessons

LESSON 1

TACTICAL PROBLEM: Attacking as a team.

LESSON FOCUS: Team serve receive.

OBJECTIVE: Serve receive and transition to attack.

A. GAME: 6 v 6.
   Goal: Setting up to attack.
   Conditions: Full court; regulation rules. Initiate game from a free ball. Free ball toss from server position, rally score.

Questions

Q: What formation will give you the best chance to attack your opponent?

A: *W* serve receive, playing positions.

Q: Why should your team use a serve receive formation?

A: To help with communication; all players know their roles.

B. PRACTICE TASK: Serve receive using free ball.

Goals: Team A has three trials at three serve receive positions (rotations); then switch to team B. Base player returns to a *home* or recovery position when the ball passes over the net.

Conditions: Two teams and three balls. Part 1 (see figure 5.26), server easy serves ball to team A; team A sets up to attack and transitions to base. Part 2 (see figure 5.27), server tosses a free ball; team A sets up to attack.

C. GAME: 6 v 6 game.

Goal: Same as initial game.

Condition: Regulation game.

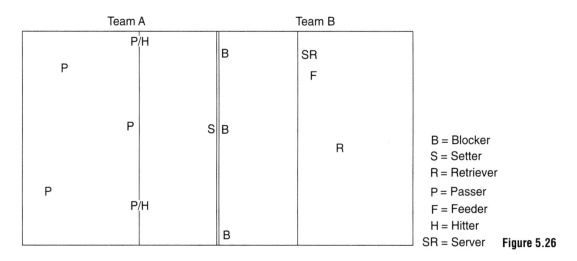

B = Blocker
S = Setter
R = Retriever
P = Passer
F = Feeder
H = Hitter
SR = Server   **Figure 5.26**

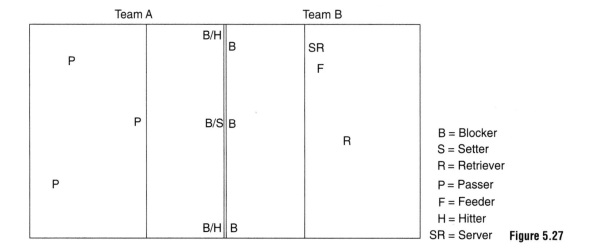

B = Blocker
S = Setter
R = Retriever
P = Passer
F = Feeder
H = Hitter
SR = Server   **Figure 5.27**

LESSON 2

TACTICAL PROBLEM: Winning the point.

LESSON FOCUS: Spiking (crosscourt and down the line).

OBJECTIVE: To use attack variations.

A. GAME: 6 v 6.

Goal: Winning the point by attack.

Conditions: Regulation court; regulation rules. Initiate game from a free ball. Free ball toss from server position, rally score.

Note: Teams can implement the no-ace serving rule as a variation.

Questions

Q: What do you ultimately want to do when you attack (spike) the ball to win a point?

A: Kill the ball; spike so players cannot return.

Q: What are the different types of spiking?

A: Tip, crosscourt, down the line, roll shot.

B. PRACTICE TASK: Attack variations.

Goal: Hitters get four trials then rotate.

Conditions: Two teams and three or four balls. Tosser tosses a good pass to setter 1, then tosses a pass to setter 2. Setter 1 sets a high outside for hitter to spike, down the line, crosscourt, tip, roll shot (see figure 5.28).

C. GAME: 6 v 6.

Goal: Same as initial game.

Condition: No-ace serve game or regulation.

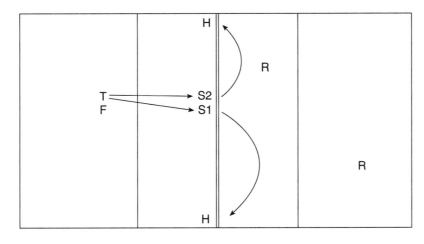

S = Setter
R = Retriever
T = Tosser
H = Hitter
F = Feeder   **Figure 5.28**

LESSON 3

TACTICAL PROBLEM: Defending against an attack.

LESSON FOCUS: Solo block.

OBJECTIVE: Attempt to front the hitter and block.

A. GAME: 3 v 3.

Goal: Defend against a spike.

Conditions: Narrow court, slightly lower net, regulation rules. Initiate game from a free ball. Free ball toss from server position, rally score.

Questions

Q: What is the first line of defense against an attack?

A: Block.

Q: How do you block?

A: Arms up before hit or spike.

B. PRACTICE TASK: Solo block against a spike.

Goal: Blocker stays for four trials then rotate.

Conditions: Two teams and three or four balls. Setter tosses high outside sets for hitter to hit or spike. Blocker blocks (see figure 5.29).

Cues: Hands high.

Front the hitter.

Jump on the arm swing of the hitter.

Press to center court.

C. GAME: 3 v 3.

Goal: Same as initial game.

Conditions: No-ace serve, rally score, or regulation game.

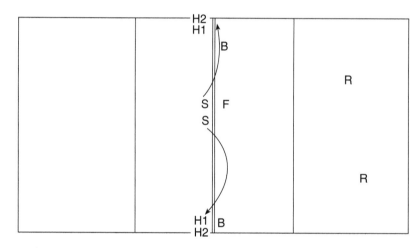

B = Blocker
S = Setter
R = Retriever
F = Feeder
H = Hitter

Figure 5.29

LESSON 4

TACTICAL PROBLEM: Attacking as a team.

LESSON FOCUS: Team serve receive.

OBJECTIVE: Serve receive and transition to attack.

A. GAME: 6 v 6.

Goal: Serve receive and setting up to attack.

Conditions: Full court, regulation rules, no-ace serve, rally score.

Question

Q: What is the goal of the game?

A: Serve receive, setting up to attack, winning the point, and so on.

B. PRACTICE TASK: Free ball *wash.*

Goal: To earn two points in a row.

Conditions: Two teams and three or four balls; initiate game from a free ball.

A *wash* is an attempt by one team to earn two consecutive points. Here is an example using teams A and B. Team A starts by receiving a free ball. Team A wins the rally and earns the right to receive the next free ball. Team B has the opportunity now to *wash out* or nullify team A's second point. If team A wins the second point they win the game, but if team B is successful in washing team A's second point the game begins again. If team A does not win the first point then the game starts over with team B receiving the first free ball.

Note: Implement a game manager to toss free balls from the sideline near the net standard. You can manage and coach one game while the other court manages itself; then switch after five to seven minutes.

C. GAME: 6 v 6.

Goal: Serve receive and setting up to attack.

Conditions: Full court, regulation rules, no-ace serve, rally score.

LEVEL V

The problem of defending as a team becomes the primary focus at level V, with the introduction of defensive systems. If the students are ready, you can introduce the double block and complete the tactical levels by introducing attack coverage (players supporting their hitter if he were blocked). An additional challenge for your students is to introduce different set plays for setting up to attack.

Level V Lessons

LESSON 1

TACTICAL PROBLEM: Setting up to attack.

LESSON FOCUS: Play sets.

OBJECTIVE: Setter comes from the back row to work on play sets.

A. GAME: 6 v 6.

Goal: Setting up to attack.

Conditions: Full court, regulation rules. Initiate game from a free ball or no-ace serve rule. Free ball toss from server position, setter plays server position. Rotate around setter, rally score.

Questions

Q: What do teams do to vary their tactics in setting up to attack?

A: Change sets.

Q: How do you do this?

A: Setter comes from the back row, set height.

B. PRACTICE TASK: Play sets.

Goal: Three or four setter trials then rotate.

Conditions: Two teams and three or four balls. Tosser slaps ball (prompts) for hitters to transition off the net and setter 1 to transition to the net. Tosser tosses good pass to setter target spot. Setter calls and sets four, two, red. Hitter hits; repeat for setter 2 (see figure 5.30).

Play sets: Four ball is high outside set (left front hitter). Two ball is two feet high and two feet out from the setter (middle hitter). Red is high ball back (right front hitter).

C. GAME: 6 v 6.

Goal: Same as initial game.

Conditions: No-ace serve, rally score, or regulation games.

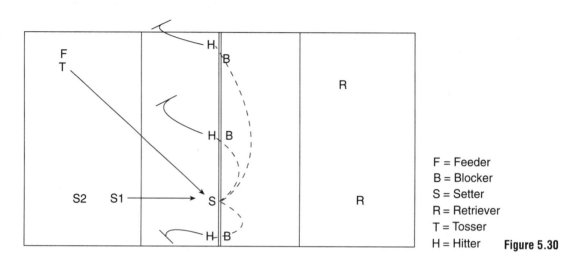

F = Feeder
B = Blocker
S = Setter
R = Retriever
T = Tosser
H = Hitter

Figure 5.30

LESSON 2

TACTICAL PROBLEM: Attacking as a team.

LESSON FOCUS: Attack coverage.

OBJECTIVE: Play sets and attack coverage.

A. GAME: 6 v 6.

Goal: Set and hit or spike two and red earns one point.

Conditions: Full court, regulation rules. Initiate game from a free ball or no-ace serve rule. Free ball toss from server position; setter plays server position. Rotate around setter, rally score.

Question

Q: What do teams do to protect their hitter if she gets blocked?

A: Cover the hitter.

B. PRACTICE TASK: Free ball transition and attack coverage.

Goal: Three or four trials then rotate.

Conditions: Two teams and three or four balls. Tosser slaps ball for team to call "free" and hitter to transition off the net and setter to transition to the net. Passer passes free ball to setter target spot. Setter calls and sets four, two, red; hitter hits. Team covers the hitter.

Cue: Form a funnel around the hitter.

PART 1: Base positions (see figure 5.31).

Note: Numbers represent position in rotation.

PART 2: Transition to attack (see figure 5.32).

PART 3: Attack coverage if hitter 4 hit or spiked (see figure 5.33).

C. **GAME:** 6 v 6.

   Goal: Same as initial game.

   Conditions: Same as initial game.

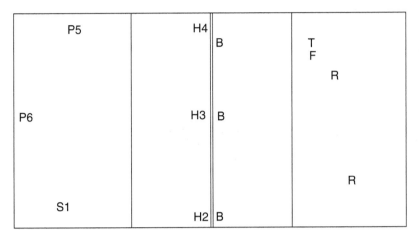

P = Passer
F = Feeder
B = Blocker
S = Setter
R = Retriever
T = Tosser
H = Hitter   **Figure 5.31**

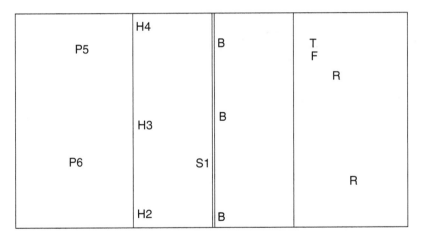

P = Passer
F = Feeder
B = Blocker
S = Setter
R = Retriever
T = Tosser
H = Hitter   **Figure 5.32**

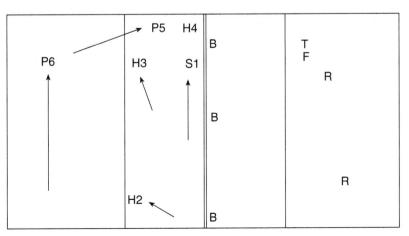

P = Passer
F = Feeder
B = Blocker
S = Setter
R = Retriever
T = Tosser
H = Hitter   **Figure 5.33**

LESSON 3

TACTICAL PROBLEM: Defending as a team against an attack.

LESSON FOCUS: Floor defense.

OBJECTIVE: Floor defense against an attack.

A. GAME: 6 v 6.

Goal: Defend against the attack and a dig-set-hit or a block earns one point.

Conditions: Full court, initiate game from a free ball or no-ace serve rule. Free ball toss from server position.

Question

Q: What do teams do to defend against an attack?

A: Organize a defense, play positions.

B. PRACTICE TASK: Attack defense.

Goal: Three or four trials then rotate.

Conditions: Two teams and three or four balls. Tosser slaps ball (prompts) for hitter to transition off the net and setter to open up to set. Tosser tosses good pass to setter. Setter calls and sets four, two, red. Hitter hits. Defense plays the ball out (pass, dig-set-hit) (see figure 5.34).

Cues: Base.

Read.

Adjust.

Play.

A player starts in *base*, *reads* the play, *adjusts*, then makes the *play*.

Floor Positions: Digger 1 and digger 5 cover primarily crosscourt and line. Digger 6 has tip and roll shot patrol. Blocker 2 and blocker 4 block when on the ball and cover the angle shot when off the ball. Setter or blocker 3 solo or double blocks and transitions to set.

C. GAME: 6 v 6.

Goal: Defend against the attack and a dig-set-hit or a block earns one point.

Conditions: Full court, initiate game from a free ball or no-ace serve rule. Free ball toss from server position.

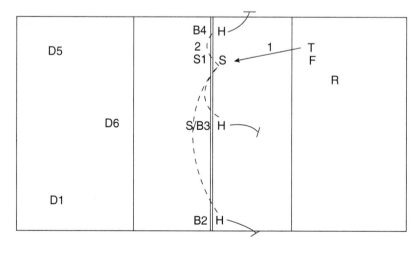

D = Digger
F = Feeder
B = Blocker
S = Setter
R = Retriever
T = Tosser
H = Hitter

Figure 5.34

LESSON 4

TACTICAL PROBLEM: Attacking and defending as a team.

LESSON FOCUS: Team tactics and communication.

OBJECTIVE: Successful implementation of team concepts.

A. GAME: 6 v 6.

    Goal: Team tactics.

    Conditions: Full court, regulation rules, no-ace serve rule, rally score.

    Question

    Q: What is the goal of the game?

    A: Serve receive, setting up to attack, winning the point, and so on.

B. PRACTICE TASK: Free ball wash (refer to level IV, lesson 4 for game description).

    Goal: Earn two points in a row.

    Conditions: Two teams and three or four balls, initiate game from a free ball.

    Note: Implement a game manager to toss free balls from the sideline near the net standard. You can manage and coach one game while the other court manages itself; then switch after five to seven minutes.

C. GAME: 6 v 6.

    Goal: Serve receive and setting up to attack.

    Conditions: Full court, regulation rules, no-ace serve, rally score.

GAMES VARIATIONS

An additional motivating game or game form to introduce to your students is known as *Continuous* or *King or Queen* of the court or beach. It uses one-point games either in quick score method (every point scores) or regulation volleyball scoring. You can use one or more courts, labeling one side of the court winners and the other challengers. If a team wins, they move to or stay on the winner's court. If a team loses, they try again by joining the challengers' line. The game can focus on various components of the total game.

1. It can begin from a serve, modified or no-ace serve, free ball, down ball, or spiked ball.

2. You can teach other critical elements of game play, such as pursuit (for a ball out of control), transition off the net, serve receive, or floor position for defense.

3. Students can gain control of skills by playing a form of triples known as *Cheap Shot,* changing the end line boundary to the 10-foot line.

4. Regulating the offense is another modification of triples. You can accomplish this by creating rules such as using only back row attack, attack must go beyond 10-foot line, attack must be from middle or back row only, and any other combinations of these ideas. This enables the teams to focus on specific offensive strategies.

SUMMARY

The levels of tactical complexity and lessons are the building blocks for your unit. Our intent is to offer you lessons specifically designed to solve tactical problems at different levels of tactical complexity, *not* organized units from first lesson to last lesson. For example, we encourage you to include tournament play in your units. The following are suggestions for score keeping during tournament play.

1. Use goals from earlier game forms.

2. Rally score games.

3. Use regulation games but initiate games from a free ball or using a no-ace serving rule.

4. Games can either be scored (i.e., 5, 11, 15 points) or can be timed (i.e., 5, 7, 10 minutes).

We encourage you to make these materials meet the contextual needs of you, your students, facilities, and equipment. You can mix levels and lessons. For example, you might organize a unit primarily around level IV but do parts or variations of earlier level lessons to serve as review.

The possibilities for lessons at each level are endless and these materials are tools to get you started. We advise you to implement the levels as a way of sequencing your games curriculum. Don't get trapped teaching the same lessons to each grade level or you will be perpetuating the existing problem in games teaching (introducing the same skills over and over). Remember the theme is to teach games through games!

CHAPTER 6

Badminton

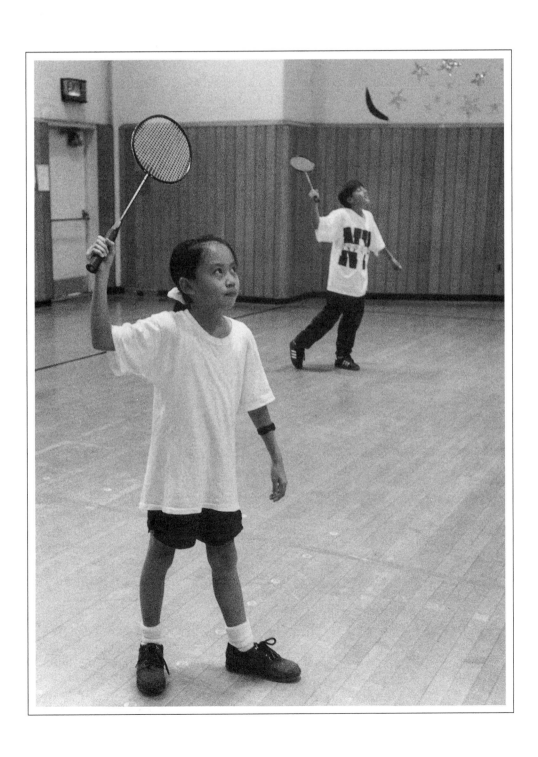

Badminton is a game for students of all abilities. You can play it at any level and it is well suited to teaching students of varying ability. Unfortunately some students believe at an early stage that badminton is a technically difficult game they cannot play. This was the case for a number of fifth grade students in a class just beginning a badminton unit.

The first lesson began with verbal instruction (lecture) concerning the parts of the racquet, which was not stimulating and not something these students needed or wanted to know. An introduction to the underhand serve followed, selected because it is *necessary* to begin a point with this skill. Many students had difficulty performing the underhand serve, either mishitting the shot or missing the shuttle completely. The teacher continued instruction until students reached a satisfactory level of competence at which point he would teach the next skill. This badminton unit ended early after two days of frustration for both teacher and students, many of whom had come to believe they lacked the necessary skills to play the game.

The tactical approach we suggest in this chapter avoids scenarios such as this one. Students are placed in modified, or conditioned, game situations immediately. They initially begin a point in whichever way they find successful—even by placing the shuttle on the racquet and throwing it over the net or by a hand toss if necessary. The singles game is the primary focus of instruction, because it is tactically simpler than the doubles game and it ensures maximum participation. As in other chapters, the tactical complexity of the game increases as students progress. New skills are taught *after* students have seen the necessity of these skills for solving tactical problems presented by the game. Bear in mind that tournament play can take place at any level, but the type of game used in a tournament should not exceed the tactical complexity that students have experienced. For example, tournament play at level I should focus on the half-court singles game. We begin with alternate serving at level I. You can introduce the correct scoring and serving rules (i.e., score on your own service) later, preferably at a point when students can return the shuttle well enough for rallies to take place.

Students will ideally work in pairs during badminton instruction. This enables them to play singles games and practice the related tactics and skills. It is also easy for the teacher to combine groups for doubles practice and competition later.

Play singles games on half a badminton court because this provides a long, thin playing area, which emphasizes the front and back of the court as primary spaces to attack during the game. One court for every four participants is ideal, though these facilities may not be available. Where space is short there are several options:

1. It is possible to set up nets down the length of a court and, with the addition of some lines, set up minicourts that go across the regulation court. Though not ideal for high school students, elementary and middle school students will have sufficient space in which to work.

2. You can use spaces between courts with the addition of some string to connect net posts.

3. You can rotate players on and off court, though this will decrease activity time for all students and clearly is not preferable.

We assume that each student will have a badminton racquet and that each pair will have a shuttle. We present the framework of tactical problems, movements, and skills in table 6.1 and the levels of tactical complexity in table 6.2.

LEVEL I

At tactical complexity level I students focus on setting up to attack by creating space on the opposite side of the net and on defending space on their own side of the net. These are the two tactical problems fundamental to badminton. Creation of space is accomplished by being aware of open areas on the court. In the half-court singles game these spaces are at the back and the front of the long, thin court. Students become aware of these spaces through appropriate teacher questioning, at which point you can introduce the skills of overhead clear and drop shot. As well as learning how to create space, students will also see the need to defend space on their own side of the net. As a player creates space by moving her opponent up and down the court, so the opponent will attempt to do the same. Hence space is created and must also be defended. This is where we introduce the concept of recovery.

The focus on these two tactical problems enables the basic form of the badminton game to take shape. At this level students can serve underarm, overarm, or any other way (even with a throw) to ensure that the point gets started with-

Table 6.1
Tactical Problems, Movements, and Skills in Badminton

Tactical problems	Movements	Skills
Scoring (offense)		
Setting up to attack by creating space on opponent's side of net		Overhead clear— forehand, backhand Overhead drop shot— forehand, backhand High service Underarm clear— forehand, backhand
Winning the point		Smash Attacking the short serve Attacking drop shot
Attacking as a pair	Front, back offense Communication	
Preventing scoring (defense)		
Defending space on own side of the net	Recovery to center court	Low service
Defending against an attack		Returning the smash Returning the drop shot
Defending as a pair	Side-to-side defense Communication	

out a failed serve. We introduce the service line in lesson 3 because students might begin to see the value of dropping a short service into the front court.

Notice that we do not recommend discussing specifics of racquet parts or grip. Most students will hold the racquet in a way that is comfortable for them, which approximates an Eastern (shake hands) grip, and so can be left alone. You can take care of grip problems early on an individual basis by observing students with grip problems and quietly correcting them. Most grip problems take the form of an exaggerated Western (frying pan)

grip, where the back of the hand points to the sky when the head of the racquet is parallel to the floor. To correct the grip ask students to rotate the racquet grip a quarter turn clockwise (right-hander) or counterclockwise (left-hander). Individual grip corrections prevent all students listening to a lecture on grip that many of them may not need. Likewise we do not recommend teaching the underhand serve at first. For many novice players this is a difficult skill. Allow them to start the rallies by whatever means they find successful so they get to play.

Table 6.2
Levels of Tactical Complexity for Badminton

Tactical problems	Levels of tactical complexity		
	I	II	III
Scoring			
Setting up to attack by creating space on opponent's side of net	Clears—overhead Drop shot—forehand	High serve Clears—underarm	
Winning the point		Smash Attacking the short serve	Attacking drop shot
Attacking as a pair			Front, back offense Communication
Preventing scoring			
Defending space on own side of net	Recovery to center court	Low serve	
Defending against an attack		Returning the smash	Returning the drop shot
Defending as a pair			Side to side defense Communication

Level I Lessons

LESSON 1

TACTICAL PROBLEM: Creating space.

LESSON FOCUS: Half-court singles game.

OBJECTIVE: Keeping the shuttle in play.

A. GAME: Half-court singles, use any serve (see figure 6.1).

   Goal: Keep a rally going as long as possible using overarm and underarm shots.

   Questions

   Q: How do you score a point in badminton?

   A: Make the shuttle hit the floor on your opponent's side.

   Q: How can you stop your opponent from scoring?

   A: Keep the shuttle in play.

   Q: Is it easier to do this with overhead or underhand shots?

   A: Overhead (this is the case for most novices).

B. PRACTICE TASK: Half-court singles.

   Goal: Keep a rally going as long as possible using *only overhead* shots.

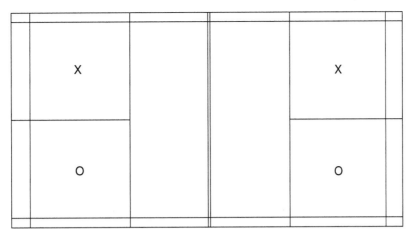

Figure 6.1

C. GAME: Half-court singles.

Goal: Awareness of what spaces can be used on other side of net.

Conditions: Alternate service (any type); score one point if shuttle hits floor in court on opponent's side of net. Score every service (not only when serving).

LESSON 2

TACTICAL PROBLEM: Creating space.

LESSON FOCUS: Pushing the opponent back, overhead clear.

OBJECTIVES: Understanding value of forcing opponent back.

Ability to push opponent back using overhead clear (forehand).

A. GAME 1: Half-court singles.

Goals: Awareness of what spaces can be used on other side of net.

Understanding that it is harder to attack from the back of the court so it is useful to push your opponent back.

Conditions: Alternate service, score one point if shuttle hits floor in court on opponent's side of net. Score every service (not only when serving).

Questions

Q: Where are the available spaces on the court?

A: Front and back.

Q: Is it harder for your opponent to attack you from the front or from the back?

A: Back.

Q: Why?

A: Because the opponent is farther from the net.

Q: So is it best to send your opponent to the back or to the front?

A: Back.

Q: Is it easier to send your opponent back by using an overhead or underhand shot?

A: Overhead (use analogy of throwing for distance if necessary).

GAME 2: Half-court singles.

Goals: Understanding that more power can be generated from overhead shots.

Play overhead shots only.

Push opponent back.

Condition: Use only overhead shots.

B. PRACTICE TASK: Half-court technique practice (cooperative).

Goal: Push opponent back.

Conditions: Maintain forehand overhead rally; hand feed if necessary.

Cues: Snap the wrist.

Get under the shuttle using long strides to move.

Line up the shuttle with nonhitting arm.

Break the elbow.

Throw the racquet head at the shuttle.

C. GAME: Half-court singles.

Goal: Use skillful overhead clear to push opponent back in game situation.

Conditions: Alternate service, score one point if shuttle hits floor in court on opponent's side of net. Score every service (not only when serving).

LESSON 3

TACTICAL PROBLEM: Creating space.

LESSON FOCUS: Pushing the opponent back, backhand overhead clear.

OBJECTIVE: Use backhand where necessary to push opponent back.

A. GAME: Half-court singles.

Goal: Maintain rally and push opponent back.

Conditions: Alternate service, score one point if shuttle hits floor in court on opponent's side of net. Score every service (not only when serving).

Question

Q: How can you push your opponent back if the shuttle does not come to your strong (forehand) side?

A: If possible, lean across and play a forehand anyway. Otherwise you need to play a backhand.

B. PRACTICE TASK: Half-court technique practice (cooperative).

Conditions: Maintain backhand rally; hand feed to start if necessary.

Cues: Contact the shuttle at high point.

Move your front foot (same side as hitting hand) toward the shuttle (this turns you sideways).

Keep the elbow high.

Flick the wrist.

C. GAME: Half-court singles game, introduce underarm service.

Goal: Use of forehand and backhand overhead clears to push opponent to back of court.

Conditions: Alternate service, score on every serve. Each point to begin with underarm serve. Introduce service line; must serve beyond service line.

LESSON 4

TACTICAL PROBLEM: Creating space.

LESSON FOCUS: Introducing the drop shot.

OBJECTIVE: Use drop shot to move opponent forward.

A. GAME 1: Half-court singles, underarm serve (if some students still cannot do this, allow a second serve by any method).

Goals: Push opponent back with overhead clears.

Awareness of available space at front of opponent's court.

Conditions: Alternate service, score on every serve. Each point to begin with underarm serve.

Must serve beyond service line.

Questions

Q: Now that you can push your opponent back, where is the space you can attack to win a point?

A: Front.

Q: How do you attack this front space?

A: Use a drop shot.

GAME 2: Half-court singles.

Goal: Win point by dropping shuttle into front court space.

Conditions: Same as game A.

B. PRACTICE TASK: Half-court technique practice. One feeds to back of court; partner hits drop shots back.

Goals: Land shuttle as close to net as possible.

Specific number to land inside service line.

Cues: Disguise, prepare as for overhead clear.

Stiff wrist on contact.

C. GAME: Repeat game 2.

LESSON 5

TACTICAL PROBLEM: Defending space.

LESSON FOCUS: Recovery to center court.

OBJECTIVE: Recovering to center court between shots.

A. GAME: Half-court singles.

Goals: Move opponent.

Awareness of need to retain position at center court.

Questions

Q: Where should you go between your shots?

A: Back to the center of the court.

Q: Why?

A: So you can get to either the front or back of the court for your next shot.

B. PRACTICE TASK: Partner practice, one feeder, one hitter. Feeder has two shuttles; feeds first to back of hitter's court. Hitter returns and immediately recovers to center court. Feeder feeds second shuttle to either front or back of hitter's court. Hitter returns and recovers; rotate.

Cues: Recover immediately after the shot.

Use long strides to recover.

Stay on your toes.

C. GAME: Half- or full-court singles, minitournament.

Goals: Recover to center court between shots.

Take up position between service line and back alley.

Condition: One coach per player to encourage and reinforce movement.

LEVEL II

Tactical complexity level II further develops student's ability to create and defend space by introducing high and low service, and underarm clears, skills introduced in the context of the tactical problem at hand. The skills are presented, again through appropriate teacher questioning, as potential solutions to the tactical problems of creating and defending space. Students at level II also can explore solutions to the problem of winning a point. Although players can win points in badminton by simply moving the opponent about the court until he cannot reach the next shot, this will become less likely as the opponent's tactical awareness and skill level increase. Students will seek ways to win points when the opportunity arises, making introduction of the smash appropriate. Having been introduced to the smash, students will see the need to defend against this attack, another tactical problem. We now give attention to solving this problem. Finally, during level II students encounter the doubles game, which presents them with added tactical and technical complexities.

Level II Lessons

LESSON 1

TACTICAL PROBLEM: Creating space.

LESSON FOCUS: Starting the point on the attack.

OBJECTIVE: Use the high service to put opponent on the defensive at the start of a point.

A. GAME: Half-court singles.

Goal: Push opponent back with service.

Condition: Alternate service.

Questions

Q: Where is a the best place to serve to in the singles game?

A: The back of your opponent's court.

Q: Why?

A: Because you will put your opponent on the defensive.

B. PRACTICE TASK: Half-court technique practice.

Goals: Serve high and to opponent's backhand side.

Specific number to land in back alley.

Condition: Alternate serving (no rallying).

Cues: Drop shuttle.

Flick wrist.

Follow through.

Land shuttle as close as possible to baseline.

C. GAME: Repeat game A.

LESSON 2

TACTICAL PROBLEM: Creating space.

LESSON FOCUS: Underarm shots for maintaining depth.

OBJECTIVE: Use underarm forehand and backhand clears to keep opponent in back court.

A. GAME: Half-court singles, introduce correct serving and scoring rules (i.e., can only score on own service).

Goal: Awareness that it's not always possible to play overhead shots to back court, therefore need to develop underarm clear.

Condition: Use low serve to front of court.

Question

Q: If the shuttle is low, how can you get it to the back of your opponent's court?

A: Use the wrist, underarm clear.

B. PRACTICE TASK: Half-court partner practice.

Goals: Clear shuttle underarm to back court.

Specific number to land in back alley.

Conditions: One feeds to front court, one hits underarm clears to back of feeder's court. Alternate feeds to forehand and backhand.

Cues: Step to the shuttle (opposite foot on forehand, same foot on backhand).

Snap the wrist to give power.

C. GAME: Repeat game A.

LESSON 3

TACTICAL PROBLEM: Winning the point.

LESSON FOCUS: Winning the point with a smash.

OBJECTIVE: Using a smash to win a point.

A. GAME: Half-court singles.

Goals: Move opponent.

Win the point.

Awareness of need to attack weak clear.

Questions

Q: What is the best way to make a shot unreturnable?

A: Hit it hard and straight to the ground—smash.

Q: Where can you use a smash from most easily?

A: Front or middle of your own court.

Q: So what kind of shot are you looking for from your opponent?

A: Weak clear or high drop shot.

B. PRACTICE TASK: Half-court partner practice.

Goal: Shuttle to hit floor as close to net as possible.

Conditions: One feeds high serves to midcourt; partner smashes.

Cues: Prepare as for clear.

Contact shuttle high and in front of you.

Snap wrist for power.

C. GAME: Repeat game A, competitive game.

LESSON 4

TACTICAL PROBLEM: Defending against an attack.

LESSON FOCUS: Returning the smash.

OBJECTIVE: Returning the smash positively (i.e., not providing a second attacking opportunity for opponent).

A. GAME: Half-court singles game.

Goals: Win point with a smash if possible.

Awareness of need to return the smash without setting up an easy kill for opponent.

Condition: Each point must start with a high serve.

Question

Q: How can you return a smash without setting up your opponent for another smash?

A: With a block return or drop shot.

B. PRACTICE TASK: Half-court partner practice.

Conditions: One feeds with high serve to midcourt; partner smashes. Continue point; alternate service.

Cues: Feet square and racquet head up to receive smash (ready position).

Block smash, firm wrist.

Drop shuttle into front court.

C. GAME: Repeat game A.

LESSON 5

TACTICAL PROBLEM: Defending space.

LESSON FOCUS: Low service, introduction of doubles game.

OBJECTIVE: Prevent attack against the serve by keeping it low (i.e., opponents will be unable to hit a downward return).

A. GAME: Full-court doubles.

    Goals: Awareness of potential risk of using the high serve, particularly in doubles where service box is shorter.

        Awareness of potential value of a short, low serve.

    Condition: Alternate serving (i.e., change every point).

    Questions

    Q: Why is a high serve more risky in doubles than in singles?

    A: Shorter service box makes smash of high serve more likely.

    Q: What serve can you use instead?

    A: Short and low.

    Q: What is the danger with a short serve?

    A: Hitting the net or hitting it too high and setting up an easy smash for your opponent.

B. PRACTICE TASK: Half-court partner practice, diagonal.

    Goal: Shuttle to land just the other side of the service line, specific number within two feet.

    Cues: Drop the shuttle late; this helps disguise the serve.

        Serve from waist height; this can give the shuttle a flat trajectory.

        Firm wrist.

        Stroke the shuttle.

C. GAME: Repeat game A.

LESSON 6

TACTICAL PROBLEM: Winning the point.

LESSON FOCUS: Attacking the short serve.

OBJECTIVE: To punish a weak, short serve.

A. GAME: Full-court doubles game.

    Goal: Awareness of attacking opportunity if short serve is too high.

    Condition: Each point to start with a short serve.

    Question

    Q: How can you attack a short serve?

    A: Get low and hit it straight back overhead with a flick of the wrist; look for the poor serve that goes a bit too high.

B. PRACTICE TASK: Half-court partner practice, singles.

    Goals: Attack the serve and put opponent on the defensive.

        Hit return of serve flat or downward.

    Conditions: One feeds short serves from service line; partner attacks the serve.

    Cues: Ready position, weight forward, racquet up.

        Punch with the arm and flick the wrist.

        Downward (if possible) or horizontal trajectory on the return.

C. GAME: Full-court doubles game.

    Goal: Attack the short serve to put opponents on defensive.

    Condition: Each point to start with short serve.

LEVEL III

Level III involves a further shift from the half-court singles game to the more tactically complex doubles game. Students can develop more technically advanced means of winning the point and defending against attack before exploring tactical problems presented by the doubles game, specifically attacking and defending as a pair. Students are guided to solutions involving different formations of play and practice these in game situations. The last two lessons of level III are doubles tournament play.

Level III Lessons

LESSON 1

TACTICAL PROBLEM: Winning the point.

LESSON FOCUS: The *attacking* drop shot.

OBJECTIVE: To play an effective, fast attacking drop shot.

A. GAME: Half-court singles game.

   Goal: Awareness of need to play a drop shot that will reach the floor quickly.

   Condition: A player cannot play two consecutive smashes.

   Questions

   Q: Why is it best not to use two smashes in a row?

   A: This is probably what the opponent is expecting.

   Q: If two smashes are not a good idea, how else can you get the shuttle to the floor quickly?

   A: Faster, attacking drop shot.

B. PRACTICE TASK: Half-court partner practice.

   Goals: Continual downward trajectory of drop shot.

       Specific number of shots to land inside service line.

   Conditions: One feeds high to midcourt; partner plays drop shots into front court.

   Cues: Prepare as for smash.

       Contact shuttle high and in front of you.

       Keep the wrist open and firm.

C. GAME: Repeat game A.

LESSON 2

TACTICAL PROBLEM: Defending against an attack.

LESSON FOCUS: Returning the attacking drop shot.

OBJECTIVE: Return the drop shot from below net height without giving an attacking opportunity to the opponent.

A. GAME: Half-court singles game.

Goals: Proficient drop shots.

Awareness of need to return drop shot in attacking manner.

Condition: No smashes from behind service line.

Question

Q: How can you return the drop shot? Remember you don't want to give an easy smash to your opponent.

A: Underarm clear or *touch* return.

B. PRACTICE TASK: Half-court partner practice for keeping shuttle low to net.

Goal: Touch return, shuttle to *roll* over net.

Condition: Both players inside service line, rally.

Cues: Firm wrist.

Let shuttle hit your racquet, no racquet movement.

C. GAME: Repeat game A.

LESSON 3

TACTICAL PROBLEM: Attacking as a pair.

LESSON FOCUS: Front and back offense.

OBJECTIVE: Attacking in a front and back formation.

A. GAME: Full-court doubles game.

Goal: Recognition of most effective attacking formation (front and back).

Condition: Alternate formations between front and back and side to side.

Questions

Q: What formation (front and back or side to side) will give you the best chance to attack your opponents with a smash, particularly if you are serving?

A: Front and back (see figure 6.2).

Q: Why?

A: It gives the best opportunity for the easy smash at the front of the court. This is the best place to *put the point away*.

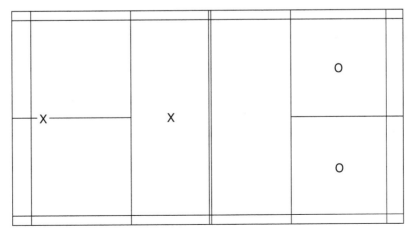

X = Attacking pair   O = Defending pair   **Figure 6.2**

B. PRACTICE TASK: Full-court doubles.

    Goal: Keep serve low and attack the return.

    Conditions: Alternate serving on every point. Use low serve and follow to the net.

    Cues: Server keep serve low and follow in to the net with racquet up.

        Partner cover the middle of the back court to get any high, deep returns.

C. GAME: Competitive doubles game, normal rules.

    Goal: Attack where possible.

    Condition: Regulation doubles rules.

LESSON 4

TACTICAL PROBLEM: Defending as a pair.

LESSON FOCUS: Side-to-side defense.

OBJECTIVE: Effective defense against the smash by a doubles pair.

A. GAME: Full-court doubles.

    Goal: Awareness that front and back is not an effective formation to defend against the smash.

    Conditions: Start every point with high serve; play front and back formation.

    Questions

    Q: How can you cover as much court as possible if you are being smashed at?

    A: Side-to-side formation (see figure 6.2)

    Q: Why is this formation best for defense?

    A: Covers all the court and gives *both* players as much time as possible to see the shuttle coming toward them.

B. PRACTICE TASK: Full-court doubles.

    Goal: Movement to side-to-side formation to receive smash.

    Conditions: Alternate serving, must be high serve.

    Cues: Serve high and drop back to side to side.

        Ready position to defend against smash.

C. GAME: Full-court doubles, normal rules.

    Goal: Effective movement of defending pair to receive smash whether from a service return or during the point.

    Conditions: Vary serves, regulation rules.

LESSON 5

TACTICAL PROBLEM: Attacking as a pair.

LESSON FOCUS: Review and tournament play to practice attacking as a pair.

OBJECTIVE: Attack and communication.

A. GAME: Full-court doubles play, rotating opponents.

   Goals: Effective attack as a pair.

       Communication to move each other about the court.

       Movement to front and back formation to attack.

   Condition: Vary serves, high and low.

LESSON 6

TACTICAL PROBLEM: Defending as a pair.

LESSON FOCUS: Review and tournament play to practice defending as a pair.

OBJECTIVE: Effective defense and communication.

A. GAME: Full-court doubles play, rotating opponents.

   Goals: Effective defense as a pair.

       Communication to move partner from attacking (front and back) to defending (side-to-side) formation.

       Cover at net for partner pushed back to receive high serve.

   Condition: Vary serves, high and low.

SUMMARY

If your students complete the three levels of tactical complexity provided in this chapter, they will have progressed from simple to complex understanding of the game. Again we recommend that you base instructional units on one level of tactical complexity and use material from other levels to individualize instruction as necessary.

From an offensive point of view badminton is about setting yourself up to attack by creating space on your opponent's side of the net, then winning the point in the most effective way possible. You can easily combine these tactical problems in an instructional unit. Having learned to solve these tactical problems, students will appreciate defending space on their own side of the net and defending against the attack. Presented in this way the sequencing of instruction is logical and makes good sense to students.

An understanding of what to do within game situations will enable players to select the appropriate movements and skills to solve the tactical problems presented by the game and by the opponent. Some material in this chapter will assist your students in playing other net games, particularly tennis, which has much in common with badminton from a tactical perspective.

CHAPTER 7

Tennis

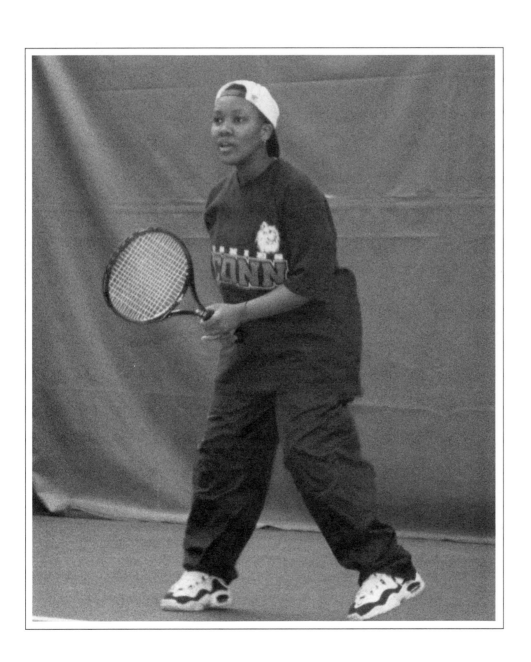

Tennis is a popular lifetime activity and if played on public courts with moderately priced equipment is relatively inexpensive. As the teacher your focus should be having your students experience success and appreciation for the *game* of tennis. Your challenge is to hook your students into the *game* through games!

Tennis, like badminton, is an easy game to understand tactically. Both games are played 1 v 1, with players having limited alternating roles of striker and receiver. Two basic conditions guide players tactically—shot selection and court position. The premise behind a tactical approach is that students can play games with limited skill (technique) and these games can be interesting, challenging, and even competitive.

Similar to the badminton chapter, this chapter will focus instruction primarily on the singles game. Singles is tactically simpler and will maximize game-play opportunities. Consider the game-play opportunities of four students who share a court but play singles on half of that court (i.e., long and narrow). If these four students play doubles they would have only half the game-play opportunities. We believe that doubles should be taught and played but encourage you to start your students playing singles.

Your teaching challenge will be to modify or arrange conditions in games that will enable students to successfully solve the tactical problems of net games. We offer frameworks of tactical problems, movements, and skills. Table 7.1 can help you organize the game and provide solutions to tactical problems. Table 7.2 presents the levels of tactical complexity, which assist you in matching skills and movements with your students' development.

Students will work in pairs during most tennis instruction, which will enable practice of tactics and skills related to a singles game. We also implement a *triad formation,* advocated in the volleyball chapter, for some practice tasks. In the triad formation you would have (a) an initiator to toss or hit balls off the racquet, (b) a performer to hit ground strokes, volleys, and so forth, and (c) a retriever to collect tennis balls for repeated trials. Ideally, you want one court for every four students, but where space is short you may consider some options suggested in the badminton chapter.

TIPS FOR TACTICAL TENNIS TEACHING

1. *Use badminton courts.* We have had success using badminton courts with lower nets, providing you with tennis indoors.

2. *Use foam tennis balls.* Foam tennis balls help increase tactical understanding and game performance early in a unit because they slow down game play.

3. *Use racquetball racquets.* Racquetball racquets help lower ability students master difficult techniques because they are shorter and easier to manipulate.

4. *Use alternatives to a regulation game.* As you will read in the following lessons we encourage implementing one-point games into teaching. We also suggest deuce games and no-ad games (four-point games) as alternatives to regulation scored games.

LEVEL I

At tactical complexity level I, students focus on setting up to attack by creating space on the opposite side of the net, winning the point, and defending space on their own side of the net. These tactical problems provide the basics for a tennis game to take shape. Creating space is accomplished by being aware of open areas on the court. When playing in a half-court singles game, these spaces are at the back and the front of a long and narrow court (minicourt). Through teacher questions, students become aware of these spaces and focus practice on ground strokes (forehand and backhand), approach shot, and volley. As players create space by moving their opponents up and down the court, they will also see the need to defend space on their side of the court. To defend space, we introduce the off-the-ball movement of recovery. When implementing level I lessons you can alternate service and use a bounce-hit forehand stroke of the racquet.

Table 7.1
Tactical Problems, Movements, and Skills in Tennis

Tactical problems	Off-the-ball movements	On-the-ball skills
Scoring (offense)		
Setting up to attack by creating space on opponent's side		Ground stroke • forehand • backhand • crosscourt • line Lob • forehand • backhand Serve
Winning the point	Footwork • approach shot • volley	Volley • forehand • backhand • crosscourt • line Approach shot Passing shot Attacking drop shot Smash Serve
Attacking as a pair (doubles)	Side-to-side offense Communication	
Preventing scoring (defense)		
Defending space on own side of the net	Recovery	
Defending against an attack		Lob • forehand • backhand
Defending as a pair (doubles)	Side-to-side defense Communication	

Table 7.2
Levels of Tactical Complexity for Tennis

Tactical problems	Levels of tactical complexity		
	I	II	III
Scoring			
Setting up to attack by creating space on opponent's side	Ground stroke • forehand • backhand Approach shot Footwork	Flat serve Ground stroke • crosscourt • line Lob • offensive	
Winning the point	Volley • forehand • backhand	Smash Volley • crosscourt • line	Passing shot Attacking drop shot
Attacking as a pair		Up and back formation	Both up both back Communication
Preventing scoring			
Defending space on own side of net	Recovery to center court	Lob • defensive	
Defending against an attack			Returning the • drop shot
Defending as a pair	Up and back formation		Side to side Communication

Level I Lessons

LESSON 1

TACTICAL PROBLEM: Setting up to attack by creating space on opponent's court.

LESSON FOCUS: Awareness of court.

OBJECTIVE: Understanding the concept of creating space.

A. GAME: No-racquet game.

    Goal: Increase court awareness.

    Note: You may choose to have your students do either or both of the following no-racquet games.

    Conditions: Short-court game (see figure 7.1). Short and narrow court, toss-bounce-catch game, underhand toss.

    Conditions: Half-court game (see figure 7.2). Long and narrow court, toss-bounce-catch game, underhand toss.

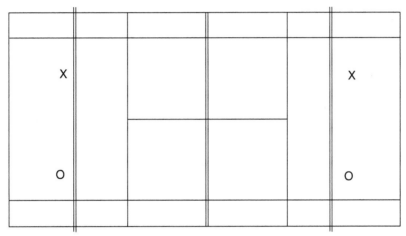

Figure 7.1

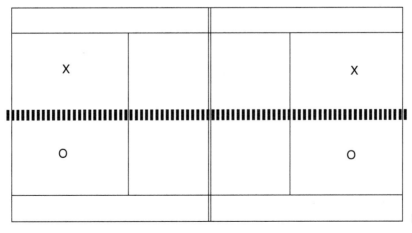

Figure 7.2

Question

Q: What do you do to move your opponent?

A: Toss to an open space.

B. PRACTICE TASK: Forehand ground stroke, triad (see figure 7.3).

Goal: Three to five trials and rotate.

Conditions: Tosser tosses or hits ball from racquet to hitter; hitter hits ground strokes. Retriever retrieves tennis balls. Students can say "bounce-hit-bounce" as a cue.

Note: You can practice in pairs and use a long and narrow court if you feel your students can have success. Although pairs will maximize participation we advocate a triad formation for novice players.

Cues: Side to net.

Racquet back.

Swing parallel.

Follow through.

Hit to space.

C. GAME: Half-court singles.

Goal: Awareness of space on other side of the net.

Conditions: Long and narrow court, bounce-hit serve. Player with ball starts (see figure 7.2).

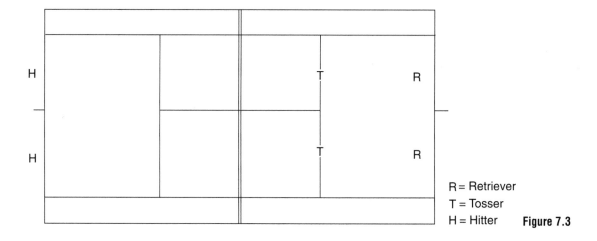

R = Retriever
T = Tosser
H = Hitter

Figure 7.3

LESSON 2

TACTICAL PROBLEM: Setting up to attack by creating space on opponent's court.

LESSON FOCUS: Awareness of court.

OBJECTIVE: Creating space using ground strokes.

A. GAME 1: Rally game, short-court singles.

Goal: Keep rally going for as long as possible using *only* ground strokes.

Conditions: Short and narrow court, bounce-hit serve. Player with ball starts (see figure 7.1).

Question

Q: What do you do to keep the rally going?

A: Hit to each other.

GAME 2: Short-court singles.

Goal: Awareness of space on either side of the net.

Conditions: Short and narrow court. Alternate serve, bounce-hit serve, one point games (see figure 7.1).

Questions

Q: What did you do to win a point?

A: Hit to an open space.

Q: What spaces are there on your opponent's side of the net into which you can hit the tennis ball?

A: Front and back, side to side.

Q: How do you return the ball if it does not come to your forehand side?

A: Backhand.

B. PRACTICE TASK: Backhand ground stroke, triad (see figure 7.3).

Goal: Three to five trials and rotate.

Conditions: Tosser tosses or hits ball from racquet to hitter; hitter hits ground stroke. Retriever retrieves tennis balls.

Note: You can practice in pairs and use a long and narrow court if you feel your students can have success. Pairs will maximize participation.

Cues: Side to net.

Racquet back.

Swing parallel.

Follow through.

C. GAME: Half-court singles.

Goal: Awareness of space on other side of the net.

Conditions: Long and narrow court. Alternate serve, bounce-hit serve, four-point games, ground strokes only (see figure 7.2).

LESSON 3

TACTICAL PROBLEM: Setting up to attack by creating space on opponent's court.

LESSON FOCUS: Understanding the value of forcing opponent back to the baseline.

OBJECTIVE: Ability to push opponent back with strong ground strokes.

A. GAME: Half-court singles.

Goals: Awareness of space on other side of the net.

Understanding that it is harder to attack from the back of the court so it is useful to push your opponent back to the baseline.

Conditions: Long and narrow court. Alternate serve, bounce-hit serve, four-point games, ground strokes only (see figure 7.2).

Questions

Q: Is it harder for your opponent to attack from the baseline or at the net in the front court?

A: Baseline.

Q: Is it best to send your opponent to the baseline or to the front court at the net?

A: Baseline.

Q: How do you send your opponent back?

A: Ground stroke to baseline.

B. PRACTICE TASK 1: Ground stroke mixer, triad (same as figure 7.3).

  Goal: Six to eight trials and rotate.

  Conditions: Tosser tosses or hits ball from racquet, mixes forehand and backhand to hitter. Hitter hits ground strokes; retriever retrieves tennis balls.

  Note: You can practice in pairs and use a long and narrow court if you feel your students can have success. Although pairs will maximize participation, we advocate a triad formation for novice players.

  PRACTICE TASK 2: Half-court singles.

  Goal: Maintain ground stroke rally from the baseline.

  Condition: Cooperation between pairs.

C. GAME: Half-court singles.

  Goal: Use skillful ground strokes to push opponent back in game situation.

  Conditions: Alternate service, long and narrow court, bounce-hit serve, four-point games, ground strokes only.

LESSON 4

TACTICAL PROBLEM: Winning the point.

LESSON FOCUS: Getting to the net to attack.

OBJECTIVE: Approach shot to net.

A. GAME: Half-court singles game.

  Goals: Move opponent.

  Win the point.

  Awareness of need to punish short ground stroke.

  Conditions: Play no-ad score games (4-point games). Can play the ball before it bounces after serve.

  Questions

  Q: What did you do to a short ground stroke?

  A: Move up to play the ball.

  Q: After you move up is it easier to run back or keep moving toward the net?

  A: Toward the net.

  Note: You can choose to use the following practice task B 1 or B 2.

B. PRACTICE TASK 1: Approach shot practice (see figure 7.4).

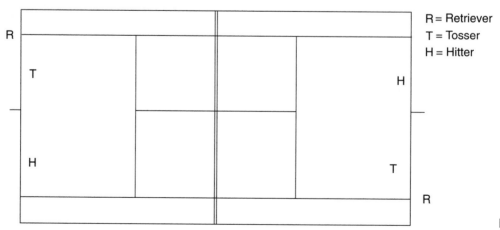

R = Retriever
T = Tosser
H = Hitter

Figure 7.4

Goals: Three to five trials and rotate.

Use half court or full court.

Conditions: Tosser feeds a short ground stroke ball (hits off the racquet). Hitter executes an approach shot and continues to net. Hitter then returns to the baseline to repeat practice task. This can be practiced as a triad (tosser-hitter-retriever).

Cues: Medium to low posture.

Approach ball side to net.

Racquet back.

Swing parallel.

Move to net.

PRACTICE TASK 2: Half-court technique practice.

Goal: Specific number to land in back court.

Conditions: One player feeds short ground strokes; one player hits approach shots. Switch roles.

C. GAME: Half-court singles game.

Goals: Move opponent.

Win the point.

Awareness of need to punish weak ground stroke.

Conditions: Play deuce games. One person serves for complete deuce game, long and narrow court. Can play the ball before it bounces after serve.

LESSON 5

TACTICAL PROBLEM: Winning the point.

LESSON FOCUS: Winning the point using the volley.

OBJECTIVE: Using a volley to win a point.

A. GAME: Half-court singles game.

Goals: Move opponent.

Win the point.

Awareness of need to punish weak ground stroke.

Conditions: Play deuce games. One person serves for complete deuce game, long and narrow court. Can play the ball before it bounces after serve.

Questions

Q: What shot would you use if you keep moving toward the net?

A: Volley.

Q: What did you do to play the ball before it bounces?

A: Move closer to the net, to front court.

Note: You can choose to use the following practice task B 1 or B 2.

B. PRACTICE TASK 1: Volley technique practice (see figure 7.5).

Goals: Three to five trials and rotate.

Use half court or full court.

Conditions: One player feeds (either a toss or off the racquet). One player hits volley. Repeat three times by practicing forehand, backhand, and mixing both. This can be practiced as a triad.

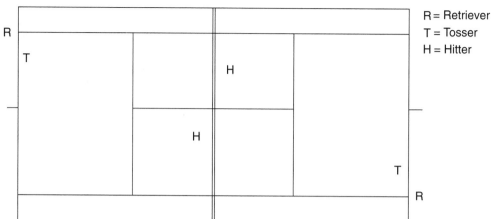

R = Retriever
T = Tosser
H = Hitter

Figure 7.5

Cues: Make yourself light (weight on balls of feet).

Short backswing.

Turn side to net.

Reach forward to hit.

Recover.

PRACTICE TASK 2: Half-court technique practice.

Goal: Specific number to land in back court.

Conditions: One player feeds ground strokes to front court or net. One player hits volley (backhand and forehand).

C. GAME: Half-court singles game.

Goals: Move opponent.

Win the point.

Awareness of need to punish weak ground stroke.

Conditions: Play deuce games. One person serves for complete deuce game, long and narrow court. Can play the ball before it bounces after serve.

LESSON 6

TACTICAL PROBLEM: Defending space on your own court.

LESSON FOCUS: Recovery to center baseline.

OBJECTIVE: Recovering to center baseline between shots.

A. GAME: Half-court singles game.

Goals: Move opponent.

Awareness of the need to recover to center court.

Conditions: Alternate service. Bounce-hit serve, long and narrow court.

Question

Q: Where should you go between your shots?

A: Back to the center of the baseline.

B. PRACTICE TASK: Full-court singles minitournament.

Goal: Recover to center baseline between shots.

Conditions: One coach per player or court. Bounce-hit serve, no-ad scoring (four-point games). Change roles after each game.

C. GAME: Continue minitournament.

LESSON 7

TACTICAL PROBLEM: Defending as a pair.

LESSON FOCUS: Two-back formation.

OBJECTIVE: Using a two-back formation in doubles.

A. GAME: Full-court doubles.

   Goal: Two-back formation.

   Conditions: Bounce-hit serve, each person serves two points.

   Questions

   Q: Do you have more time to see the open court standing in the back or front court?

   A: Back court, baseline.

   Q: If a shot comes down the middle what do you and your partner have to do?

   A: Communicate, talk.

B. PRACTICE TASK: Full-court doubles practice.

   Goal: Awareness of doubles positions and responsibilities.

   Conditions: Each person serves two bounce-hit serves. Play points to completion.

C. GAME: Doubles game.

   Goal: Two-back formation.

   Conditions: Bounce-hit serve, each person serves full game. No-ad scoring (four-point game).

LEVEL II

Level II continues to develop your students' abilities to create and defend space. You can introduce shots such as the crosscourt or down-the-line ground stroke, and an offensive lob. Students should also begin serving. As in all net games, players can win points by moving the opponent around the court until they cannot reach the next shot. Nonetheless, this solution will have limitations as opponent's tactical awareness and ability improve, so at this level students will explore winning a point. After your students have practiced the volley, approach shot, and smash their awareness for the need to defend against these attacks will increase.

Level II Lessons

LESSON 1

TACTICAL PROBLEM: Setting up to attack by creating space in opponent's court.

LESSON FOCUS: Starting the point on the attack.

OBJECTIVE: Use the flat service to put opponent on the defensive at the start of a point.

A. GAME: Half-court singles game.

   Goal: Push opponent into back court with service.

Conditions: Alternate service. Push opponent back, long and narrow court.

Question

Q: Where is the best place to serve to put your opponent on the defensive?

A: Deep service court.

B. PRACTICE TASK 1: Toss practice.

Goals: Accurate toss into (near) racquet head.

Five to eight trials.

Conditions: Students stand along baseline. Place racquet butt next to front foot with racquet extended in front of student's body. Toss ball for serve so it lands in or near head of racquet on the court.

PRACTICE TASK 2: Half-court technique practice.

Goals: Serve deep and to opponent's backhand side.

Specific number (three or four) to land in back service court.

Condition: Alternate serving (no rallying).

Cues: Face net post.

Racquet behind head.

Toss up and forward.

Reach high.

Swing through.

C. GAME: Half-court singles game, same as in A.

LESSON 2

TACTICAL PROBLEM: Setting up to attack by creating space in opponent's court.

LESSON FOCUS: Ground stroke variations.

OBJECTIVE: Use crosscourt and down-the-line ground strokes.

A. GAME: Full-court singles game.

Goal: Awareness to vary ground strokes.

Conditions: Two serves per person, ground strokes only, move opponent around court.

Questions

Q: What do you do to move your opponent along the baseline?

A: Vary your ground strokes.

Q: What are the types of ground stroke placement?

A: Crosscourt or down the line.

B. PRACTICE TASK 1: Crosscourt and line practice (see figure 7.6).

Goals: Crosscourt and down-the-line ground stroke placement.

Specific number crosscourt and down the line.

Conditions: One player feeds to other player's forehand in the corner of the baseline; one player hits crosscourt. Switch roles; repeat task going down the line.

Cues: Step into shot.

Follow through to target.

Note: This task can also be accomplished using half-court singles.

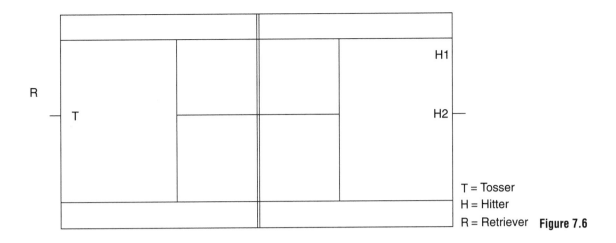

T = Tosser
H = Hitter
R = Retriever   **Figure 7.6**

PRACTICE TASK 2: Crosscourt and line practice (see figure 7.6).

Goals: Crosscourt and down-the-line ground stroke placement.

Specific number crosscourt and down the line.

Conditions: One player feeds to player in the corner of the baseline. Other player starts in the middle of the court and moves to hit crosscourt. Switch sides of the court. Switch roles. Repeat task going down the line.

C. GAME: Full-court singles game.

Goal: Use crosscourt or down-the-line placement to move opponent.

Conditions: Two serves per person, ground strokes only, move opponent around court.

LESSON 3

TACTICAL PROBLEM: Setting up to attack by creating space in opponent's court.

LESSON FOCUS: Lob shots for maintaining depth.

OBJECTIVE: Use lob (forehand and backhand) to keep opponent in back court.

A. GAME: Half- or full-court singles game.

Goal: Awareness for the need to develop lob shot.

Conditions: Play deuce games. One person serves for complete deuce game. Push opponent back.

Question

Q: What do you do to keep opponent back if you cannot use a ground stroke?

A: Open face of racquet and use a lob.

B. PRACTICE TASK: Half-court partner lob practice (see figure 7.7).

Goals: Clear to back court using lob.

Specific number to land deep to baseline (back court).

Conditions: One player feeds to back court. One player hits lobs back to feeder's court. Switch or alternate forehand, backhand, and lobs.

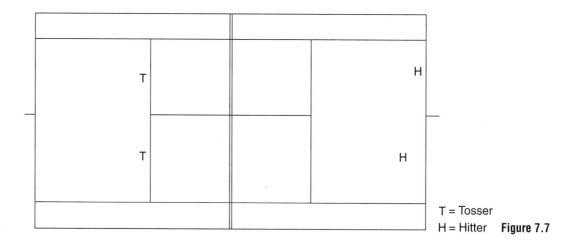

T = Tosser
H = Hitter   **Figure 7.7**

Cues: Full backswing.
Open face racquet.
Swing low to high.
Finish high.

C. GAME: Half- or full-court singles game, same as in A.

LESSON 4

TACTICAL PROBLEM: Winning the point.

LESSON FOCUS: Winning the point using an approach shot and volley.

OBJECTIVE: Approach shot to volley.

A. GAME: Half- or full-court singles game.
Goals: Move opponent.
Win the point.
Awareness of need to punish short ground stroke.
Conditions: Play no-ad score games; can play the ball before it bounces after serve.
Questions
Q: What did you have to do to a short ground stroke?
A: Move up to play the ball.
Q: After you move up is it easier to run back or keep moving toward the net?
A: Toward the net.
Q: What shot would you use if you kept moving toward the net?
A: Volley.
Q: Where should you place your volley?
A: In an open space, angles of the court, move your opponent.

B. PRACTICE TASK: Approach shot to volley practice (see figure 7.8).
Goals: Three to five trials and rotate.
Use half court or full court.
Conditions: Tosser will feed two balls (hits off-the-racquet). First ball is short ground stroke. Hitter executes an approach shot and continues to net for volley. Tosser hits another ground stroke for hitter to volley. This can be practiced in pairs or in a triad.

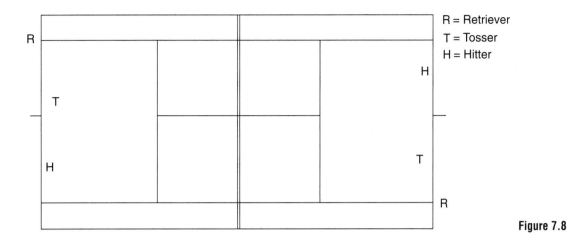

R = Retriever
T = Tosser
H = Hitter

Figure 7.8

Note: This task can be extended to include forehand and backhand of both approach shot and volley.

C. GAME: Half- or full-court singles game, same as in A.

LESSON 5

TACTICAL PROBLEM: Winning the point.

LESSON FOCUS: Winning the point using the smash.

OBJECTIVE: Using the smash to win a point.

A. GAME: Half- or full-court singles game.

    Goals: Move opponent.

        Win the point.

        Awareness of need to punish weak lob.

    Conditions: Play deuce games. Can play the ball before it bounces after serve.

    Questions

    Q: What is the best way to make a shot unreturnable?

    A: Hit it hard and straight to the ground—smash.

    Q: Where can you smash from on your own court?

    A: Front or middle of your court.

    Q: What kind of shot are you looking for from your opponent?

    A: Weak lob.

    Q: Where should you place your smash?

    A: In an open space, angles of the court, move your opponent.

B. PRACTICE TASK: Half-court partner practice.

    Cues: Prepare as serve.

        Point to ball.

        Reach high, hit down.

        Finish swing after contact.

    Goal: Ball hits court angle and deep.

    Conditions: One feeds high ground strokes to midcourt; partner smashes.

C. GAME: Half- or full-court singles as in A.

    Condition: Competitive no-ad score game.

LESSON 6

TACTICAL PROBLEM: Defending against an attack.

LESSON FOCUS: Returning the smash.

OBJECTIVE: Returning the smash with success (i.e., not providing a second attacking opportunity for opponent).

A. GAME: Half- or full-court singles game.

    Goals: Win point with a volley or smash if possible.

        Awareness of need to return the smash without setting up an easy winner by opponent.

    Conditions: Play no-ad score games (four points). One person serves for complete game, playable serve (no-ace rule).

    Question

    Q: How can you return a volley or smash without setting up your opponent for another smash?

    A: With a defensive lob.

B. PRACTICE TASK: Half-court partner practice.

    Goals: Specific number of trials.

        Practice both shots.

    Condition 1: One player feeds with high ground stroke to midcourt; partner smashes. Continue point; player executes defensive lob.

    Condition 2: One player feeds with ground stroke; partner volleys. Continue point; player executes defensive lob.

    Cues: Short backswing.

        Open face.

        Swing low to high.

        Finish high.

C. GAME: Half- or full-court singles, same as in A.

LESSON 7

TACTICAL PROBLEM: Attacking as a pair.

LESSON FOCUS: Up and back formation.

OBJECTIVE: Using up and back formation in doubles.

A. GAME: Full-court doubles.

    Goal: Up and back formation.

    Conditions: Flat serve, each person serves two points.

    Questions

    Q: What are the roles and responsibilities of the back player?

    A: Serve, serve receive, ground strokes, all shots the up person does not take.

    Q: What are the roles and responsibilities of the up player?

    A: Net play, communication.

B. PRACTICE TASK: Full-court doubles practice.

   Goal: Awareness of doubles roles and responsibilities.

   Conditions: Each person serves two bounce-hit serves; play points to completion.

C. GAME: Doubles game.

   Goal: Up and back formation.

   Conditions: Flat serve, each person serves full game. No-ad scoring (four-point game).

LEVEL III

Tactical complexity level III will shift you from a primarily half-court singles game to a more tactically complex doubles game. Students will have the opportunity to challenge themselves by discovering more advanced ways of winning the point and defending against attack. The final phase of level III is to solve the tactical problems presented by the doubles game (attacking and defending as a pair). Once again, questions guide students to solutions they practice in game situations.

Level III Lessons

LESSON 1

TACTICAL PROBLEM: Winning the point.

LESSON FOCUS: Attacking the short serve.

OBJECTIVE: Punishing a weak, short serve.

A. GAME: Half- or full-court singles game.

   Goal: Awareness of attacking opportunity if serve is short.

   Conditions: Each point starts with a short serve; play deuce game.

   Questions

   Q: How can you attack a short serve?

   A: Passing shot down-the-line or crosscourt shot.

   Q: What should you do after attacking a short serve?

   A: Move to the net.

B. PRACTICE TASK: Half-court partner practice.

   Cue: Same as ground stroke.

   Goal: Attack the serve and put opponent on the defensive.

   Conditions: One player feeds short serves from service line; partner attacks the serve. Specific number of successful returns.

C. GAME: Half- or full-court singles game.

   Goal: Awareness of attacking opportunity if serve is short.

   Conditions: Each point starts with a short serve; play deuce games.

LESSON 2

TACTICAL PROBLEM: Winning the point.

LESSON FOCUS: The *attacking* drop shot.

OBJECTIVE: To play an effective, fast, attacking drop shot.

A. GAME: Half- or full-court singles game.

Goal: Awareness of need to play a drop shot that will reach the ground quickly.

Conditions: A player cannot play two consecutive volleys; play deuce games.

Question

Q: What else can you do besides the volley to get the tennis ball to the floor quickly?

A: Faster, attacking drop shot.

B. PRACTICE TASK: Half-court partner practice.

Goals: Fast attacking drop shot.

    Specific number of shots to land inside service court.

Conditions: One player feeds ground stroke to midcourt; partner plays drop shots into front court.

Cues: Drop shot.

    Disguise the shot.

    Open face.

    Swing high to low.

C. GAME: Half- or full-court singles game.

Goal: Awareness of need to play a drop shot that will reach the ground quickly.

Conditions: A player cannot play two consecutive volleys, no-ad scoring game.

LESSON 3

TACTICAL PROBLEM: Defending against an attack.

LESSON FOCUS: Returning the attacking drop shot.

OBJECTIVE: Return the drop shot without giving an attacking opportunity to an opponent.

A. GAME: Half- or full-court singles game.

Goals: Proficient drop shots.

    Awareness of need to return drop shot in attacking manner.

Conditions: No volley or smashes; play deuce games.

Question

Q: How can you return the drop shot? Remember you don't want to give an easy volley to your opponent.

A: Passing shot on the run, either cross court or down-the-line.

B. PRACTICE TASK: Half- or full-court partner practice.

Goal: Passing shot return.

Conditions: In pairs; one player feeds drop shots to the other, who attempts a passing shot; 4-6 trials then switch roles.

Cues: Keep ball low.

    Out of reach of opponent at net.

C. GAME: Half- or full-court singles game.

> **Goals:** Proficient drop shots.
>
> > Awareness of need to return drop shot in attacking manner.
>
> **Conditions:** No volley or smashes, no-ad scoring game.

LESSON 4

TACTICAL PROBLEM: Attacking as a pair.

LESSON FOCUS: Side-to-side offense.

OBJECTIVE: Attacking in a side-to-side formation.

A. GAME: Full-court doubles game.

> **Goal:** Recognition of most effective attacking formation (both up, both back).
>
> **Conditions:** Alternate formations between up and back, both up and both back; play no-ad scoring games.
>
> **Question**
>
> *Q: What formation (both up, both back, or up and back) will give you the best chance to attack your opponents with a volley or a smash, particularly if you are serving?*
>
> A: Both up.

B. PRACTICE TASK: Full-court doubles.

> **Cues:** Server keeps serve wide and follows in to the net with racquet up.
>
> > Partner sets up at the net protecting the alley.
>
> **Goal:** Keep serve low and attack the return.
>
> **Conditions:** Alternate serving on every point. Use low serve and follow to the net.

C. GAME: Competitive doubles game.

> **Goal:** Attack where possible (both up).
>
> **Condition:** Regulation game.

LESSON 5

TACTICAL PROBLEM: Attacking as a pair when serving.

LESSON FOCUS: Setting up a winning volley (the poach).

OBJECTIVE: Attacking in a two-up formation.

A. GAME: Full-court doubles game.

> **Goal:** Setting up a winning volley.
>
> **Conditions:** Two up or up and back formation, play no-ad scoring games.
>
> **Questions**
>
> *Q: What type of serve will set up a volley for your partner?*
>
> A: Wide, deep serve.
>
> *Q: What is the responsibility of the player at the net?*

A: Poach: hit a winning volley.

Q: How do you do this?

A: Anticipate, be ready, footwork, racquet up, volley use angles.

B. PRACTICE TASK: Full-court doubles.

Goal: Hitting a winning volley.

Conditions: Team A serves to team B six to eight serves; serve wide. Set up net player to poach; switch roles.

C. GAME: Competitive doubles game.

Goal: Attack where possible.

Condition: Regulation game.

LESSON 6

TACTICAL PROBLEM: Defending as a pair against a serve.

LESSON FOCUS: Serve receive tactics.

OBJECTIVE: Effective defense against the serve in doubles.

A. GAME: Full-court doubles.

Goal: Focus on service receive tactics.

Condition: Two serves per person.

Question

Q: What are the possible serve receive tactics in doubles?

A: 1. Return ball to the feet of the net player or advancing server.

    2. Pass the net player.

    3. Lob the net player.

    4. Hit crosscourt angled toward the server.

B. PRACTICE TASK: Full-court doubles.

Goal: Attempt each serve receive tactic.

Conditions: Doubles team A alternates serves to doubles team B. Rotate after six to eight serves. Do not play points to completion.

C. GAME: Full-court doubles.

Goal: Focus on service receive tactics.

Condition: No-ad scoring.

SUMMARY

We advocate tournament play to challenge your students' tactical awareness and problem-solving skills. You can arrange scoring in tournaments by the tactical problems taught, game forms played, or ability groups. Here are three illustrations to guide you. First, if your unit focus was to solve the tactical problem of setting up to attack, you may limit tournament play to using ground strokes (i.e., forehand, backhand, crosscourt, down the line). Second, you can choose the game form you or your students use throughout the tournament, such as half-court singles, no-ad scoring, or deuce games. Third, students can self-select into ability group tournaments (e.g., rookie, recreation, and all-pro leagues).

Team tennis is another tournament option. Ideally team tennis involves teams of eight players. Each team will organize players to play a male and a female doubles team, mixed doubles team, male and female singles. Each contest would be a six-game set using a no-ad scoring rule. We encourage you to modify team tennis to meet the needs of your situation.

This chapter provides you with a scheme for teaching tennis using a tactical approach. We want you to make it yours! This may mean modifications to the lessons provided. The following are possible ways to modify lessons and units.

1. Use court rotations. If you have limited court space you can rotate students on and off half-court singles, full-court singles, and doubles games.

2. Use stations. A great change of pace is to organize stations. Stations could focus on specific skills and movements as well as a tournament play station.

3. Use student choice. Students may choose to focus on either singles or doubles only. You can accomplish this by mixing singles or doubles practice throughout the unit but still focusing on tactical problems.

4. Use coaches or statisticians. If you have few courts you may want to have students involved in roles such as coach or statistician. This can be helpful when assessing game performance.

Remember to focus on limited tactical problems in your unit. In other words do a few things well and work to keep the *game* in tennis!

CHAPTER 8

Softball

Softball is generally taught in upper elementary through high school curriculums. At the secondary level, softball tends to be the last unit of the school year and often serves as more of a recreational activity than a series of instructional lessons. This is perhaps as much because of the nature of the game as the nature of the teacher at the end of a school year. As a game, softball does not lend itself to an instructional setting. The 10 v 10 game provides few opportunities for students to field or hit and run. Furthermore, the best players tend to dominate key positions (i.e., shortstop, pitcher, first base), with outfield positions filled with four or more players who can't or won't even run to a ball, let alone field it.

The tactical approach promotes small-sided (i.e., 3 v 3, 4 v 4, etc.) conditioned games, which allow students to focus on specific situations and the tactics required during those situations, whether as a fielder or as a batter and base runner. Not only do small-sided games foster student involvement, they highlight what players should do and how to do it. Dividing the class into three or four small-sided games allows the teacher to individualize instruction, as the focus of each game can vary according to the level of students participating. Less experienced students can focus on fundamental skills and tactical problems. More experienced students can focus on complex skills and tactical problems they are likely to encounter as a function of their game-play ability.

The small-sided games require no more room than the regulation softball or baseball diamond and are best arranged in an open field. We have found the cloverleaf arrangement to be the most efficient method for managing three or four small-sided games of softball. First, lay out four playing areas in a cloverleaf, with the home plate areas at the center (see figure 8.1). Stagger the playing areas a bit to prevent overthrows from endangering players on adjacent fields. The center should allow a large enough area (safety zone) for students to safely stand as they wait their turn to bat. Safety rules are necessary and should include areas where students must stand while others are batting and rules about what batters should do with the bat after they hit the ball.

You can divide students into teams of 6, 8, 10, or 12, allowing small-sided games of 3 v 3, 4 v 4,

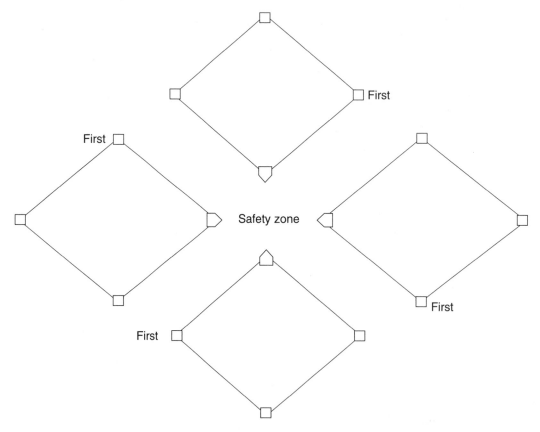

Figure 8.1 The cloverleaf arrangement is an efficient method for managing multiple softball games.

5 v 5, or 6 v 6 on each field. We have found it best to assign students to teams and fields for an entire unit, eliminating the need for organizing teams and fields daily. At the minimum, each team and field should have three softballs and one bat. If possible, at least half of the students should have gloves.

We present the framework of tactical problems, situations, movements, and associated skills in table 8.1 and the levels of tactical complexity in table 8.2. The lessons that follow serve only as examples and are not intended to encompass every detail of a lesson or every lesson of a unit.

LEVEL I

You can use kickball, T-ball, or softball to introduce level I tactics. We have found kickball appropriate for sixth graders, as many have not developed adequate skills in softball or baseball. This lack of skill development tends to prohibit students from fully exploring many fundamental tactical problems. If you use kickball to present level I tactics in sixth grade, you may want to use T-ball or softball in seventh grade to review level I tactics. Another option is to use level I lessons to teach kickball in fifth grade and T-ball in sixth grade, then use some level I and II lessons to introduce slow-pitch softball in seventh grade. Don't be afraid to use batting tees at any level. In our softball classes, many of the college students use batting tees during practices and games.

Tactics at level I focus on situations in which there are zero to two outs, no runners on base, grounder to the infield and zero to two outs, runner on first, grounder or line drive to the outfield. The tactics to prevent scoring in these situations include defending space by infield position, defending space by outfield position, and defending bases, specifically first and second. The tactics related to scoring include getting on base and advancing to the next base, specifically first to second base.

By the end of the unit, students should know the infield and outfield positions as well as the boundaries and features of the playing area. By solving tactical problems, students will understand what to do at infield and outfield positions when there are no runners or a runner on first, and how to cover first and second base on a force play. They will review catching skills as they field grounders, line drives, and fly balls as well as reviewing or refining throwing skills.

Offensively, students will review kicking or batting skills and refine these skills as they solve tactical problems related to getting on base when there are zero to two outs and no runners on base. The need to place the ball to the left side of the infield will motivate students to work on accuracy and placement. The need to hit and run will refine kicking and batting because this hit-and-run movement requires a fluid motion in the follow-through of the swing to the drive step toward first base. Base running is also a focus of level I tactics, and conditioned games and practices will help students understand when to run past or round first base as well as how to advance quickly and safely to second base.

Although not specifically the focus of a lesson, you can incorporate support play, which involves calling for the ball, signaling the number of outs, and backing up when teaching other elements of game play. As students are ready or as teachable moments arise, you can introduce or reinforce tactical problems through pinpointing, that is highlighting critical aspects of a skill, movement, or play.

In this chapter we use the term *practice situation* rather than *practice task*. In softball and baseball the situation (e.g., no outs, runner on first and one out, runners on first and second, ground ball to shortstop) is the essence of the game and prompts players about what to do, whether a fielder, batter, or base runner.

Table 8.1

Tactical Problems, Movements, and Skills in Softball

Tactical problems	Movements	Associated skills
Scoring (outs, runners)		

Getting on base
  0-2 outs, no runners
  0-2 outs, runner on second
  0-2 outs, runner on second
      or third
		Hitting to left side
		Grounders between
		  left infielders
		Line drives over
		  left, center
		  infield

Moving the runner
  0-2 outs, runner on first
  0-2 outs, runner on second
  0-2 outs, runner on second
      or third
	Delaying the throw
	Lead off to draw throw
		Place hitting
		Hitting between
		  right infielders
		Line drives over
		  right side of
		  infield

0-1 out, runner on first
  0-1 out, runner on second
  0-1 out, runner on second
      and third
		Sacrifice fly

0-2 outs, runners on first
      and second
  0-2 outs, bases loaded
		Hitting to outfield
		Line drives
		  between gaps

Advancing to next base From home to first		Step and drive Running past first Rounding first

From first to second
  From second to third
  From third to home
	Delaying the throw	Take-off or
		  starting position
		Sliding
		  • pop-up slide
		  • hook slide
		  • head first
		Rounding second, third

On a fly ball		Tagging up
Preventing scoring (outs, runners, ball placement)		

Defending bases on throw
from outfield
  0-1, on first, line drive or fly
  0-1, numerous situations
    where runner not forced
    to advance to next base
  0-2, runner caught between
    bases
		Base coverage
		
		Throwing from outfield
		  • to a cutoff
		  • to a base
		
		Rundowns

Defending space as a team
  0, no runners
  0-2, pull hitter
  0-2, right-handed batter
	Positioning
	• starting (base positions)
	• shift for pull hitter
	• shift for right-handed hitter	

Communicating	Calling the ball Informing fielding player of situation Signaling number of outs	

Table 8.2
Levels of Tactical Complexity for Softball

Tactical problems	Levels of tactical complexity			
	I	II	III	IV
Scoring				
Getting on base	Kick or hit grounders to infield Situation is 0-2 outs, no runner	Ball placement to get on first	Hit grounders left, center, right Hit line drives Situation is 0-2 outs, runner on second or third	Hit between infield and outfield positions
Moving the runner		Sacrifice fly Moving runner from first to second	Hitting behind the runner Situation is 0-2 outs, runner on first	Drawing a throw to advance lead runner Situation is runners on first and third
Advancing to next base	Run through first Rounding first	Running from first to second Tagging up	Running from first to third Breaking up double play	Slide, hook slide
Preventing scoring				
Defending space by infield, outfield position	Fielding grounders Fielding fly balls Situation is 0-2 outs, no runner	Throwing to a base from outfield Throwing to a relay Situation is 0-2 outs, runner on first or second 0-1 out, runner on third	Cutoff plays Situation is 0-2 outs, ball hit to outfield with one or more runners on base	
Defending bases	Base coverage on force play at first	Cutting lead runner	Second-first double play Rundowns	Third-first double play
Defending space as a team	Positioning straight away Back-ups	Shift for left, right hand		Positioning outfield to prevent run from scoring
Communicating	Call the ball Signal number of outs		Informing teammate of play	

Level I Lessons

LESSON 1

TACTICAL PROBLEM: Defending space by infield position.

LESSON FOCUS: Situation is zero outs, no runners on base, grounder to left side of infield.

OBJECTIVES: Field grounders from third base and shortstop positions.

Make an accurate throw to first base.

A. GAME: Zero-Zero, zero runners on base, zero outs.

Goals: Defensive team get runner out at first.

Offensive team get to first before throw.

Conditions: Number of players is 3 v 3 minimum, 6 v 6 maximum. Kicker or batter must kick or hit a ground ball to left side of the infield. (Ground ball is any ball that hits the ground before reaching an infielder, pitcher excluded.) Player scores a run by reaching first base safely. Inning is over after three runs or three outs, whichever comes first.

Questions

Q: What was the goal of the game for the team on offense?

A: Get to first before throw.

Q: What was the goal of the game for the team on defense?

A: Get runner out at first.

Q: Today we are going to focus on the defensive team's performance. How were you able to get the runner out at first?

A: Move feet to the ball; watch ball into glove. Catch ball; throw to first. Keep feet moving toward first.

B. PRACTICE SITUATION: Three players in the field (minimum), shortstop, third base, first base; three players kicking or hitting (the *battery*—pitcher, catcher, batter). Extra players serve as pitcher and catcher. From a ball rolled from pitcher's mound or batting tee, kicker or hitter kicks or hits grounder to left side of infield, then runs hard and fast to first. After fielding three balls from each position (third and shortstop), rotate to first base or into the battery. Fielding player always calls the ball. Nonfielding player always backs up fielding player.

Goals: Successfully field three balls in a row from third and from shortstop.

Throw batter out at first five of six times.

Cues: Feet to the ball.

Watch it in.

Catch and cover.

Recover to throw.

C. GAME: Repeat Zero-Zero game A.

LESSON 2

TACTICAL PROBLEMS: Defending space by infield position.

Defending first base.

LESSON FOCUS: Situation is zero outs, no runners on base, grounder to right infield.

OBJECTIVES: Field grounders from second base and first base positions.

Make an accurate throw to first base.

A. GAME: Zero-Zero, zero runners on base, zero outs.

Goals: Defensive team get runner out at first.

Offensive team get to first before throw.

Conditions: Number of players is 3 v 3 minimum, 6 v 6 maximum. Kicker or hitter must kick or hit a ground ball to right side of the infield. Player scores a run by reaching first base safely. Inning is over after three runs or three outs, whichever comes first.

Questions

Q: What was the goal of the game for the team on offense, defense?

A: Get to first ahead of throw; get runner out at first.

Q: Today we are going to focus on the defensive team's performance. What did you do to get the runner out at first?

A: Feet to the ball; watch ball into glove. Throw quickly to first.

Q: Were you successful? If not, let's practice.

B. PRACTICE SITUATION: Two players in the field (minimum), second base, first base, pitcher (optional); three players kicking or hitting (the battery). Extra players serve as catchers. From a ball rolled, pitched, or hit from tee, kicker or hitter kicks or hits grounder to right side of infield, then runs hard and fast to first. Field three balls from each position. Can also focus on footwork used to cover first base on a force play.

Goals: Successfully field three balls in a row from second and from first base.

Throw batter out at first five of six times.

Cues: Feet to the ball.

Watch it in.

Catch and cover.

Recover to throw.

C. GAME: Repeat Zero-Zero game A.

LESSON 3

TACTICAL PROBLEM: Getting on base.

LESSON FOCUS: Situation is zero to two outs, no runners on base.

OBJECTIVES: Kick or hit a grounder to the left side of the infield.

Kick or hit and run to first base.

Run to first as quickly as possible (running through or past first).

A. GAME: Gotta Get There.

Goal: Get on first base safely.

Conditions: 4 v 4 minimum, 5 v 5 optimum, 6 v 6 maximum. Defensive players play first base and as many other infield positions as possible. Kicker or hitter must kick or hit a ground ball to the infield and get to first before the throw. Player scores a run by reaching first base safely. Inning is over after three runs or three outs, whichever comes first.

Questions

Q: Where did you have to kick or hit the ball to get on first base?

A: Third baseline, left side of infield, close to third.

Q: So, when there are zero to two outs and no runners on, where would be the best place on the left side of the infield to kick the ball?

A: Third baseline.

Q: How did you run to get to first before the throw?

A: Fast, don't look at ball; run past first base.

B. PRACTICE SITUATION: Three players in the field (minimum), shortstop, third base, first base; three players kicking or hitting (the battery). Extra players serve as pitchers and catchers. From a ball rolled or thrown from pitcher's mound or a batting tee, kicker or batter kicks or hits grounder to left side of infield, then runs hard and fast over first, to a cone 20 feet past first on the first baseline. Kicker or batter will kick or hit and run five times, attempting to knock down cones (one big cone on third baseline 10 feet past third and the other cone just beyond but between the third base player and shortstop). After five kick-and-runs, the kicker replaces a defensive player. Defensive players make a play on every ball and attempt to throw runner out at first (all rules related to backups, calling the ball, etc., remain in effect).

Note: You may use three or four cones as targets, depending on ability of players.

Goals: Angle bat or approach to kick or hit toward third baseline or between third and short.

Run hard and fast through first base.

Cues: Kick or hit; step and drive.

Run hard.

Run through first base.

Don't watch the ball.

Adjust angle of approach (if kicking) or angle of bat (if batting) to kick or hit ball toward left field line.

C. GAME: Repeat Gotta Get There game A; match final score with score of previous game.

LESSON 4

TACTICAL PROBLEM: Defending space by outfield position.

LESSON FOCUS: Situation is zero to two outs, runner on first, ball hit to left side of outfield.

OBJECTIVES: Field grounders, line drives, and fly balls in outfield.

Back up adjacent outfielder.

Make an accurate throw to second base.

A. GAME: Movin' On Up.

Goals: Defensive team get runner out at second.

Offensive team move runner to second safely.

Conditions: Number of players is 4 v 4 minimum, 6 v 6 maximum; defensive players play left field, left center field, second base, and first base. Offensive team must have a runner on first at all times. Kicker or hitter must kick or hit ball to left side of outfield and run to first base. Balls kicked to the right of second base are considered outs. Player scores a run by reaching second base safely. Inning is over after three runs or three outs, whichever comes first.

Questions

Q: What was the goal of the game for the offensive team, defensive team?

A: Move runner to second safely; get runner out at second.

Q: Today we're going to focus on the defense. How were the defensive players, left fielder and left center fielder, able to get the ball to second base ahead of the runner?

A: Get to ball quickly and throw to second as quickly as possible.

Q: Why is it important for the outfielders to get the ball to the infield as quickly as possible?

A: To keep runners from advancing or scoring.

Q: What should the nonfielding outfielder do and why?

A: Back up player fielding the ball; be ready in case fielder misses ball to stop ball and get it to the infield as quickly as possible.

B. PRACTICE SITUATION: Four players on defense (minimum), left fielder, left center fielder, second base, first base; four players on offense, the battery and a base runner. Kicking or hitting a ball from pitcher, kick or hit to left side of outfield, then run hard and fast to first base. Runner on first advances to second, except on a fly ball caught by the left or left center fielder. After fielding three balls from each position (left and left center) rotate to second base, then to first or into battery. Fielding player calls the ball and nonfielding player offers backup.

Goals: Successfully field the ball and throw runner out at second base.

Perform proper backup on every play.

Cues: Feet to the ball.

Watch it in.

Catch and cover over throwing shoulder.

Recover and throw quickly.

Back up to get appropriate angle; pretend fielder isn't there or assume he will miss the ball.

C. GAME: Repeat Movin' On Up game A. Defense scores bonus run for every base runner thrown out at second base on a throw from an outfielder.

LESSON 5

TACTICAL PROBLEM: Defending space by outfield position.

LESSON FOCUS: Situation is zero to two outs, runner on first, ball hit to right side of outfield.

OBJECTIVES: Field grounders, line drives, and fly balls in outfield.

Back up adjacent outfielder.

Make an accurate throw to second base.

A. GAME: Movin' On Up.

Goals: Defensive team get runner out at second.

Offensive team move runner to second safely.

Conditions: Number of players is 4 v 4 minimum, 6 v 6 maximum; defensive players play right center field, right field, second base, and first base. Offensive team must have a runner on first at all times. Kicker or batter must kick or hit ball to right side of outfield and run to first base. Balls kicked or hit to the left of second base are considered outs. Player scores a run by reaching second base safely. Inning is over after three runs or three outs, whichever comes first.

Questions

Q: Today we're going to focus on the defense. How were the defensive players, right fielder and right center fielder, able to get the ball to second base ahead of the runner?

A: Field ball quickly and throw quickly to second base.

Q: How were you able to quickly catch and throw the ball?

A: Catch ball over throwing shoulder, running forward if possible.

Q: Why is it important to get the ball to the infield quickly?

A: Keep runners from advancing or scoring.

Q: What should the nonfielding outfielder do?

A: Back up player; field the ball or bases.

Q: What's the best angle to take when backing up the player fielding the ball?

A: Cut behind her so if she misses the ball you'll be in a position to catch it.

B. PRACTICE SITUATION: Four players on defense (minimum), right fielder, right center fielder, second base, first base; four players on offense, the battery and a base runner. Kicking or hitting ball from pitcher or from a tee, kick or hit to right side of outfield; then run hard and fast to first base. Runner on first advances to second, except on a fly ball caught by the right or right center fielder. After fielding three balls from each position (right and right center) rotate to second base, then to first, or into the battery. Fielding player calls the ball and nonfielding player offers backup.

Goal: Successfully field the ball and throw runner out at second base.

Cues: Feet to the ball.

Watch it in.

Catch and cover over throwing shoulder.

Recover and throw quickly.

Back up to get appropriate angle; pretend fielder isn't there or assume he will miss the ball.

C. GAME: Repeat Movin' On Up game A. Defense scores bonus run for every base runner thrown out at second base on a throw from an outfielder.

LESSON 6

TACTICAL PROBLEM: Defending bases on throw from outfield positions.

LESSON FOCUS: Situation is zero to two outs, runner on first, ball hit to outfield.

OBJECTIVE: Demonstrate proper positioning and footwork when covering second base on a throw from the outfield.

A. GAME: Movin' On Up.

Goals: Defensive team get runner out at second.

Offensive team move runner to second safely.

Conditions: Number of players is 5 v 5 minimum, 6 v 6 maximum; defensive players play all four outfield positions, second base, and shortstop. Offensive team must have a runner on first at all times. Kicker or batter must kick or hit ball to right side of outfield and run to first base. Balls kicked to the left of second base are considered outs. Player scores a run by reaching second base safely. Inning is over after three runs or three outs, whichever comes first.

Questions

Q: When the ball is hit to the left side of the outfield, which infielder covers second?

A: Second base player.

Q: When the ball is hit to the right side of the outfield, which infielder covers second?

A: Shortstop.

Q: What part of the base should you tag with your foot?

A: Outside edge closest to person throwing ball.

Q: Why?

A: Keep from interfering with the runner.

B. PRACTICE SITUATION: Six players on defense (minimum), left fielder, left center fielder, right fielder, right center fielder, second base, shortstop; six players on offense, the battery and a base runner. Kicking or hitting a ball from pitcher, kicker or batter kicks or hits to the outfield, then runs hard and fast to first base. Runner on first advances to second, except on a fly ball caught by the right or right center fielder. Runner can tag up on a fly ball. After catching three balls from each position (second base and shortstop) thrown by an outfielder, rotate to the battery; then from the battery, rotate to second base or shortstop. Players use speed of incoming runner and position of incoming throw to adjust their foot position when covering second base.

Goals: Keep runner from advancing to second base.

Appropriate player (second base player) covers second.

Cover second using proper footwork and outside edge of base.

Cues: Give them a target.

Foot on edge closest to the incoming throw.

Use incoming runner and incoming throw to adjust position used to cover second base.

Catching the ball is first priority.

C. GAME: Repeat Movin' On Up game A. Defense scores a bonus run when they throw base runner out at second base.

LESSON 7

TACTICAL PROBLEM: Advancing to second base.

LESSON FOCUS: Situation is zero to two outs, runner on first, ball hit to outfield.

OBJECTIVES: Take off from first at appropriate time; run to second base and execute proper stop.

Tag up and run to second base on a fly ball to outfield.

A. GAME: Movin' On Up.

Goals: Defensive team get runner out at second.

Offensive team move runner to second safely.

Conditions: Number of players is 5 v 5 minimum, 6 v 6 maximum; defensive players play all four outfield positions, second base, and shortstop. Offensive team must have a runner on first at all times. Kicker or hitter must kick or hit ball to right side of outfield and run to first base. Balls kicked or hit to the left of second base are considered outs. Player scores a run by reaching second base safely. Inning is over after three runs or three outs, whichever comes first.

Questions

Q: As a runner, when should you leave first base?

A: When batter steps.

Q: How should you stop at second base?

A: Slide; lean backward as you approach; hang on to base with foot.

Q: Can the runner on first advance to second on a fly ball to the outfield?

A: Yes, but must tag up.

Q: What should the runner do to tag up?

A: Wait until fielder touches the ball; then run as fast as possible to next base.

Q: What if she is unable to make it to the next base; does the runner have to run?

A: No. Runner does not have to advance if less than two outs.

B. PRACTICE SITUATION: Six players on defense (minimum), left fielder, left center fielder, right fielder, right center fielder, second base, shortstop; six players on offense, battery and a base runner. Kicking or hitting a ball from pitcher or from tee, kicker or batter kicks or hits to the outfield, then runs hard and fast to first base. Runner on first advances to second, except on a fly ball caught by the right or right center fielder. Runner can tag up on a fly ball. Kicker or batter kicks or hits and runs to first three times. The base runner runs from first to second three times (the kicker or hitter should attempt to kick or hit at least one fly ball so the runner can practice tagging up). After running, the player should rotate to an infield position, then from an infield position to an outfield position.

Goals: Runner *take off* as soon as any defensive player touches the ball.

Fielders try not to let ball touch the ground.

Get to ball as quickly as possible; then keep runner at first base.

Cues: Ready position.

Take off (or step off) on batter's step.

Watch the ball through the infield.

Fly; go when ball contacts glove of any offensive player.

Run hard, prepare to slide.

C. GAME: Repeat Movin' On Up game A. Defense scores bonus run when base runner thrown out at second base.

LEVEL II

Students that have had level I or previous playing experience, such as on a recreational team, should be ready for level II lessons. Most of the lessons in level II focus on the situation with zero to one out and a runner on first base. This allows defenders to focus on force plays at second base, including plays from outfield throws and double plays, second to first. Many of these plays require what we call *crossover* play. In crossover play the shortstop covers second base when ball is hit to right side of the infield or outfield. The second base player covers second base when balls are hit to the left side of the infield or outfield. We also introduce relays during level II lessons and focus on when to use a relay, how to perform a relay, and how to line up a relay.

In level II lessons, students solve the problem of where to hit the ball to get on base or to advance the runners. The zero to one out, runner on first base situation provides opportunities for students to learn about base running, specifically how to hit and run to first and advance from first to second quickly and safely.

Level II Lessons

LESSON 1

TACTICAL PROBLEM: Getting on base.

LESSON FOCUS: Situation is zero to two outs, no runners on base, grounder to left infield.

OBJECTIVES: Hit a ground ball to the left side of the infield.

Hit and run hard to first base.

A. GAME: First Things First.

Goals: Offensive batter focus on placing ball to an area of the field that would allow him to get on first base.

Defense throw ball to first, ahead of the runner.

Conditions: 4 v 4 minimum, 5 v 5 optimum, 6 v 6 maximum; defensive players play first, second, third, and shortstop. Batter must hit a ground ball to the infield and get to first before the throw. Player scores a run by reaching first base safely. Inning is over after three runs or three outs, whichever comes first.

Questions

Q: When there are zero to two outs and no runners on, where would be the best place to hit the ball?

A: Left side of infield, down third baseline.

Q: Why?

A: Longer throw, more likely to get to first safely.

Q: How did you have to run to get to first before the throw?

A: Fast, don't look at ball.

B. PRACTICE SITUATION: Cones placed on left field line (three or four abreast), between third and shortstop positions, and between shortstop and second base. Hitting from a batting tee or pitch, batter attempts to hit cones. Batter gets five tries. Batter runs to first following fifth attempt. Remaining players field at third, shortstop, and first base; others can back up infielders from outfield positions. Remaining players can practice running to first base as the batter hits the first four of her five attempts.

Goals: Angle bat or approach to hit toward third baseline or between third and short.

Hit and run *hard.*

Cues: Normal to open stance.

Contact in the power zone.

Bat angled toward target.

Follow through target.

C. GAME: Repeat First Things First game A. Defensive team scores bonus run for every base runner thrown out at first base by third base and shortstop.

LESSON 2

TACTICAL PROBLEMS: Advancing to the next base (second).

Defending bases (second).

LESSON FOCUS: Situation is zero to one out, runner on first, grounder to left infield.

OBJECTIVES: Run from first to second base.

Coverage of second by second base player.

A. Game: Double Up.

Goals: Offensive team get runners to first and second safely.

Defensive team turn a double play.

Conditions: Number of players is 3 v 3 minimum, 6 v 6 maximum. Batter must hit a ground ball to left side of the infield. Player scores a run by reaching first base safely. Inning is over after three runs or three outs, whichever comes first.

Questions

Q: *Who covered second base when the shortstop or third base player fielded the ball?*

A: Second base player.

Q: *Why?*

A: Shortstop may be making a play on ball. Second base player is in better position to make double play.

Q: *How did the second base player cover second base when the ball was fielded in front of the base path?*

A: Inside pivot, moves to inside edge of base, then steps with left foot (pivots) to make throw to first base.

Q: *How did second base player cover second base when ball was fielded behind the base path?*

A: Outside crossover, moves to outside edge of base, then crosses feet on throw to first.

Q: *What if there is a chance that the runner will interfere?*

A: Second base player should use a *rocker step,* steps on base then pushes off, away from base to make throw.

B. PRACTICE SITUATION: Ball hit to left side of infield, play at second base. Second base player covers second base. Additional players serve as base runners. Offense should always have a runner on first base. Runners practice proper base running techniques.

Goals: Use proper footwork when covering second.

Turn the double play.

Cues: Time approach to second.

Adjust to position of ball, incoming throw, and incoming runner.

Crossover if coming from behind base.

Inside pivot if covering inside base.

Rocker step if there is no need to cross base.

Catch ball first, get sure out.

C. GAME: Repeat Double Up game A. Defensive team scores three bonus runs for every double play turned by second base player.

LESSON 3

TACTICAL PROBLEMS: Advancing to the next base (second).

Defending bases (second).

LESSON FOCUS: Situation is zero to one out, runner on first, grounder to right infield.

OBJECTIVES: Run from first to second base.

Cover second from shortstop position.

A. GAME: Double Up.

Goals: Offensive team get runners to first and second safely.

Defensive team turn a double play.

Conditions: Number of players is 3 v 3 minimum, 6 v 6 maximum; batter must hit a ground ball to right side of the infield. Player scores a run by reaching first base safely. Inning is over after three runs or three outs, whichever comes first.

Questions

Q: Who covered second base when the first or second base player fielded the ball?

A: Shortstop.

Q: How did the shortstop cover second base when the ball was fielded in front of the base path (path from first to second)?

A: Inside crossover, came toward base and touched base while catching throw, then used crossover step to throw to first.

Q: How did the shortstop cover second base when the ball was behind the base path?

A: Outside crossover, crossed over base and touched base while catching throw, then used crossover step to throw to first.

B. PRACTICE SITUATION: Ball hit to right side of infield. Play at second base; shortstop base player covers second base. Additional players serve as base runners. Offense should always have a runner on first base. Runners practice proper base running techniques.

Goals: Use proper footwork to cover second.

Turn the double play.

Cues: Move quickly to cover bag.

Tag bag with left foot.

Plant right and pivot.

Keep feet moving to first after throw.

Tag left, step right, and pivot.

Adjust to position of ball, incoming throw, and incoming runner.

C. GAME: Repeat Double Up game A. Defensive team scores three bonus runs for double play turned by shortstop.

LESSON 4

TACTICAL PROBLEMS: Moving the runner.

Defending space by outfield positions.

LESSON FOCUS: Situation is zero to one out, runner on first, fly ball to outfield.

OBJECTIVES: Batter hit a fly ball to the outfield.

Fielder field a fly ball and throw to second quickly.

Base runner tag up and run from first to second.

A. GAME: Fly Bye.

Goals: Offensive players

Batter hit long fly ball to an outfield area most likely to allow the runner to advance to second.

Runner tag up on the catch and run as quickly as possible to second base.

Defensive players

Catch the ball on the fly and make a throw to second ahead of the runner tagging up from first.

Conditions: Number of players is 6 v 6 minimum. Defensive players play all four outfield positions plus shortstop and second base. Offensive team starts with a runner on first. Batter must hit a ball out of the infield (cannot touch the ground in front of the base path). Runner scores when he reaches second safely. Inning is over after three runs or three outs, whichever comes first.

Questions

Q: When would be the best time to hit a fly ball?

A: When there are fewer than two outs and you want to move or score runner.

Q: How did you have to swing the bat to hit a fly ball?

A: Hard and fast, hit through center of ball and follow through up.

Q: What is the best way to field a fly ball so you can make a quick throw?

A: Catch ball over throwing shoulder.

Q: On a fly ball, when can the runner advance to second?

A: When a fielder touches the ball.

Q: When should the runner leave the base?

A: As soon as a defensive player touches the ball.

B. PRACTICE SITUATION: Batter hits fly balls to outfield, with runner on first base. Each batter attempts to hit five fly balls, then rotates. Runner must tag up and run on a fly ball to provide a throwing situation for outfielders. Students may have to move up in the infield so they can hit a fly ball to the outfield.

Goal: Reach second base safely after tagging up on a fly ball hit to the outfield.

Cues: Hitting a fly ball

Hit through center of ball.

Follow through toward outfield.

Throw from outfield

Catch over throwing shoulder.

Recover and throw immediately.

Tagging up

Ready position.

Listen for coach to go.

Run hard.

C. GAME: Repeat Fly Bye game A. Defensive team scores one bonus run for putout at second base on throw from outfielder.

LESSON 5

TACTICAL PROBLEM: Defending bases.

LESSON FOCUS: Situation is zero to one out, runner on first, grounder or line drive to outfield.

OBJECTIVE: Proper coverage of second base when ball hit to left side and right side of outfield.

A. GAME: Fly Bye.

Goal: Defensive players have the appropriate player cover second base on a ball hit to the outfield.

Conditions: 6 v 6 minimum; defensive players play all four outfield positions plus shortstop and second base. Offensive team starts with a runner on first. Batter must hit a ball out of the infield (cannot touch the ground in front of the base path). Runner scores when she reaches second safely. Inning is over after three runs or three outs, whichever comes first.

Questions

Q: What was the goal of the game?

A: Have appropriate player cover second base on hit to outfield.

Q: Which infield player should cover second base on a hit to the left side of the infield?

A: Second base player.

Q: Which infield player should cover second base on a hit to the right side of the infield?

A: The shortstop.

Q: Which infield player should cover second base on a hit from center field?

A: Shortstop.

Q: Why?

A: They will be moving for a possible play on the ball and opposite player will be off the ball, allowing them to easily cover second base.

B. PRACTICE SITUATION: 3 v 3 to 8 v 8; use two to four outfielders, shortstop, and second base player. Batter hits or throws fly balls to outfield, three left, three right. Extra players run from first to second. Review proper footwork for base coverage on throw from outfield.

Goals: Shortstop covers second on ball hit to right side of outfield.

Second base player covers second on ball hit to left side of the outfield.

Cues: Shortstop covers when ball hit right.

Second base player covers when ball hit left.

C. GAME: Repeat Fly Bye game A. Defensive team scores bonus run for a putout at second base on throw from outfielder if appropriate player is covering second.

LESSON 6

TACTICAL PROBLEM: Defending bases.

LESSON FOCUS: Situation is zero to one out, runner on first, long ball to outfield.

OBJECTIVE: Use cutoff to get ball to infield from the outfield.

A. GAME: Rubber Band.

Goal: Use cutoff to get ball to the infield from the outfield.

Conditions: Number of players is 6 v 6 minimum. Defensive players play all four outfield positions plus shortstop and second base. Offensive team starts with a runner on first. Batter must hit a ball out of the infield (cannot touch the ground in front of the base path). Runner scores when he gets to second and or third safely. Inning is over after three runs or three outs, whichever comes first.

Questions

Q: When should a shortstop or second base player move out toward the fielding outfielder to cut ball off?

A: When runners have already advanced and you need to keep them from running to next base.

Q: Which player is responsible for cutoff when ball hit to left?

A: Shortstop.

Q: Which player is responsible for cutoff when ball is hit to right?

A: Second base player.

Q: What should the other infielders be doing while cutoff is being taken?

A: Cover bases (except pitcher).

Let's practice using a cutoff player to keep runners from advancing.

B. PRACTICE SITUATION: Use two or three outfielders, shortstop, second, third, and first base players. Extra players run from first base. Batter attempts six hits to outfield. Runners advancing to second safely, stay and advance to third on next hit. Runners must continue running until cutoff player throws ball to a base. Outfielders throw to cutoff. Cutoff player is only player who can throw a player out at a base.

Goals: Do not let runners score.

Throw to keep lead runner from advancing.

C. GAME: Repeat Rubber Band game. Defensive team scores a bonus run every time they keep a runner from advancing to third base.

LESSON 7

TACTICAL PROBLEM: Defending bases.

LESSON FOCUS: Situation is zero to one out, runner on first, long ball to outfield.

OBJECTIVE: Use relay to get ball to infield from the outfield.

A. GAME: Rubber Band.

Goal: Use relay from shortstop or second base player to get runners out at bases.

Conditions: Number of players is 6 v 6 minimum. Defensive players play all four outfield positions plus shortstop and second base. Offensive team starts with a runner on first. Batter must hit a ball out of the infield (cannot touch the ground in front of the base path). Runner scores when she gets to second and or third safely. Inning is over after three runs or three outs, whichever comes first.

Questions

Q: What is the difference between a cutoff and a relay?

A: Cutoff is used to stop runners; relay is used to get ball in quickly and possibly make play at a base.

Q: How does the shortstop or second base player know where to stand to set up the relay?

A: Player covering the base (or pitcher) should tell him to move left or move right to help him adjust position.

Q: Should you throw the ball to the relay the same as to a cutoff and why?

A: Yes, if throw is or will be late and she needs to cut the ball to hold runners.

Q: How will she know whether to cut or relay the ball?

A: Player covering the base (or pitcher) should call, "Cut!"

B. PRACTICE SITUATION: Students in threes stand about 10 to 15 yards apart. Middle player practices receiving throw and pivoting to throw to other player. End players practice receiving throw over throwing shoulder and throwing quickly and accurately to pivot player.

Goal: Relay as quickly as possible from one player to another (compete with another group of three players).

Cues: Catch and cover over throwing shoulder.

Pivot left on right foot (right dominant).

See target (glove).

Step and throw *through* target.

C. GAME: Repeat Rubber Band game. Defensive team scores a bonus run every time they keep a runner from advancing to third base.

LEVEL III

Tactical complexity advances in level III lessons by increasing the complexity of conditioned games. This requires players to use more refined skills and tactics. Offensively, students need to work on situations that require a batter to place the ball (e.g., down the right field line, between infielders, and down the left field line) to get himself on base and to advance runners. Use situations with a runner on second to provide players opportunities to advance runners into scoring position, practice looking back the runner, and covering third base. We provide a few examples of these types of lessons in the next section.

Level III Lessons

LESSON 1

TACTICAL PROBLEM: Defending space by infield position.

LESSON FOCUS: Situation is zero to two outs, no runners, grounder to infield.

OBJECTIVES: Determine best place to hit ball in this situation.

Hit and run hard to first; understand when to run through or round first base.

A. GAME: Gotta Get There.

Goal: Given the situation zero to two outs, no runners on base, runner should advance to as many bases possible.

Conditions: 4 v 4 minimum, 5 v 5 optimum, 6 v 6 maximum. Batter must hit a ground ball. Runs scored for each base reached safely following the initial hit. Inning is over after three runs or three outs, whichever comes first.

Questions

Q: How did you run to first when there was absolutely no chance of advancing to second?

A: Ran hard and fast, through or over first base.

Q: How did you run to first when there was a possibility of advancing to second base?

A: Rounded base and observed position of ball (or listened to coach).

Q: What would be the advantage of listening to a coach?

A: Would not have to hesitate before advancing to second; would know how to run without having to watch the ball.

B. PRACTICE SITUATION: Three players in the field (minimum), first base, second base, third base, shortstop; three players batting. Have one player serve as coach. Batter should hit grounder to left side of infield, then run hard and fast to first base. Coach should tell runner whether to round or go to second.

Goal: Do what the coach says.

Cues: Coach let runner know what to do as soon as possible.

Runners *listen.*

Don't watch the ball.

C. GAME: Repeat Gotta Get There game A. Coach gets bonus run for her team for every base runner able to advance safely (if runner out at any base, no bonus runs are earned).

LESSON 2

TACTICAL PROBLEM: Moving the runner.

LESSON FOCUS: Situation is zero to one out, runner on first, grounder behind runner.

OBJECTIVES: Determine best place to hit ball in this situation.

Base running from first to third.

A. GAME: Score More.

Goals: Offensive batter should focus on strategic placement of the ball allowing runner to get to third safely.

Defense get the lead runner out.

Conditions: 4 v 4 minimum, 5 v 5 optimum, 6 v 6 maximum. Defensive players play first base, second base, shortstop, pitcher, and as many other infield positions as possible. Player scores a run by reaching third base safely. Inning is over after three runs or three outs, whichever comes first.

Questions

Q: What area of the field should you place the ball if the batter is trying to advance the runner?

A: Behind the runner.

Q: As a batter (if you are a right-handed hitter), how do you have to position yourself in the batter's box if you want to hit to right field?

A: Angled toward right side of field.

Q: At what point in the power zone should you contact the ball if you're attempting to hit down the right field line?

A: Outside toward right field side of plate, between plate and the area of the field you want to hit to.

Q: How should you follow through?

A: Follow through toward right field.

B. PRACTICE SITUATION: Batter hit three balls from a batting tee, attempting to hit down right field line. Then hit three pitched balls, attempting to hit down right field line. Repeat drill, but batter attempts to hit ball between players covering first and second.

Goals: Hit balls down right field line.

Hit balls between first and second base players.

Cues: Pick a target.

Angle body and bat toward target.

Follow through toward target.

Know where in the power zone you want to contact the ball before it is pitched.

Contact ball in the power zone.

C. GAME: Repeat Score More game A. Batter scores two bonus runs for grounder hit behind runner and through right side of infield.

LESSON 3

TACTICAL PROBLEM: Defending bases.

LESSON FOCUS: Situation is zero to one out, runner on second, grounder down right field line.

OBJECTIVE: Hold the lead runner.

A. GAME: Score More.

Goal: Get the lead runner out.

Conditions: 4 v 4 minimum, 5 v 5 optimum, 6 v 6 maximum. Defensive players play first base, second base, shortstop, pitcher, and as many other infield positions as possible. Offensive team must always have a runner at second base. Batter must hit a ground ball. Player scores a run by reaching third base safely. Inning is over after three runs or three outs, whichever comes first. Defensive team scores an additional run if they keep lead runner from advancing to third base.

Questions

Q: After fielding the ball, what did you do to keep the runner from advancing?

A: Look runner back.

Q: Once throw is made to first base, what should first base player do if runner is advancing to third?

A: If they have a play, step off first and throw to third. If no play, get sure out at first; then put ball in throwing hand and move toward third base to hold runner there.

Q: When runner attempts to advance, what does the third base player need to do?

A: Cover third base; give a good target.

Q: How should the third base player position herself to make a tag on the runner?

A: Straddle bag.

Q: How should the third base player tag the runner? Why?

A: Sweep low across edge of base closest to runner; if sweep at runner they may move and avoid tag.

B. PRACTICE SITUATION: Defensive team needs four or five infield players. Offensive team must have a runner on second base. Batter hits and runs. On hit, runner must run to third, hesitating if player *looks them back*, but proceeding to third if throw is made to first.

Goal: Get lead runner out at third using sweep tag.

Cues: Look runner back.

Players covering bases provide target.

Sweep tag at base.

C. GAME: Repeat Score More game A. Offensive team scores bonus run when player safely advances to third. Defensive team scores two bonus runs for putout at third and five bonus runs for double play (first to third).

LESSON 4

TACTICAL PROBLEMS: Moving the runner.

Advancing to the next base.

LESSON FOCUS: Situation is two outs, runner on second, line drive to outfield.

OBJECTIVE: Hitting a line drive from left to middle of field.

A. GAME: Stayin' Alive.

Goal: Offense get on base and move runner to third.

Conditions: 8 v 8 (can have fewer players if you place restrictions on where batters can hit, e.g., left field hitting only). Batter can hit ball anywhere on playing field. Player scores a run by reaching first safely and scores another run if the runner on second reaches third safely.

Questions

Q: What did the batter do to advance the runner from second to third and get on base?

A: Line drive from middle to the left side of the outfield.

Q: Why would this be the best place to hit the ball?

A: If outfield, infield still has long throw to get batter at first and runner still has a chance to advance to third base.

Q: Where in the power zone is the best place for batters to contact the ball if they're trying to hit from left to left center?

A: Between plate and left or left center field.

Q: *How should the batter contact the ball?*

A: Hit through middle of ball; swing level. Follow through to target; know where you want to hit the ball before the pitch.

Q: *What should the runner do in this situation?*

A: Watch to be sure ball gets through infield before running; watch to be sure ball won't be caught on fly by outfield. If ball is caught, runner should act as a decoy for as long as possible to give batter a chance to get to first safely.

B. PRACTICE SITUATION: From batting tee or pitched ball, practice hitting (5 to 10 times in a row) line drives over or between infielders on left side of infield. Base runners practice running from second to third as batters hit line drives.

Goal: Hit line drives between or over infielders and in front of or between outfielders.

Cues: Contact in the power zone.

Swing level through target.

Know where you want to hit and where you want to make contact.

Watch the ball.

C. GAME: Repeat Stayin' Alive game A. Line drives score two bonus runs. Line drives over infield and in front of or between outfielders score five bonus runs.

LEVEL IV

Level IV lessons are for students with extensive experience in softball or baseball. Structure lessons to provide many competitive experiences to motivate these players. For example, students can play the conditioned games against another team. They can perform practice situations with another team or within their own team. You can add some element of competition that would allow players to compete against themselves or other members of their team.

Situations in level IV lessons should provide opportunities for players to work individually and as a team. More advanced situations include batting and fielding with a runner on second, a runner on third, or even runners on second and third. These situations require more complex tactical play such as positioning for rundowns, backups, and defending space as a team. Hitting during these situations requires placement of the ball, which allows the runner to get on base and to score or advance runners already on base. Students can refine base running skills, as sliding and maneuvering to draw a throw are often considered a part of advanced play.

Level IV Lessons

LESSON 1

TACTICAL PROBLEM: Getting on base.

LESSON FOCUS: Situation is zero to two outs, no runners, grounders to left side of infield.

OBJECTIVE: Batter will place ball between players on the left side of the infield.

A. GAME: Tweeners.

Goal: Offense hit grounders between infielders.

Conditions: 4 v 4 minimum; defensive players play first, second, third, and shortstop. Batter must hit a ground ball. Player scores a run by reaching first base safely. Offensive team scores an additional run if the grounder goes through the infield.

Questions

Q: Where in the infield was the best place for the batter to hit the ball to get on base?

A: Right side of infield, down third baseline or between third and shortstop.

Q: How should the batter position her body to place the ball?

A: Open stance, slightly toward left field.

Q: Where in the power zone should the batter make contact if he is trying to hit through left side of infield?

A: Out in front, but contact point and follow-through should be in direction of target.

Q: How many players were able to consistently hit where they were aiming?

A: Most players could not.

B. PRACTICE SITUATION: Put large cones or hoops between each infield position and one on foul line, behind the base. Batter attempts to hit cone or hoop with ball, scoring five bonus runs if successful. Each player should get five balls hit from a tee, soft toss, or pitch, and hit and run on the fifth trial.

Goal: Place ball between players on left side of the infield.

Cues: Mentally see (visualize) where you want to hit the ball.

Contact ball in power zone.

Follow through toward target.

Watch ball contact bat.

C. GAME: Repeat Tweeners game A. Offensive team scores two bonus runs when ball hit between or past third base player and shortstop.

LESSON 2

TACTICAL PROBLEM: Getting on base.

LESSON FOCUS: Situation is zero to two outs, runner on first, grounder to right side of the infield.

OBJECTIVE: Batter will place ball between players on right side of the infield.

A. GAME: Tweeners.

Goal: Offense hit grounders between infielders.

Conditions: 4 v 4 minimum; defensive players play first, second, third, and shortstop. Batter must hit a ground ball. Runner scores when she reaches second safely. Offensive team scores an additional run if the grounder goes through the infield.

Questions

Q: Where in the infield was the best place for the batter to hit the ball to advance runner to second base?

A: Right side of infield, down first baseline, or between first and second.

Q: How should the batter position his body to place the ball?

A: Closed stance, slightly toward right field.

Q: Where in the power zone should batter make contact if she is trying to hit through the right side of infield?

A: Out in front, but contact point and follow-through should be in direction of target.

Q: How many players were able to consistently hit where they were aiming?

A: Most players could not.

B. PRACTICE SITUATION: Put large cones or hoops between each infield position and one on foul line, behind the base. Batter attempts to hit cone or hoop with ball, scoring five bonus runs if successful. Each player should get five balls hit from a tee, soft toss, or pitch, and hit and run on the fifth trial.

Goal: Place ball between players on right side of the infield.

Cues: Mentally see (visualize) where you want to hit the ball.

Contact ball in power zone.

Follow through toward target.

Watch ball contact bat.

C. GAME: Repeat Tweeners game A. Offensive team scores two bonus runs when ball hit between or past first and second base players.

LESSON 3

TACTICAL PROBLEM: Defending bases.

LESSON FOCUS: Situation is zero to two outs, runner on first, grounder fielded by first base player.

OBJECTIVE: Pitcher coverage of first base.

A. GAME: Pitcher's Pride.

Goals: Offense get to first ahead of the pitcher.

Defense get ball to pitcher (covering first base) ahead of the runner.

Conditions: 3 v 3 minimum; defensive players play first, second, and pitcher. Batter must hit a grounder to the right side of the infield. Only the pitcher can make the play at first base. Player scores a run by reaching first base safely. Inning is over after three runs or three outs, whichever comes first.

Questions

Q: What did the pitcher do to make the play at first base?

A: Run to first ahead of the runner.

Q: How did the pitcher need to run to avoid a collision with the runner?

A: Parallel along the base path.

Q: Where should the ball be thrown so the pitcher has the best opportunity to make the play?

A: Directly over the base.

B. PRACTICE SITUATION: Batters hit grounders to right side and run to first base. Pitcher covers first and attempts to make play ahead of the runner. Each player gets three to five attempts as pitcher. Each player should get at least three attempts to field and throw to first.

Goal: Pitcher to get runner out at first.

Cues: Run parallel with runner.

Get to first ahead of runner.

Give a good target.

Throw to base.

Time throw.

C. GAME: Repeat Pitcher's Pride game A. Pitcher scores a bonus run for his team for every putout at first base.

LESSON 4

TACTICAL PROBLEM: Defending bases.

LESSON FOCUS: Situation is zero to one out, runner on second, line drive through the middle.

OBJECTIVES: Double play from third to first.

Perform sweep tag and throw.

A. GAME: Hold 'Em at 2.

Goals: Offense advances runner by hitting a line drive over or through middle of infield.

Defense get lead runner out, hold at second base, or turn three-to-one double play if runner tries to advance.

Conditions: 4 v 4 minimum. Defensive players play first, second, third, shortstop, and pitcher. Batter must hit grounder or line drive between the shortstop and second base positions (place cones behind infield positions to mark area). Batter scores a run by reaching first *and* runner reaching third safely. The defensive team gets five bonus runs for a three-to-one double play. The inning is over after three runs or three outs, whichever comes first.

Questions

Q: When a three-to-one double play occurred, what type of tag was or should have been used by the third base player?

A: Sweep tag.

Q: Why is sweep tag best for a three-to-one double play?

A: Keeps person covering base out of the way of the runner and keeps runner from knocking ball out of third base player's glove.

Q: What's the advantage of a three-to-one double play?

A: Cut lead runner; keeps runner from getting into scoring position.

B. PRACTICE SITUATION: Third base player practices three-to-one double play, sweep tag, and throw. Set up runner at second. Member of battery hits or throws ball toward or over second base and runs to first base. Infielders attempt to field and throw to third base. Provide at least five opportunities for each player to cover third base and to field and throw to third.

Goals: Successfully complete the three-to-one double play.

Use sweep to tag runner.

Cues: Sweep with two hands.

Sweep and step toward first (play).

Sweep ball toward throwing shoulder (if possible).

Follow through toward play at first.

C. Game: Repeat Hold 'Em at 2 game A. Defensive team scores five bonus runs for three-to-one double play.

LESSON 5

TACTICAL PROBLEMS: Advancing to the next base.

Moving the runner.

LESSON FOCUS: Situation is zero to one out, runner on second, grounder or line drive to right side.

OBJECTIVES: Base runner to serve as a decoy to delay throw.

Player fielding ball looks runner back before throwing.

A. GAME: Runner's Trick.

Goals: Offense get on base and move runner to third.

Defense get batter out and hold runner at second.

Conditions: 8 v 8 (can have fewer players if you place restrictions on where batters can hit, e.g., left field hitting only). Offensive team must have a runner at second. Batter must hit to the right side of the field. Batter scores a run when she gets to first *and* the runner advances to third safely. The inning is over after three runs or three outs, whichever comes first.

Questions

Q: What should the runner on second do to delay throw to first base?

A: Act like he is going to run.

Q: Where's the best place to hit to move the runner from second to third?

A: Hit toward left side of infield, between third baseline and shortstop.

Q: Why?

A: Longer throw, batter more likely to move runner and get to first safely.

Q: If runner gets to third and throw is made to first, what should the third base runner do?

A: Lead off toward home. Run home if first base player throws to third, and if you can't make it return to third.

Q: What should runner on first do if throw goes to third?

A: Run to second.

Q: As a defender, what would you have to do to hold runners?

A: Stand next to one of the runners with ball in throwing hand, looking at other runner; call for time-out.

B. PRACTICE SITUATION: Use minimum of four infielders. Batter hits ball to right side of infield and runs to first. Runner at second and attempts to advance to third. After batter gets to first, runner on third attempts to lead off to draw throw. Runners advance depending on throw or until offense has ball under control and has called for time-out.

Goals: Base runners advance to as many bases possible.

Fielders keep runners from advancing past second base.

Cues: Have ball ready to throw as you look runner back.

Fake or take quick steps toward next base to delay or draw throw.

Be ready to run.

Keep moving or running until offense controls ball.

C. GAME: Repeat Runner's Trick game A. Offensive team scores five runs for every runner reaching home safely. Defensive team scores five bonus runs for three-to-one double play and three bonus runs for holding runner at second base.

LESSON 6

TACTICAL PROBLEM: Defend bases.

LESSON FOCUS: Situation is zero to one out, runner on first, grounder or line drive to right side.

OBJECTIVE: Execute a rundown.

A. GAME: Runner's Trick.

Goals: Offense get on base and move runner to third.

Defense get batter out and hold runner at second.

Conditions: 8 v 8 (can have fewer players if you place restrictions on where batters can hit, e.g., left field hitting only). Offensive team must have a runner at second. Batter must hit to the right side of the field. Batter scores a run when he gets to first *and* the runner advances to third safely. The inning is over after three runs or three outs, whichever comes first.

Questions

Q: What should you do when the runner is caught between bases?

A: Attempt to run her back to the base she came from.

Q: What should off-the-ball players do during a rundown?

A: Back up to closest base.

Q: What if someone else is backing up a base?

A: Move in behind him.

Q: Why is support important in a rundown?

A: Keeps runners from advancing and scoring.

B. PRACTICE SITUATION: Groups of three with two bases and one runner. Play running bases; when player caught between bases, attempt to tag runner or run her back to other base. Repeat on base path with other players moving into backup.

Goals: Get runner out.

If you can't get runner out, keep him from advancing to the next base.

Cues: Run the runner *back* to original base.

Have ball ready to throw while running runner back.

Know when to step out (and let backup continue rundown).

Support, support, support.

C. GAME: Repeat Runner's Trick game A. Defensive team scores five bonus runs for tagging runner out while in a rundown.

SUMMARY

Chapter 8 has provided you with sample lessons you could use to teach softball tactically. You can extend or refine many of these lessons to create new ones focusing on a variety of off-the-ball movements and on-the-ball skills. The key to creating new lessons is to remember that for each situation (e.g., one out, runner on first), every offensive and defensive player has a role. As you examine a situation, ask yourself what off-the-ball movements or on-the-ball skills are required for a player to adequately perform her role? Having identified these movements and skills, you can create game and practice conditions to help your students understand what to do and how to it.

If you find that a particular game is not working, try to identify where the game is breaking down. Then devise and implement a condition (or rule) that will force students to do what you want them to do. For example, if a throw is not being made to second base to cut the lead runner, give the defensive team two additional runs each time they successfully get the lead runner out. If a game is breaking down because students are unable to perform a particular skill, stop the game and ask students why they think the game is breaking down. Students know when things are not going well and are usually able to identify why. Having identified poorly executed skills as the reason for the breakdown in the game, students will be more motivated to practice these skills. Now they'll know *why* skill drill practice is necessary. Play ball!

CHAPTER 9

Golf

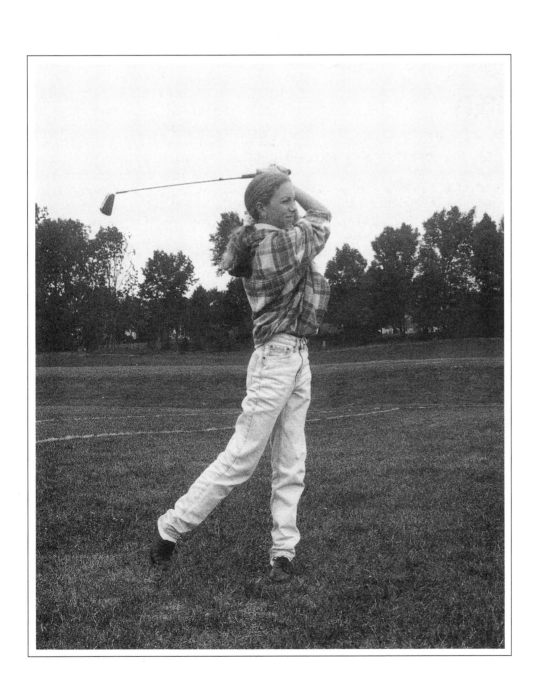

Golf is a target game with many unique tactical problems. Approximately one-third of all shots taken during a game of golf require a full swing, a complex skill. The complexity of a full swing increases when the golfer uses drivers and fairway woods. As you will see in the next section, we recommend starting with the putt and working up through short, middle, and long distance irons, and using the driver and fairway woods only with advanced players. In fact, a full swing with a middle iron is all that players need off the tee and, in the long run, will add to the novice's success and enjoyment of the game. Encourage novice players to play short par three courses to help them gain confidence, skill, and tactical understanding of the game.

SAFETY

Safety is a major consideration when teaching golf to a whole class. Arranging students so they are far enough apart yet close enough to monitor and instruct is not an easy feat. Here we offer a few suggestions for organizing students and equipment. First, you can arrange putting runners or strips of carpet like spokes of a wheel (see figure 9.1), with putting cups at center for easy management and observation of students. You can use the same arrangement for chipping practice, except you can position small pieces of artificial turf or carpet squares about 10 feet beyond

the end of the runner. This allows students to chip onto the green.

Partners are a must. They are not only useful for providing feedback to their peers, partners can serve as the primary observer for safety infractions. Select a safety cue such as *freeze*, *fore*, or *no*. When a safety cue is given, everyone should stop and wait for your command to restart activity. Practice this safety cue with your students. Periodically yell out this safety cue to ensure that students are alert and safety conscious.

Check club heads after every class. The constant pounding caused by multiple swings into the floor or ground can cause club heads to loosen. Also, be sure to check grips periodically. Grips can become slippery after many uses. Replacing grips is an easy task, and grip replacement kits are inexpensive. Get to know the owner or manager of a local golf course. They can often provide club repair tips and may even volunteer their services. Local courses are also a good source of score cards, pencils, tees, and other golf gadgets you can use in class or as prizes for that Reeses Cup Putt-Putt Golf Classic, for example.

TIPS FOR INSTRUCTION

We do not advocate teaching the grip, the club parts, or the history of the game, at least not right away. Let students acquire their own grip. Only

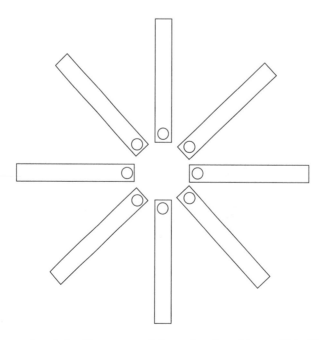

Figure 9.1 Arranging putting cups in a circle with runners radiating outward provides an efficient layout for observing students.

intervene when you observe a dysfunctional grip. Use proper terminology as you demonstrate each swing, referring to the *sweet spot* on the *club face*, for example, as you describe each swing. As for the history of the game, assign students the task of finding out how golf got its start. They can ask parents, grandparents, or look it up in the library. Get the clubs in their hands and let them play. Once students are engaged and having fun, they will want to learn about the game and how to be successful playing it.

TACTICAL REALITY GOLF

To grasp tactical concepts of golf (learn golf tactically), students will need to understand the conditions under which they are making each shot. How far the ball is from the hole, obstacles between the ball and the hole, and the lie of the ball are all important aspects of a golf shot. The decisions made before the shot, preshot preparation, are as important as the shot itself. We recommend using visual aids to help students understand how to use each type of shot within the game of golf. You can use posters, colored chalk drawings, overheads, and so forth to illustrate a situation on the golf course. Be sure to include bunkers, hazards, trees, and so on to illustrate the reality of a golf course. We have often copied diagrams of golf holes found in magazines, score cards, and golf resort promotional material. If the diagram is too small, enlarge it. Then laminate these enlarged diagrams. You can use them as instructional aids or let the students pretend to play a few holes in class, thus Tactical Reality Golf (see figure 9.2).

We present the tactical framework and levels of tactical complexity for golf in tables 9.1 and 9.2. We describe each level before lesson outlines.

LEVEL I

Level I lessons begin with the putt and end with a full swing using a middle iron. The foci are on club selection, setup, preshot routine, selection of intermediate target, stance, and swing. Through a number of games and practices, students encounter many problem-solving experiences to help them understand the relationship between loft of the club and placement of the ball within the stance.

Many drills require partners to observe their partner's swing or the flight characteristics of their partner's ball. This requires keen observation skills that must be taught. Take time to provide instruction about how to observe (i.e., where to *stand*, watch *one* critical element at a time, and view multiple trials). Use a marker to stripe the golf balls, because the direction of spin can provide feedback about the swing. By becoming competent observers and evaluators, students can improve their own skill and game performance.

Tactical Reality Golf
(Directions)

Player A _____   Player B _____

Instructions

1. Select a partner and have at least one bag of clubs between you.

2. Choose a hole to play (diagrams of golf holes).

3. Begin with a tee shot from a rubber tee using a whiffle ball, and hit remaining shots from turf mats.

4. Your partner is responsible for deciding how far and in which direction your ball has gone. She will tell you where you will play your next shot from.

5. For each shot you will have to select the appropriate club. The club you select will depend on your distance from the hole and any obstacles in your path (i.e., you might have to hit over a bunker so you will need to get plenty of height).

6. When you reach the green, take your regulation ball and putter to the artificial green and putt the hole out.

7. For each player, record the number of strokes from tee to green, the number of putts, and add these two for the score on the hole.

Maximum distances allowed with each club

Driver - 230 yds	3 wood - 210 yds
3 iron - 190 yds	4 iron - 180 yds
5 iron - 170 yds	6 iron - 160 yds
7 iron - 150 yds	8 iron - 140 yds
9 iron - 130 yds	Wedge - 120 yds

Name	1	2	3	4	5	6	7	8	9	Score

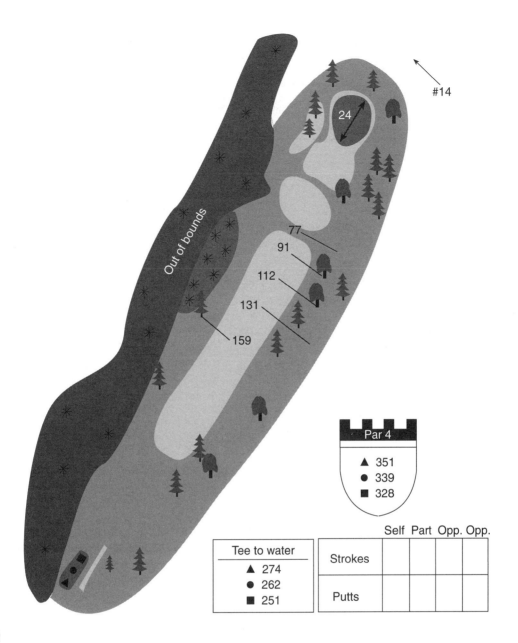

Figure 9.2

Table 9.1
Tactical Problems, Decisions, and Skills in Golf

Tactical problems	Preshot preparation	Shot execution
Reduce number of strokes		
Hitting ball the proper distance	Club selection Ball placement Judge distance Tee the ball Determine swing length	Setup routine Stance Swing plane Drive Putt 1-1, 2-2 Swing 6-8, 3-9, 2-10, full
Hitting the ball in the intended direction	Select target Intermediate target Read green	Setup Stance Swing plane Putt
Hitting out of hazards	Ball placement Read lie	Stance Swing plane for sand shot
Uphill, downhill, sidehill, and uneven lies	Club selection Ball placement Read angle of the lie	Stance Swing plane
Hitting the ball with spin	Backspin Left to right Right to left Hook Slice	Setup Stance Swing plane

Table 9.2
Levels of Tactical Complexity for Golf

Tactical problems	Levels of tactical complexity	
	I	II
Reduce number of strokes		
Hitting ball the proper distance	Club selection Ball placement Setup routine Determine swing length Putt 1-1, 2-2 Swing 6-8, 3-9, 2-10, full with midiron	Full swing • long irons • with woods Fairway woods
Hitting the ball in the intended direction	Select intermediate target Read green Setup Swing plane	
Hitting out of hazards	Ball placement Read lie Deep, dense grass	Sand shot
Uphill and downhill lies Sidehill lies and uneven lies		Club selection Stance Ball placement Swing plane
Hitting the ball with spin		Backspin Left to right Right to left

Level I Lessons

LESSON 1

TACTICAL PROBLEM: Hitting for proper distance.

LESSON FOCUS: Putt, club selection.

OBJECTIVE: Putt ball into hole in fewest number of strokes.

A. GAME: Putt 10 balls at 3 feet and 10 balls at 10 feet, keep score.

Goal: Put ball in hole in fewest number of strokes.

Conditions: See figure 9.1 for equipment setup. Ask students to select club that will best allow them to complete the task. Impose a safety rule that students should not raise club head higher than their feet. Balls lie 3 feet and 10 feet from hole on a green, a smooth, flat surface. Use diagram, poster, overhead, and so on. to give students a mental picture of the green and ball position relative to the hole (see figure 9.3 for an example).

Questions

Q: What was the goal of the game?

A: Put ball in hole in fewest number of strokes.

Q: What stance, grip, and body position helped you best achieve this goal?

A: Square and balanced, comfortable grip, ready position with head and nose over ball.

Q: How did you swing your club to achieve the goal?

A: Smooth, blade straight.

Q: How was your swing for the 3-foot putt different from your swing for the 10-foot putt?

A: Three-foot putt swing was shorter than 10-foot putt swing.

Q: Why would it be important to know how long your swing should be when you're attempting a three-foot putt?

A: So that every time you had a three-foot putt the swing would be the same.

B. PRACTICE TASK: Putt between rulers, yard sticks, or measured boards. Putt 10 strokes 1-1 (with a one- to two-foot backswing and forward swing) and have partner measure distance ball travels on last five strokes (use measuring tape). Switch roles with partner. Repeat task for 2-2 stroke (two- to three-foot swings) and 3-3 stroke (three- to four-foot swings) . Partner also serves as coach, repeating cues and giving feedback. Have students calculate average distance ball traveled at each stroke length.

Goal: Develop a consistent swing for the 1, 2, and 3 putts.

Cues: For stance and swing

    Balanced.

    Square blade.

    Comfortable grip.

    Quiet body.

    Nose over ball.

    Smooth, even stroke.

C. GAME: Repeat game A.

Goal: Same.

Conditions: With balls at 3 feet, 10 feet, and 15 feet, keep score. Compare scores at 3 feet and 10 feet with scores of first game.

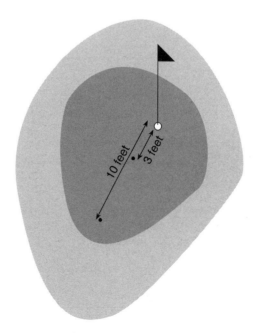

Figure 9.3

LESSON 2

TACTICAL PROBLEM: Hitting ball in proper direction.

LESSON FOCUS: Reading the green.

OBJECTIVE: Use an intermediate target to putt ball into hole in fewest number of strokes.

A. GAME: Putt 10 balls at 8 feet and 10 balls at 15 feet, keep score.

Goal: Put ball in hole in fewest number of strokes.

Conditions: See figure 9.1 for equipment setup. Ask students to select club that will best allow them to complete the task. Impose a safety rule that students not raise the club head higher than their feet. Balls lie 8 feet and 15 feet from hole on a green, an uneven surface (place rope under green to change surface).

Questions

Q: What was the goal of the game?

A: Put ball in hole in fewest number of strokes.

Q: What made today's game more difficult than yesterday's game?

A: Curves and bumps in the green.

Q: What did you do to be successful?

A: Look at green and decide which way ball would roll.

Q: Where did you aim to get the ball in the hole?

A: Left or right of the hole.

Q: Did anyone use a target between the ball and hole to help them reach the goal, and where was your target?

A: One, two, or three feet ahead of the ball or a spot next to hole.

Q: When you use a target between the ball and the hole, we refer to it as an intermediate target. Where is the best place for this intermediate target, closer to the ball or closer to the hole?

A: Don't know.

Let's experiment to find out the best place for an intermediate target.

B. PRACTICE TASK: Using same conditions as game, students use stickers, stars, or small markers to find the best place for an intermediate target when attempting 8-foot and 15-foot putts. Have them first place their markers between the ball and hole, then move marker gradually closer to the hole. When they think they have selected a good place for an intermediate target at 8 feet and 15 feet, let them move to another green to try their target placement.

Goal: Determine the best location for an intermediate target when putting.

Cues: Quiet body, quiet stroke.

Line it up, then focus on the swing length.

Questions

Q: What was the goal of the practice task?

A: Find the best place for an intermediate target.

Q: What did you determine to be the best place for an intermediate target?

A: Fairly close to the ball.

Q: Why would this be better than an intermediate target at a farther distance?

A: Closer target is easier to hit, less error.

C. GAME: With balls at 8 feet and 15 feet, keep score and compare with score of first game.

LESSON 3

TACTICAL PROBLEM: Hitting the ball the proper distance and in the intended direction.

LESSON FOCUS: Club selection, selection of intermediate target, and chipping.

OBJECTIVE: Select and execute a chip shot from 20 feet, landing ball within one short putt of the hole.

A. GAME: Ball 3 feet off green on first cut; ball 10 feet off green in rough. Hit ball onto green, then putt out.

> **Goals:** Put ball in hole in the fewest number of strokes.
>
> Chip ball within three feet of hole.
>
> **Conditions:** Ask students to select club that will best allow them to complete the task. Impose a safety rule that students should not raise the club head higher than their knees. Both lies are 20 feet from hole, one 3 feet off green, the other 10 feet off the green. (Use diagram, poster, overhead, etc. to give students a mental picture of the green, the surrounding area, and ball position relative to the hole.) Students record scores.

Questions

Q: Did you use the same club for both shots or did you find different clubs better for one shot than the other?

A: You can use the 3-7 iron for 3-foot and 9 or wedge for 10-foot shot because of deep grass.

Q: How did that club influence the flight of the ball?

A: Let ball fly up in air enough to land on green.

Q: What stance, grip, and body position did you find best for successfully reaching the goal?

A: Open stance, comfortable and choked down, ready position with head over ball.

Q: What swing was best for successfully reaching the goal from three feet?

A: Square, smooth, follow-through toward hole.

Q: How did your swing from the 3-foot distance differ from your swing at the 10-foot distance?

A: Longer swing at 10-foot distance.

Q: How were you able to control the direction your ball traveled?

A: Select an intermediate target.

Q: What about the flight of the ball; were you more successful when your ball landed close to the hole or farther from the hole?

A: Farther from the hole, then let it roll.

B. PRACTICE TASK: Chip ball from between two-yard or meter sticks into a target about one-third the distance between ball and hole (use a small rope or cord to mark a target). Chip 10 balls each from the 3-foot and 10-foot distances. Then select a longer distance (between 12 feet and 20 feet) and adjust your swing and target.

> **Goal:** Use appropriate form to chip ball into a target.
>
> **Cues:** For chip
>
> > Open stance, keep hands ahead of blade.
> >
> > Weight on front foot, hands to target.
> >
> > Lag club face, quiet body.

C. GAME: Repeat game A; compare score with score of first game.

LESSON 4

TACTICAL PROBLEM: Hitting ball with proper distance, direction, and trajectory.

LESSON FOCUS: Club selection, pitch shot.

OBJECTIVE: Use one-quarter (6:00 to 9:00) and one-half (6:00 to 12:00) swing with a short iron to pitch ball over a hazard and close to the hole 10 feet from that hazard.

A. GAME: Ball 30 feet and 60 feet from hole, sand trap between ball and hole, hole within 10 feet of hazard. Hit 5 to10 balls from each distance.

Goals: Put ball in hole in fewest number of strokes.

Land ball within five feet of hole.

Conditions: Ask students to select club that will best allow them to complete the task. Impose a safety rule that students not raise the club head higher than their shoulders. Ball lies are 30 feet from hole and 60 feet from hole with sand trap between ball and hole. Hole is 10 feet on other side of trap. (Use diagram, poster, overhead, etc. to give students a mental picture of the green, the surrounding area, and ball position relative to the hole.) Students record scores.

Questions

Q: What club was best for reaching the goal?

A: Wedge or 9 iron.

Q: Why were these clubs better than higher numbered clubs?

A: More loft and more control.

Q: Why did you need the ball to go higher?

A: To get over sand and to have less roll when ball lands; hole is close to trap so you need high fly ball with backspin.

Q: What stance, grip, and body position did you find best for successfully reaching the goal?

A: Square stance, comfortable grip, overlapping, interlocking, and natural, ready position.

Q: What was the best way to swing to hit from 30 feet and how was that different from 60 feet?

A: Bigger swing than chip, needed bigger backswing for 60-foot hit and needed more body to get ball to target.

Q: In our putt swing concept, the farther from the hole the longer the swing. How would that concept apply to pitching?

A: The farther from the hole the longer the backswing.

Q: Some people use the face of a clock to refer to the distance of a backswing. How could we use the face of the clock to measure the length of our backswing?

A: A quarter swing would be 6:00-9:00; 6:00-12:00 would be a half swing.

B. PRACTICE TASK 1: Use game situation to practice one-quarter and one-half swing to pitch ball onto the green. Use partner checklist to evaluate swing form and length. Each partner takes 10 practice swings, then 10 more swings for their partner to evaluate their form. Rotate after 20 swings, then go to the other distance (30 feet or 60 feet).

Goals: Use good form on one-quarter and one-half swings to perform a pitch shot.

Evaluate partner's pitch shot performance.

Questions

Q: What about your setup routine, selection of intermediate target, and ball placement? Were these similar or different from the chip and putt?

A: Setup and selection of intermediate target would be same; ball placement would be different.

Q: Relative to the stance, what was the best place for the ball to be?

A: Don't know.

Let's find out

PRACTICE TASK 2: Use game situation to practice ball placement from 30-foot or 60-foot distance. Each student hits two balls placed off the front, middle, and rear foot. Partners chart the trajectory of each shot. Partners switch roles and repeat task.

Questions

Q: How does the placement of the ball in the stance influence its flight?

A: The farther the ball is forward the lower the trajectory.

Q: What other factor influences the trajectory of the ball?

A: The loft of the club.

Q: If you want the ball to have a high trajectory, what should you do?

A: Place ball toward middle of stance and select a club with a lot of loft (9 iron or wedge).

C. GAME: Repeat game A; compare results with first game.

LESSON 5

TACTICAL PROBLEM: Hitting ball the proper distance, direction, and trajectory.

LESSON FOCUS: Hitting over a lake and landing on the green.

OBJECTIVE: Use three-quarter and full swing with a short iron to pitch the ball within 15 to 20 feet of the hole.

A. GAME: Ball 90 feet and 120 feet from hole, lake between ball and hole, hole within 20 feet of hazard.

Goals: Put ball in hole in fewest number of strokes.

Land ball within 10 to 15 feet of hole.

Conditions: Ask students to select club that will best allow them to complete the task. Impose a safety rule that students should not raise the club head unless their partner gives the all clear signal. Ball lies are 90 feet from hole and 120 feet from hole with a lake between ball and hole. Hole is 20 feet on other side of lake. Hit 5 to 10 balls from each distance. Record number of balls landing within 15 feet of hole (see figure 9.4).

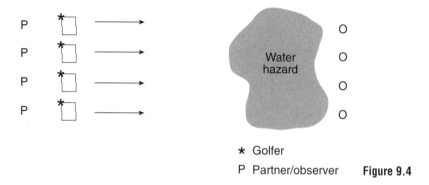

★ Golfer

P Partner/observer   **Figure 9.4**

Questions

Q: What club was best for these shots?

A: Wedge or 9.

Q: How did your swing differ from 90 feet to 120 feet?

A: Bigger swing needed for 120 feet.

Q: How was this swing similar to the one-quarter or one-half swings?

A: Same, but longer with a greater range of motion.

Q: How does the rhythm of the full swing compare with the one-quarter and one-half swings?

A: Same rhythm, smooth, fluid.

B. PRACTICE TASK: Use game situation to practice three-quarter to full swing to pitch ball onto the green. Use partner checklist to evaluate swing form and length. Each partner takes 10 practice swings, then 10 more swings for their partner to evaluate their form. Rotate after 20 swings, then go to the other distance (90 feet or 120 feet).

Goals: Use good form to perform three-quarter to full swing pitch shot.

Evaluate partner's swing.

C. GAME: Repeat game A; compare score with score of first game.

LESSON 6

TACTICAL PROBLEM: Hitting ball the proper distance and direction.

LESSON FOCUS: Hitting ball with low trajectory.

OBJECTIVE: Use a three-quarter to full swing with a middle distance iron to approach the green.

A. GAME: Ball under a tree and 150 feet from hole.

Goal: Get ball into hole in fewest number of strokes.

Conditions: Ask students to select club that will best allow them to complete the task. Impose a safety rule that students should not raise the club head unless their partner gives the all clear signal. Hit 10 balls, then hit 3 to 5 balls, playing each all the way out. (Use diagram, poster, overhead, etc. to give students a mental picture of the green, the surrounding area, and ball position relative to the hole.) Students record scores of last three to five balls.

Questions

Q: Where was the best place to land the ball and why?

A: Short of green, then let it roll to avoid penalty for losing ball in woods.

Q: Which club was best for achieving the goal?

A: Middle distance iron or individual preference; use the club that works.

Q: What was the best trajectory for achieving this goal?

A: Low to avoid tree.

Q: What swing length was best for achieving the goal?

A: Three-quarter to full swing.

Q: Where was the best ball placement?

A: Forward in stance to keep trajectory low.

B. PRACTICE TASK 1: Each partner takes 10 practice swings, adjusting placement to achieve proper trajectory. Then take 10 more swings for partner to evaluate form. Rotate after 20 swings. Repeat if partner needs more time to evaluate.

Goals: Adjust ball placement to get low trajectory.

Evaluate partner's full swing performance.

PRACTICE TASK 2: Use game situation to practice and full swing to get from under a tree and land in front of the green. Use partner checklist to evaluate swing errors and causes based on flight of ball.

Goal: Land ball in front of green for good approach shot.

Cues: Ball placement and club selection necessary for achieving low trajectory.

Even, smooth swing.

C. GAME: Repeat game A; compare score from first game.

LESSON 7

TACTICAL PROBLEM: Hitting ball the proper distance and trajectory.

LESSON FOCUS: Full swing with middle iron.

OBJECTIVES: Drive ball from tee.

Play five holes of golf on a Tactical Reality par three golf course.

A. GAME: From a tee box, hit the ball down the fairway so you can reach the green on your second (approach) shot.

Goals: Get ball in hole in fewest number of strokes.

Land drive within 100 feet of green.

Conditions: Ask students to select club that will best allow them to complete the task. Impose a safety rule that students should not raise the club head unless their partner gives the all clear signal. Tee box is 250 feet from hole with a lake between ball and hole; hole is 20 feet on other side of lake. (Use diagram, poster, overhead, etc. to give students a mental picture of the green, the surrounding area, and ball position relative to the hole.) Students record scores.

Questions

Q: What was the goal of the game?

A: Land drive within 100 feet of the green.

Q: Did you change any part of your setup or swing to help you achieve the goal?

A: Used a tee.

Q: How did using the tee help? Why?

A: Easier to hit ball; ball sets up, clear of grass.

Q: Did any of you try placing the ball in different places within your stance? If so, what happened?

A: No.

Let's practice to determine which ball placement will give you the best distance.

B. PRACTICE TASK 1: From tee, all students should hit two balls placed off the front, the middle, and the rear foot. Partners should chart the trajectory and approximate distance of each shot. Partners switch roles and repeat task.

Goal: Determine best placement for ball during a drive.

Questions

Q: Where was the best ball placement for obtaining the proper distance, direction, and trajectory?

A: Front foot.

Q: How high should you tee the ball?

A: Approximately an index finger's width from the ball to the ground.

Q: What is the effect of ball height on trajectory of ball?

A: If the ball is too high, the trajectory will be high. If the ball is too low, the trajectory will be low.

Let's practice to determine how high the ball should be teed.

PRACTICE TASK 2: From tee students should hit balls placed high on tee, medium height, and low (two each). Partner should chart the trajectory and approximate distance of each shot. Partners switch roles and repeat task.

Goal: Determine proper height for teeing ball.

Questions

Q: How did the height of the ball influence the trajectory?

A: Tee up ball too high you get high trajectory.

Q: What was the best tee height?

A: Low to medium for iron, medium for driver.

Cues: Work on setup and ball placement.

Swing easy, hit hard.

Fix eyes on spot (on the ball).

C. GAME: Three to five holes of Tactical Reality Golf (see figure 9.2); compare score with score of first game.

LESSON 8

TACTICAL PROBLEM: Reduce number of strokes.

LESSON FOCUS: Rules and etiquette of golf.

OBJECTIVE: Drive ball from tee. Play five holes of golf on a Tactical Reality par three golf course.

A. GAME: Play five to nine holes of Tactical Reality Golf.

Goal: Play every hole in as few strokes possible.

Conditions: Tactical Reality Golf holes (see figure 9.2), all players must follow rules or assume the appropriate penalties. Players must follow course etiquette.

Goal: Demonstrate knowledge of proper club selection, shot selection, setup, and swing length.

Questions (after three or four holes)

Q: What did you do when your ball went into the woods or other hazard, causing you to lift or pick up your ball?

A: Added penalty stroke to score.

Q: Can you describe other instances where penalty strokes are assessed?

A: Playing the wrong ball, ball moves while setting up shot, and so forth.

Q: How did you know whose turn it was?

A: Player with lowest score on previous hole.

Q: What did you do with your bag on tees and green?

A: Leave bag off tees and green. (Can include other questions about rules and etiquette.)

Let's continue play using official rules and proper etiquette.

LEVEL II

Level II lessons focus on the full swing with a driver and fairway woods. Once students have had an opportunity to develop a consistent swing pattern, they should work on altering their swing plane and club position to hit a ball left to right or right to left. Once the swing pattern has become consistent, the player can begin to work on uneven lies, uphill and downhill lies, and sidehill lies. Two of the following lessons focus on these irregular lies.

Level II Lessons

LESSON 1

TACTICAL PROBLEM: Hitting ball the proper distance and direction.

LESSON FOCUS: Full swing with a driver from the tee box.

OBJECTIVE: Use a driver to hit ball down the center of the fairway.

A. GAME: Play three to five holes of Tactical Reality Golf, par four holes.

Goals: Get ball in hole in fewest number of strokes.

Land drive in a place that will allow easiest approach to the green.

Conditions: Ask students to select club that will best allow them to complete the task. Impose a safety rule that students should not raise the club head unless their partner gives the all clear signal. Tee box is 300 yards from hole with a lake between ball and hole; hole is 20 feet on other side of lake. (Use diagram, poster, overhead, etc. to give students a mental picture of the green, the surrounding area, and ball position relative to the hole.) Students record scores.

Questions

Q: What was the goal of the game?

A: Land drive so you have an easy approach to the green.

Q: For most holes where was the best place to land the ball?

A: In the middle of the fairway, with an open shot to the green.

Q: Were you able to hit the ball straight most of the time?

A: Not many students do this consistently.

Q: How can the flight of the ball help you determine swing errors?

A: If too low or too high, then perhaps not good placement during setup; if spinning left or right, then perhaps swing plane incorrect or blade not square at impact.

Q: Let's practice swinging and reading the flight and spin of the ball. If ball too high or too low, hooking or slicing what should you do?

A: Adjust your swing.

B. PRACTICE TASK 1: Students hit whiffle balls into curtain or wall or hit real or restricted balls in a cage area or outside. As one partner practices her drive, the other partner evaluates, using a checklist and providing feedback. Partners should rotate after 10 to 20 swings.

Goals: Improve full swing performance.

Evaluate partner's full swing performance.

PRACTICE TASK 2: Students hit whiffle balls into curtain or wall or hit in cage or outside area. As one partner hits 5 to 10 balls, other partner evaluates the direction and trajectory of the ball and gives feedback.

Goal: Read trajectory and spin of ball and use it to provide feedback about swing performance.

C. GAME: Repeat game A, three to five holes of Tactical Reality Golf. Compare score with score of first game.

LESSON 2

TACTICAL PROBLEM: Hitting ball the proper distance and direction.

LESSON FOCUS: Full swing with a fairway wood, club selection.

OBJECTIVE: Use a fairway wood to hit ball to intended target.

A. GAME: Play three to five holes of Tactical Reality Golf, par five holes.

Goals: Get ball in hole in fewest number of strokes.

Land all shots to allow easiest approach to the green.

Conditions: Ask students to select clubs that will best allow them to complete the task. Impose a safety rule that students should not raise the club head unless their partner gives the all clear signal. Tee box is 450 yards from hole with a lake between ball and hole; hole is 30 feet on other side of lake. (Use diagram, poster, overhead, etc. to give students a mental picture of the green, the surrounding area, and ball position relative to the hole.) Students record scores.

Questions

Q: When you had 200 or more yards to the green after your drive, what club did you select?

A: Long iron, wood.

Q: What would be the best club to select if you were 200 or more yards from the green? Why?

A: Select 2 or 3 wood or 3 iron; longer club and larger club head give longer distance.

Q: What other factors would influence club selection?

A: Distance person can hit, lie of ball, distance to the green.

Q: How is hitting with a fairway wood different from hitting a drive from the tee?

A: Ball lies lower, not teed up.

Q: What do you think were some of the causes for mishitting the ball?

A: Setup and stance not right.

B. PRACTICE TASK 1: With a partner, use a fairway wood (2/3 or 4/5). One partner hits five balls from the forward, middle, and back positions as the other partner charts the direction and trajectory of each ball. Partners then switch roles.

Goal: Determine proper ball placement when hitting long iron or fairway wood.

Questions

Q: What was the best ball placement for hitting a fairway wood?

A: Forward, exact spot may vary from player to player.

Q: How far from your body was the ball?

A: Students will say the ball was close, medium, or far away from body.

Q: What distance did you find was best?

A: (Students will not be sure.)

Let's look at ball placement or distance ball placed from feet.

PRACTICE TASK 2: With a partner, use a fairway wood (2/3 or 4/5). One partner hits 15 to 20 balls, placing the ball at various distances from his body, from close to far from his body. After he thinks he's found the proper distance, switch with partner. Partner should provide feedback relative to form and flight of ball. (Prompt students to use findings from problem posed in practice task 1 to place ball in relation to their stance.)

Goal: Determine proper placement of ball during shot with a fairway wood.

C. GAME: Repeat game A, three to five holes of Tactical Reality Golf; compare score with score of first game.

LESSON 3

TACTICAL PROBLEM: Hitting out of hazards.

LESSON FOCUS: Sand shots.

OBJECTIVE: Hit ball out of a sand trap, landing ball in target zone.

A. GAME: Ball is in sand, hole 30 feet from trap, ball 10 feet from lip of trap, 40 feet from hole.

Goals: Get ball in hole in fewest number of strokes.

Get ball out of sand and onto the green in one stroke.

Conditions: Ask students to select clubs that will best allow them to complete the task. Impose a safety rule that students should not raise the club head unless their partner gives the all clear signal. You can use sandbox or pit to create sand trap conditions. Set up identical lies and play against partner to see who can get ball out of trap and into hole in fewest number of strokes. (Use diagram, poster, overhead, etc. to give students a mental picture of the green, the surrounding area, and ball position relative to the hole.) Students record scores.

Questions

Q: What was the goal of the game?

A: Get ball out of sand and onto green in one stroke.

Q: How were you able to do that?

A: Firm, open stance, swing through the ball.

Q: How did you know how big of a swing you needed to get ball out of sand?

A: Depended on how deep ball was lying in the sand.

B. PRACTICE TASK 1: Students work with partner to evaluate form and provide feedback. Each student takes 10 practice swings, then switches roles with partner.

Goals: Improve form during sand shots.

Evaluate partner's sand shot performance.

PRACTICE TASK 2: Students work with partner and place ball at different depths in sand. Other partner observes and provides feedback relative to point of contact in sand and swing length required to remove ball from sand.

Goal: Identify point of contact for removing ball during sand shots.

C. GAME: Repeat game A; compare scores with scores of first partner challenge.

LESSON 4

TACTICAL PROBLEM: Hitting out of hazards.

LESSON FOCUS: Hit ball lying deep in dense grass.

OBJECTIVES: Select the proper club, setup, and intermediate target.

Adjust swing plane to hit down and through the ball.

A. GAME: Hit balls out of deep, dense grass about 30 yards from the green.

Goal: Accumulate as low a score as possible.

Conditions: Ask students to select clubs that will best allow them to complete the task. Impose a safety rule that students should not raise the club head unless their partner gives the all clear signal. If dense grass is not available, use sand or loose dirt to simulate this shot. If possible, place ball 60 to 70 yards from the green. Alternate hits with a partner; score minus five every time a ball lands and stays on the green or area designated as the green. (Use diagram, poster, overhead, etc. to give students a mental picture of the green, surrounding area, and ball position relative to the hole.) Students record scores.

Questions

Q: What did you do to land the ball on the green?

A: Hit ball high and land it short.

Q: How did you adjust your swing to get the ball out of the high grass?

A: Swing down and through the ball; use firm grip, good follow-through.

Q: How many of you were able to consistently land the ball on the green?

A: Not many responses.

Let's practice.

B. PRACTICE TASK: Use game situation and add a hula hoop to provide a target to land the ball. With a partner, students take five shots each, then switch. Partner should serve as coach, providing feedback following each shot.

Goal: Adjust swing to get ball out of dense grass.

Cues: Swing down and through.

Select intermediate target.

Select place to land ball.

C. GAME: Repeat game A; compare scores at end of class.

LESSON 5

TACTICAL PROBLEM: Hitting downhill and uphill lies.

LESSON FOCUS: Setup for downhill and uphill lies.

OBJECTIVE: Determine club, setup, stance, and ball placement for uphill and downhill lies.

A. GAME: Compete with a partner. Hit five uphill lies and five downhill lies into a target area about 30 feet away.

  Goal: Score as close to 20 under par as possible.

  Conditions: Ask students to select clubs that will best allow them to complete the task. Impose a safety rule that students should not raise the club head unless their partner gives the all clear signal. If possible, place ball 10 to 20 yards from a target if hitting a whiffle ball. Score one stroke for every shot that misses the target area, minus two for every shot that lands in the target area. (Use diagram, poster, overhead, etc. to give students a mental picture of the uphill and downhill lies, surrounding area, and ball position relative to the hole.) Students record their partner's score.

  Questions

  Q: How did you adjust your preshot setup to successfully hit uphill and downhill lies?

  A: Take a practice swing to determine where to place ball in stance, ball position toward high foot.

  Q: How did you adjust your swing to successfully hit uphill and downhill lies?

  A: Adjust swing length to degree of slope; use choke-up grip (about three inches from top), shoulders parallel to slope. Uphill lie shots tend to hook; move closer to ball on downhill lies.

  Q: How successful were you at consistently making contact with the ball?

  A: Not many students respond.

    Perhaps we should practice.

B. PRACTICE TASK: Use partner evaluation, such as a checklist. Partners alternate after 10 to 20 shots. Include evaluation of preshot routine.

  Goals: Set up properly to allow for good contact.

    Improve swing used for uphill and downhill lies.

  Cues: Weight on uphill foot.

    Use practice swing to help with ball placement.

    Practice preshot routine before every practice shot.

C. GAME: Repeat game A or allow students to play two or three holes of Tactical Reality Golf, with each fairway shot played as either an uphill or downhill lie.

LESSON 6

TACTICAL PROBLEM: Hitting sidehill lies.

LESSON FOCUS: Setup for hitting sidehill lies.

OBJECTIVES: Determine club, setup, stance, and ball placement for sidehill lies.

    Refine preshot routine.

A. GAME: Compete with a partner. Hit 10 sidehill (five sloping away, five sloping toward) into a target area.

  Goal: Score as close to 20 under par as possible.

  Conditions: Ball hit from about 30 feet away; score one stroke for every shot that misses the target area, minus two for every shot that lands in the target area. Ask students to select clubs that will best allow them to complete the task. Impose a safety rule that students should not raise the club head unless their partner gives the all clear signal. If possible, place ball 10 to 20 yards from a target if hitting a whiffle ball. (Use diagram, poster, overhead, etc. to give students a mental picture of the uphill and downhill lies, surrounding area, and ball position relative to the hole.) Students record their partner's score.

Questions

Q: How did you adjust your preshot setup to successfully hit sidehill lie?

A: Took a practice swing to determine where to place ball in stance; selected an intermediate target.

Q: How did you adjust your swing to successfully hit sidehill lies?

A: Adjusted swing length to degree of slope; use choke-up grip (about three inches from top). Stand closer when ball below feet and shift weight toward heels and insteps.

B. PRACTICE TASK: Use partner evaluation, such as a checklist. Partners alternate after 10 to 20 shots. Evaluation should include a preshot routine.

Goals: Set up properly to allow good contact.

Improve swing used for sidehill lies.

Cues: Use practice swing to check for proper ball placement.

Always use preshot routine.

Close blade on downward slope (slopes away from golfer).

Open blade on upward slope (slopes toward golfer).

C. GAME: Repeat game A or allow students to play two or three holes of Tactical Reality Golf, with each fairway shot played as a sidehill lie.

LESSON 7

TACTICAL PROBLEM: Hitting a ball with spin.

LESSON FOCUS: Hitting a ball with backspin.

OBJECTIVE: Land a pitch shot on a green from 40 to 80 yards.

A. GAME: Three holes of stroke play with a foursome.

Goal: Play three partial holes in as few strokes possible.

Conditions: Pin is close to front edge of green, ball on fairway, about 60 yards from hole. Play three holes, beginning with short fairway shot.

Questions

Q: What was the best club for the first shot?

A: Nine iron, pitching wedge, or sand wedge.

Q: Where was the best spot on the green to place the ball?

A: Close to the hole so you could one putt.

Q: How were you able to get the ball to land close to the hole?

A: High trajectory.

Q: Why with a high trajectory?

A: So the ball would stay where it landed.

Q: How successful were you at landing the ball close to the hole and getting it to stay there?

A: Not very.

Let's practice!

B. PRACTICE TASK: Work on varying the loft of the ball. With a partner, one student uses a 9 iron to hit three balls, one off target heel, one off the rear heel, and one center. Partner observes ball spin and ball flight and records observation. Partners switch and repeat task. Repeat task again with a pitching wedge, then again with a sand wedge.

Goal: Observe differences in loft and flight caused by different clubs and ball placements.

Cues: Narrower stance.

Forward swing length 2:00 or 3:00.

Hands to target.

Questions

Q: How did the position of the ball influence its trajectory and spin?

A: The further back in stance the ball is placed, the lower the trajectory.

Q: How did the type of club influence the trajectory and spin of the ball?

A: The greater the loft, the higher the trajectory and the greater the spin.

C. GAME: Two to four par three holes of Tactical Reality Golf.

Goal: Few strokes as possible.

Conditions: Use visual aids to illustrate conditions of each par three hole. Do not use a tee when hitting from tee box.

LESSON 8

TACTICAL PROBLEM: Hitting a ball with spin.

LESSON FOCUS: Modifying the flight pattern of the ball.

OBJECTIVE: Determine the elements of the swing that influence the direction the ball travels.

A. GAME: Follow the Leader.

Goal: Imitate flight path of ball hit by partner.

Conditions: In a field or down the length of a gym, partners alternate shots. First partner attempts to hit ball right to left or left to right; then other partner attempts to imitate that shot. After 10 shots, switch leaders.

Questions

Q: What elements of the swing appeared to influence the direction of the ball?

A: Angle of club face at contact, angle of swing during forward swing, setup not square.

Q: What was the position of the club face when the ball rotated right (clockwise)?

A: Open.

Q: What was the position of the club face when the ball rotated left (counterclockwise)?

A: Closed.

Q: What swing plane caused the ball to move left?

A: Outside-in.

Q: What swing plane caused the ball to move right?

A: Inside-out.

Q: How many of you were successful at imitating your partner's swing?

A: Not many.

Let's practice!

B. PRACTICE TASK: One partner swings as other observes and records flight patterns. First partner attempts five full swings with an open face, then five full swings with a closed club face. Partners then switch roles. First partner attempts five full swings moving club outside-in (with club face staying square), then five full swings moving club face inside-out (again, with club face remaining square). Partners switch roles. First partner combines outside-in swing with open club face for five shots, then closed club face for five shots, as partner observes and records flight patterns. Partners switch again. First partner combines inside-out swing with open club face for five shots, then closed club face for five shots. Partners switch roles and repeat task.

Goal: To intentionally hit hook, slide, and fade shots.

Cues: Swing normal when club face open or closed.

Adjust swing plane only slightly from normal swing.

Read flight of ball for feedback.

Set up right, then let club do the work.

C. GAME: Two or three holes of Tactical Reality Golf.

Goal: Fewest strokes possible.

Conditions: During drive and long fairway shots, partners predetermine flight patterns. One stroke penalty for flight patterns not matching the predetermined flight patterns, or, if possible, select holes that require certain types of shots to approach green (i.e., narrow fairways, doglegs, strong gulf breezes).

LESSONS 9 AND 10

LESSON FOCUS: Rules and etiquette.

OBJECTIVE: Play four or five holes of golf, scoring par or better.

A. GAME: Play golf on an actual course or Tactical Reality Golf, twosomes, threesomes, or foursomes.

Goal: Play four or five holes in as few strokes possible.

Conditions: See figure 9.2.

B. PRACTICE TASK: Students analyze the four or five holes just completed. Students formulate written assessment of their game performance (i.e., skills, such as drives, approach shots, putting, etc.; and game play, such as shot selection, performance of preshot routine, selection of intermediate target).

Goal: Assess your golf game to improve play and lower score.

C. GAME: Play golf on an actual course or Tactical Reality Golf, twosomes, threesomes, or foursomes.

Goal: Play same four or five holes in fewer strokes.

SUMMARY

There are several videotapes, books, and magazines that provide information related to tactical and skill development. You can modify many drills and practice situations in these resources for your students. Experienced players enjoy working on various aspects of their game, as they realize the value of consistent, accurate shot making. Assign students the task of searching for new drills and tips to improve their games. This will help them to identify available resources for future reference. Thus, you are not only providing players with golf experience, but also offering experience identifying sources to help them develop personal skill and improve game performance.

Encourage students to play golf on a regulation course. Give them credit for a family golf outing or playing a round of golf with three of their friends. Let students know that it's OK to play, even though they may not be very skilled. After all, most golfers are far from skilled. Teach students that etiquette and courtesy count most on the golf course. As long as they allow faster groups to play through, repair divots, rake traps, and treat the golf course *gently*, they will be welcome on any golf course. You may also want to identify three or four local courses that would be best for beginners. Visit these courses yourself to see if you can get some coupons or other money-saving deals (e.g., two for one, or 18 holes for the price of 9).

Part III

ASSESSING AND IMPLEMENTING A TACTICAL APPROACH

CHAPTER 10

Assessing Outcomes

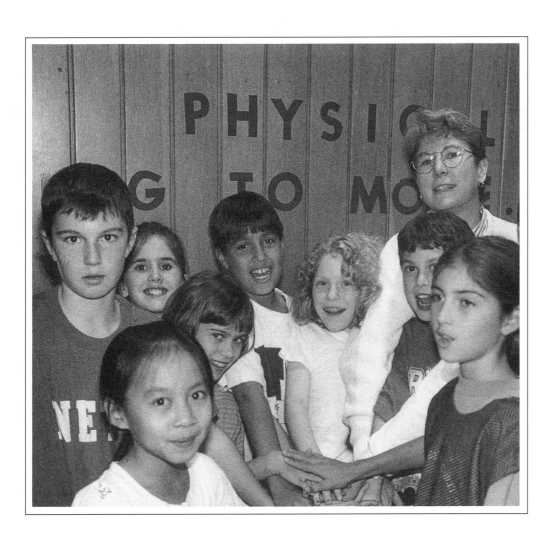

We have provided a rationale for teaching tactics and several examples of how to do this with different games and sports. We now address what learning outcomes we are looking for as a result of using a tactical approach to games teaching. Identifying specific outcomes, such as game performance, enables you as teachers to hold yourselves and your students accountable for teaching and learning. In chapter 2 we stressed that game performance is the primary goal of a tactical approach. To that end game performance should be the primary focus of assessment.

AUTHENTIC ASSESSMENT

Assessment can be for summative purposes (i.e., assigning grades) or, in particular, for formative purposes (i.e., providing feedback for diagnosing strengths and weaknesses and checking on student progress). Whichever the case, we recommend that assessment be ongoing and regular, rather than the typical beginning and end of unit or year assessment, and that it be *authentic*. That is, if the aim of games teaching is to improve students' game performance, assessment should address all aspects of performance rather than just one or two components. Assess game performance within its context. In this chapter we will elaborate on authentic assessment, which is critical to effective evaluation of students, instruction, and programs. Let us begin by identifying a potential range of outcomes.

Figure 10.1 presents anticipated learning outcomes in diagrammatic form and indicates relationships between these outcomes. Figure 10.1 suggests that improvements in game performance, the primary goal of a tactical approach, will lead to increased enjoyment, interest, and perceived competence. These affective outcomes are important if we are to motivate students to play games and sport later in life.

Improved game performance comes from increased tactical awareness. Tactical awareness is defined as the ability to identify problems and their solutions in game situations. The link between game performance and tactical awareness occurs through off-the-ball movements, skill selection, and skill execution. Improvements in one or all of these will result in enhanced game performance.

Clearly if game performance is the central outcome in a tactical approach, then we must be able to assess game performance effectively. This is difficult because game performance involves more than executing motor skills. For example, in a volleyball game consider how often your students contact the ball. Successful performance in the game involves much more than on-the-ball skills. Players spend most time making tactical decisions and moving to execute those decisions, for example setting up to attack, winning the point, or defending space on your side of the net. These aspects of game performance are not typically assessed, and it may take some time to develop a practiced eye to observe. In this chapter

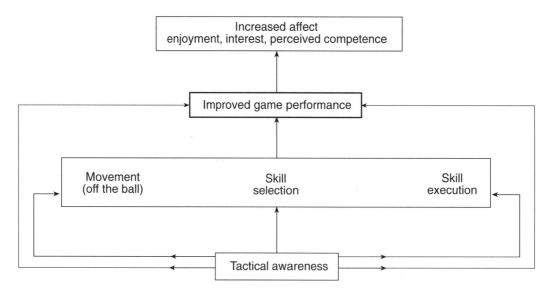

Figure 10.1 Anticipated learning outcomes.

we will provide you with some examples of how to assess off-the-ball movements and on-the-ball skills during game play.

Physical educators have typically relied on skill testing to assess student game performance, and there are many examples of common skill tests in any measurement textbook. Yet there are problems with using skill tests to assess game performance, as these tests do not predict playing performance. In addition, skill tests usually measure skills out of game context, in situations not related to game play. For example, you might be familiar with skill tests in soccer, volleyball, or softball that require students to propel a ball against a wall in some way to assess playing ability. Such skill tests fail to assess students' ability to make appropriate decisions about what to do, nor do they assess the ability to execute skill under game conditions. Given this, tests of isolated skill cannot constitute valid assessment of game-playing ability. These assessment methods do not reflect the broader view of game performance advocated in chapter 2 and thus do not provide a means of authentic assessment. Veal (1993) makes the case for authentic assessment in games teaching when she states "if the teacher's goals for students center around successful game play, then assessment must also center around game play." (p. 95)

As the teacher you must be aware of student development when you identify appropriate learning outcomes. For example, referring to the tactical framework for soccer, you might expect students at level I to understand the need to pass and control the ball quickly and accurately. You must discern critical points, including the degree to which students look for teammates to pass to, the appropriateness of the selected receiver (i.e., an open teammate rather than one who is marked or guarded), and the quality of execution (i.e., the accuracy, pace, and timing of the pass). As the teacher, you can observe the quality of the receiver's ball control by paying attention to the technique she uses to receive the ball and the speed with which she is ready for the next move, whether it be a pass, shot, or dribble.

At level III you could develop and assess your students' awareness of movements that would create space in attack. For example, it is easy to observe players who make overlapping runs to the sidelines of the field. Supporting runs of this kind are valuable in creating space in attack. Students should receive credit for these efforts even if they do not receive the ball. Although a player may not receive a pass after making a strong overlapping run, space will be created for the teammate in possession because defenders must move to cover the overlapping player. In the next section we provide you with a simple and flexible observation instrument, which, we believe, allows the assessment of game performance in its broadest context.

GAME PERFORMANCE ASSESSMENT INSTRUMENT (GPAI)

The authentic assessment of game performance requires observing participants when they are not in possession of the ball. Therefore, carefully planned observation is essential. To this end we have developed the Game Performance Assessment Instrument (GPAI). We designed the GPAI to provide teachers and researchers a means of observing and coding performance behaviors. The GPAI includes behaviors that demonstrate the ability to solve tactical problems in games by making decisions, moving appropriately, and executing skills. We initially developed game performance components for the GPAI through consultation with five teacher-coaches who had expertise in each games classification category discussed in chapter 2 (see table 2.1). Our aim was to identify observable components of game performance that applied, as far as possible, across game categories. After identifying seven components, we formulated descriptions of each component and reformulated them until all experts reached consensus. We list and define these seven components of game performance in figure 10.2.

Examples will clarify the components of game performance identified in figure 10.2. In badminton, a singles player should recover to the center of his court between shots to enable easy movement to the front or back of the court for the next shot. This center court area is a *base* position. In softball, an outfielder will *adjust* position according to whether the hitter is right-handed or left-handed. Decision making occurs in all games. For example, before executing a forearm pass a volleyball player must *decide* if this is the appropriate shot to play. Having made this decision, *skill execution* might be successful or unsuccessful. Nevertheless, you should give players credit for

Game Performance Assessment Instrument (GPAI)

1. Base—Appropriate return of performer to a home or recovery position between skill attempts
2. Adjust—Movement of performer, either offensively or defensively, as required by the flow of the game
3. Decision making—Making appropriate choices about what to do with the ball (or projectile) during a game
4. Skill execution—Efficient performance of selected skills
5. Support—Off-the-ball movement to a position to receive a pass when player's team has possession
6. Cover—Providing defensive help for player making a play on the ball or moving to the ball (or projectile)
7. Guard or mark—Defending against an opponent who may or may not have the ball (or projectile)

Figure 10.2 Components of game performance.

making correct decisions about *what* to do even though they may not subsequently execute a skill efficiently. *Support* is critical to all games, particularly invasion games. Simply put, if a soccer player does not have available receivers in appropriate positions, she will not be able to pass the ball and the team will find it difficult to maintain possession. *Cover* is important in game play from the defensive point of view. Again in soccer, a defender advancing to make a tackle should have a *covering* defender (a teammate) behind him in case he misses the tackle. Lastly the ability to *guard* or *mark* opponents, particularly in invasion games, is crucial to effective defense of space. The obvious example of this is player-to-player defense in basketball.

We recognize that not all components of game performance apply to all games. For example, the categories of *base*, *adjust*, and *execute* are important variables for successful softball performance. On the other hand, the category of base applies less to an invasion game such as soccer than do the remaining six categories. An appealing feature of the GPAI is that the observer can choose to assess all components of game performance (as identified by the GPAI) or only selected components. For example, figure 10.3 shows assessment of game performance during a soccer unit that focused on maintaining possession of the ball and attacking the goal. You might choose to focus on the components of *support*, *decision making*, and *skill execution*.

You can easily build criteria for assessment into a game-specific record sheet, as we have done for soccer in figure 10.3. These criteria might vary for students who are working at different levels. So for example, we coded Matthew's supporting runs to space as appropriate, but we coded his lack of support for teammates when they needed it as inappropriate. We code appropriateness, or

lack of it, each time Matthew makes a decision about what to do with the ball. For example, when he passes to a teammate who is closely marked (guarded) we tally the decision as inappropriate. If such a pass is technically well struck, we code it as efficiently executed.

By using a simple tally system the observer can measure the number of appropriate or efficient and inappropriate or inefficient performances. After observing and recording performance, you can group the data for individual components of game performance and overall game involvement and performance. You can include both *appropriate or efficient* and *inappropriate or inefficient* responses to gain as complete a picture as possible of each student's performance. Examples of possible performance measures, using the data collection sheet in figure 10.3, are as follows:

1. Game involvement = number of appropriate decisions + number of inappropriate decisions + number of efficient skill executions + number of inefficient skill executions + number of appropriate supporting movements

2. Decision-making index (DMI) = number of appropriate decisions made ÷ number of inappropriate decisions made

3. Skill execution index (SEI) = number of efficient skill executions ÷ number of inefficient skill executions

4. Support index (SI) = number of appropriate supporting movements ÷ number of inappropriate supporting movements

5. Game performance = [DMI + SEI + SI] ÷ 3

It is important to include inappropriate decisions and inefficient skill executions in determining game involvement. This recognizes that lower ability students, who may not make appropriate

Date 4/16/96   GPAI Soccer   Class 2C

Component of game performance   Criteria for appropriate or efficient rating (to include all restarts—throw-ins, goal
                                 kicks, corners)

1. Decision made   Criteria   Player attempts to pass to an open teammate
                              Player attempts to shoot when appropriate

2. Skill education   Criteria
                     Reception—Control of pass and setup of the ball
                     Passing—Ball reaches target
                     Shooting—Ball stays below head height and is on target

3. Support   Criteria   The player appeared to support the ball carrier by being in or moving to an appropriate
                        position to receive a pass

Name	Decision made		Skill execution		Support	
	A	IA	E	IE	A	IA
Matthew	xxxxx	x	xxxxxx	x	xxxxxxx	xxxx
Bryan					xxx	xxx
Katie	xxxxx	x	xxxxx	x	xxxx	x
Kelly	xx	x	xxx	x	xxxxx	xx
Peter	xxx	xx	xx	xxx	xx	x
Alison	x	xx	x	xx	xxxxxxx	x

Key   A = appropriate   IA = inappropriate
      E = efficient   IE = inefficient

Figure 10.3 Observation of soccer performance.

decisions or execute skills efficiently, can still be highly involved in a game. We *do not* include inappropriate support in the calculation of game involvement because this clearly indicates a lack of involvement in the game. Game performance is the arithmetical average of the decision-making, skill execution, and support indices. This calculation ensures that players whose score indicates strong game performance do have contact with the ball, make good decisions, and execute skills well within the game. The data in figure 10.3 provide an example. We have observed Matthew's team playing soccer and have assessed players' decision making, skill execution, and support. Each X on the recording sheet represents one observation. After adding up his scores for each component of game performance, we applied the formulas suggested previously to give the following measures of Matthew's game play performance:

Game involvement = 6+1+6+1+7 = 21
Decision making = 6÷1 = 6
Skill execution = 6÷1 = 6
Support = 7÷4 = 1.75
Game performance = (6+6+1.75)÷3 = 4.58

Matthew has been highly involved in the game and his decision-making and skill-execution scores indicate a high degree of success, though there were some occasions in which he failed to give support to teammates. Bryan, on the other hand, was not particularly involved in the game either with or without the ball. Using the formulas, his respective measures of game performance are 3, 0, 0, 1, and 1. Katie's performance was strong overall, and Alison's scores are interesting. Though not particularly successful in either her decision making or her skill execution, Alison was involved in the game. Her scores for support provide evidence of this, suggesting that she worked hard to be in a position to receive the ball. Therefore, the GPAI provides you with useful information about the strengths and weaknesses of your students' game play. In addition, if we were to use the formulas to calculate final game performance scores for all team members, they would be as follows:

- Matthew = 4.58
- Bryan = 0.33
- Katie = 4.67
- Kelly = 2.5
- Peter = 1.39
- Alison = 2.67

A word of caution is in order if you will use these scores for summative (i.e., grading) purposes. For example, Matthew scored 4.58 but the question arises, 4.58 out of what? Scores on the GPAI are relative to each other and there is no maximum score. Consider that a game performance score of greater than one indicates that a student averaged more appropriate or efficient responses than inappropriate or inefficient responses (Matthew's ratio was four to one). You could set targets for students relative to GPAI scores, for example, "See if you can score three on decision making today." If you choose to use GPAI scores for grade assignment, we recommend combining game performance and game involvement scores to give students enough credit both for quality of performance and for their attempts to be fully involved in game play.

ALTERNATIVE GPAI FORMATS

In this section we provide another GPAI format we've found useful for assessing game performance. This format enables you to observe and assess more students in a short time. You might use this format in conjunction with the previous format, to verify data recorded by yourself or your students.

Figure 10.4 presents a group GPAI recording sheet for assessing game performance in soccer. Using this data sheet, you can focus on any or all components of game performance and observe several students within a game situation. Use a five-point scale to rate students on each component you are observing, a score of five representing effective performance. Be aware, this format provides only an overview of student's game performance and may not be as accurate as the tally system of the previous format.

Perhaps it is best to provide an example of how to use this format. To assess game performance you might observe students during game play for a specified time (e.g., five minutes). During this period, observe carefully the components of game play you have selected for assessment. It is impossible to observe every student's performance of each component at once. We recommend that you restrict observation to two or three components and to a handful of students at a time (perhaps a team). After observing one team for five minutes, record each player's level (five through one) of game performance for each selected component. Using figure 10.4, we have assessed Becky's team on the components of support and marking in soccer. Assume that the assessment took place during a level II instructional unit, which emphasizes off-the-ball movement, both offensively and defensively. You could complete the observation sheet by assessing other components of game performance during the unit.

As a further example, having focused basketball instruction on maintaining possession and creating space in the attack, you might observe the quality of passing (decisions and executions) and the use of the V-cut (support) to create space in the attack. Be aware that some lower skilled students might show good understanding by making appropriate decisions about what to do with the ball, but may lack the skill to carry out these decisions. It is possible for students to score well on decision making but not on skill execution. This suggests that the game performance of some technically competent students may suffer because of poor decision making about when and where to apply skills within the game.

Teachers commonly ask two questions about the GPAI:

1. *How do you decide on criteria?* The criteria you develop to assess game performance components, such as decision making, skill execution, and support will depend on what you have taught during your instructional unit. Make note of your criteria (i.e., what you expect to see from students who are effective performers relative to each component you are assessing) and follow the procedures described previously for the soccer example.

2. *How can we make the GPAI more objective and less subjective?* This relates to the quality of the criteria you establish. Our field trials of the GPAI indicate that, where criteria are clear and specific, two observers assessing the same performer will

Game Performance Assessment Instrument

Date 4/16/96   Class 2C   Game Soccer (6 v 6)

Data sheet scoring key   5 = very effective performance
                            4 = effective performance
                            3 = moderately effective performance
                            2 = weak performance
                            1 = very weak performance

Criteria

Support—Player tries to be in a position to receive a pass

Marking—Player marks an opponent when ball comes into the defensive half of the field

Name	Base	Adjust	Decision making	Skill execution	Support	Cover	Guard or mark
Becky					4		5
David					3		3
Carolyn					5		4
Sheila					2		3
Susan					3		2
Larry					2		4

Figure 10.4 Game performance assessment instrument.

be in close agreement (within one point) at least 80 percent of the time. We have conducted several trials of this nature, with both undergraduate students and physical education teachers of all levels as observers. Results suggest that objectivity is quite possible if the criteria you establish are clear.

GETTING STARTED

Here we provide suggestions you may find helpful in getting you and your students started with the GPAI, whichever form you might use.

1. Videotape one team involved in a small-sided game.

2. Select the components of game performance that you will observe (these should be based on what you have taught).

3. Develop criteria for appropriate and efficient performance. Ask yourself what you can reasonably expect of your students in light of what you have taught.

4. Practice from videotape so you will feel comfortable using the GPAI in a live setting.

We encourage you to get your students involved in peer assessment. We have done this with middle and high school students, and preservice and inservice teachers, who have all found the GPAI useful and easy to use. Before students use the GPAI it is important for you to review with them the selected components of game performance and the criteria you have developed. Following are a few examples of how you might use the GPAI with your students as observers.

In volleyball, assume you have four teams: A, B, C, and D. If team A is playing team B, assign each member of team C to watch one member of team A and each member of team D to watch one member of team B. Thus, each student is paired with a member of another team. As teams A and B play, C and D observe and record on the GPAI. After a five-minute or 11-point game, have the teams switch roles. Here students could use the volleyball GPAI sheet (see figure 10.5).

In softball, assume you have three permanent teams of 8 to 10 players. Assign each player to observe a member of another team. For example, players on team A observe players on team B; team B players observe team C players; and team

C players observe team A players. As teams A and B play, players on team C observe their assigned team A player and record data on the softball GPAI (see figure 10.6). Rotate teams after two or three innings, allowing each team to observe at least two innings during the same class period.

In soccer, assume you have four permanent teams of six or seven players. Assign each player a five-minute observation period during which she observes her *own* team on the selected components of game performance, using the format presented in figure 10.4. One player per team observes at a time, keeping an equal number of players per team on the field. Have players of similar ability observing at the same time to keep the playing teams equitable.

Student measures provide you several checks on your own assessments, adding to your data and holding students accountable for being knowledgeable observers of game performance. Student observations do not necessarily take place during one lesson but can take place over several lessons, making assessment an ongoing process. In addition, using students as observers maintains their involvement during downtime and integrates cooperative learning into a lesson. Students can even work with each other to develop criteria for their own assessment.

SUMMARY

The flexibility of the GPAI enables the observer to focus on specific aspects of game performance, such as support, marking, cover, decision making, and skill execution, and to develop his own criteria for what constitutes effective performance. This is advantageous because it can assist the observer in diagnosing specific strengths and weaknesses of students' game performance. It is, of course, imperative that observers have enough knowledge to make accurate judgments about what is effective performance. Criteria for these judgments should be well thought out before observing.

The GPAI provides you with an authentic means of assessing a student's ability to play games. Our intent in developing the GPAI is to redefine game performance as a *process* that takes place whether or not players are in possession of the ball, puck, or Frisbee. This encourages teachers to think more broadly about game performance and to assess it authentically.

GPAI Volleyball

Evaluator _____   Date _____

Class _____

Categories

Decisions made—criteria   two levels
        1 = pass ball over the net
        2 = pass to set up attack

Skill execution—criteria
        Forearm and overhead pass = legal contact, playable ball

Adjust—criteria
        Player moves to open up or in pursuit to save a ball

Recording procedures—Use a tally to mark the appropriate category.

Names	Decision made		Skill execution		Adjust	
	A	IA	E	IE	A	IA

Figure 10.5

GPAI Softball

Class _____   Date _____

Evaluator _____

Categories   (Note: These categories represent offensive game play.)

Start—Player is in an appropriate starting position (for example, with no runners on base and no outs, players should play straight away).

Backup—Player provides backup to player fielding a ball or a player covering a base.

Catch and throw—Player fields ball *cleanly* (without fumbling) and, if appropriate, throws accurately to base or relay.

Decision making—Player makes the appropriate play, considering the situation (for example, with no runners on base, no outs, and a grounder to short stop, the throw should go to first base).

Recording procedures   Use a tally to mark the appropriate category. Mark each player's responses during offensive game play (for example, each time a batter comes to the plate and the fielder plays the appropriate starting position, indicate that response with a tally 1 in the *Start, Appropriate* category). If the player you are evaluating fields the ball, be sure to mark whether or not she made an appropriate or inappropriate decision.

Player or inning	Start		Backup		Catch and throw		Decision making	
	A	I	A	I	E	I	A	I

Figure 10.6

CHAPTER 11

Implementing the Approach

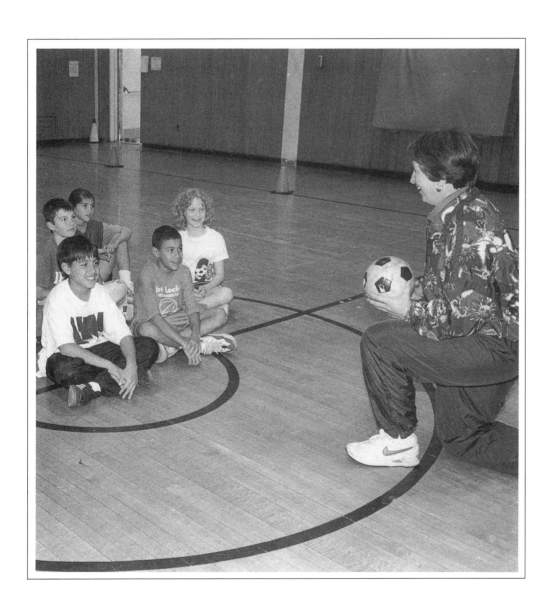

This chapter will help you examine your openness to new ideas and attitudes toward change. The question teachers most commonly ask is, "How do I get started?" We understand this to mean, how can you feel safe trying a new approach, and how do you make it your own. To address these questions and others you may have we will focus on the specific practices, attitudes, and skills teachers attempting to master new knowledge will need. We feel strongly that teachers learn the most when communication is open among teachers in K-12 schools, preservice programs, and college or university settings. You are not alone!

In the first part of this chapter we address skills and attitudes to help you as you learn a tactical approach. In the second part of this chapter we provide you with implementing practices we have learned from our experiences and the experiences of preservice and inservice teachers. These practices, attitudes, and skills add up to your own teacher development process.

We will present four skills and attitudes Joyce and Showers (1995) have identified that facilitate your learning potential as teacher. These are (a) putting your learning into action, (b) persistence, (c) meeting the cognitive demands of instruction, and (d) flexibility. We will address each issue separately.

PUTTING YOUR LEARNING INTO ACTION

You have probably attended many classes, conferences, workshops, and read books that have motivated you to consider change. The problem is how do you turn your motivation into action? In other words how do you *make* the transfer? Transfer is the ability to convey something you have learned from one situation to another. In this section we look at the *phases of transfer* every teacher goes through to make a new learning structure truly her own. This is important because making changes is never easy and seeing the phases of transfer gives you a perspective that the difficulties are a normal part of the change process. As teachers, we vary in our ability to transfer a new teaching approach to our settings. You may want to consider these phases of transfer on a continuum. The notion of a continuum provides you with a way of thinking about struggles (discomfort) you may have with new knowledge (Joyce and Showers 1995). For example, you may be uncomfortable beginning your lessons with a game (e.g., 3 v 3 in volleyball) because you have always begun your lessons with an exercise or skill-drill warm-up.

We invite you to consider where on the continuum in figure 11.1 you might be after reading this chapter and suggest you return occasionally to see how you are progressing.

1. *Imitative transfer* is an exact replication of skills, knowledge, or ideas. For example, you may use exact questions, games, or practice tasks from the lessons in the earlier part of the textbook. You may also attend a teacher development workshop and use the exact drills or games as they were presented at the workshop.

2. *Mechanical transfer* is horizontal transfer in the basic structure of lessons. For example, you start to change the format of your lesson by beginning the lesson with a game, such as playing 3 v 3 in volleyball unit.

3. *Routine transfer* is using skills and strategies at this stage with ease and comfort but not carrying them over throughout the curriculum. For example, you may choose to implement a tactical approach for teaching just invasion games (e.g., soccer, team handball, and basketball) but not net games (e.g., tennis and badminton).

4. *Integrative transfer* is taking the approach across subject areas. This means that you begin to view other teaching-learning environments through this approach. Perhaps you teach health or coach a varsity sport and implement principles of the approach in that situation.

5. *Executive control* happens when you are grounded in the theory and can select and implement materials appropriately and comfortably throughout the curriculum. You are able to make decisions and problem solve because you understand the principles. In other words you are in *charge* of the material and have completely made it yours.

Imitative	Mechanical	Routine	Integrative	Executive control

Figure 11.1 Where on the continuum do you fall in your ability to transfer a new teaching approach in your classroom setting?

We are not at all suggesting that transfer is a clean, clear, linear process. You may find yourself jumping along the entire continuum throughout one unit! We encourage you to work toward executive control.

PERSISTENCE

Persistence is what Joyce and Showers (1995) call "driving through" the initial trials in which performance is awkward. For example, as a player you know how hard it is to change your golf swing or your tennis backhand. Think about how hard it is as a teacher to give up using calisthenics as warm-ups or to use a game *before* skill practice. The key to success often is pure determination (not necessarily talent); this will go a long way to serve you in overcoming the difficulty of changing behavior.

During a project that focused on learning to teach using a tactical approach, Danielle, a middle school physical education teacher, provided an example of persistence when we asked her how she felt about using a new approach with sixth graders. Danielle states, "When you have taught one way and you are in the pressure of the moment, you have to work hard not to go back to your old way."

MEETING THE COGNITIVE DEMANDS OF INSTRUCTION

Teachers have complained that their preservice program has overemphasized theory and neglected the practical aspects of teaching (Joyce and Showers 1995). Nonetheless, teachers who acknowledge the importance of understanding theory can better *meet the cognitive demands of instruction*. When you know what to do and how to do it you can be flexible and use the new knowledge appropriately in many situations.

FLEXIBILITY

Flexibility is an *openness* to consider that alternatives have something to offer. We realize that being flexible is important in all aspects of teaching. Nonetheless it can serve you well when you participate in the teacher-as-learner process. For example, a teacher who has always used a technical approach to games teaching starts his volleyball unit by teaching the forearm pass and setting students up to practice this skill. Generally his role is *information giver* (direct instruction). Now this teacher shifts to implementing a tactical approach in the volleyball unit. Here he would place students in small-sided games and, after game play, gather them for discussion, using his questions to address the value of setting up to attack using the forearm pass. The teacher's role now shifts from information giver to *information processor* (indirect instruction). This role shift will require the teacher to be flexible.

IMPLEMENTING PRACTICES

We have developed implementing practices from our teacher and staff development efforts. These practices will help create a safe learning-by-doing climate (Stallings 1989).

1. Make explicit your core beliefs.
2. Think small.
3. Pick your favorite sport.
4. Make it yours.
5. Think gamelike.
6. Make your lessons reflect a game-practice-game cycle.
7. Plan a unit.
8. Find company.

In the following section we will discuss each of these practices in more detail.

1. *Make explicit your core beliefs.* Beliefs are highly resistant to change and serve as a filter through which our experiences must pass (Lortie 1975; Pajares 1992). Beliefs help individuals understand their world and persevere even when contradictory evidence is presented (Nisbett and Ross 1980; Peterman 1991). Core beliefs form the center of a belief system. They are the most powerful beliefs and exert a strong influence over other beliefs. Core beliefs are also the most resistant to change because they become part of us at an early stage (Nisbett and Ross 1980; Rokeach 1968).

We offer a games-teaching continuum as a way of thinking about your core beliefs on games teaching (see figure 11.2).

On the left is the technical (drill-for-skill practice) approach, on the right is a tactical approach, and in the middle a progression we refer to as a

Technical	Gamelike	Tactical

Figure 11.2 Games teaching continuum.

gamelike approach. A gamelike approach shifts skill practice from isolated drills (e.g., shuttle or circle drills in volleyball) to drills arranged within the tempo and flow of the game (e.g., triad drill in volleyball).

The games-teaching continuum acts as a gauge to (a) give you a reading of where you are and (b) offer possible progressions for moving your games teaching toward a tactical approach. One teacher from our workshops and research shares her change in her core beliefs:

"I have always been concerned about the development of my students' skills. When first beginning to teach physical education, and up until a few years ago, I taught technical skills in isolation; detached from the game or activity, such as, forearm passing to oneself or set to the wall . . . . Realizing that I made very little impact on the level of skill improvement in my students has caused me to reconsider my philosophical perspective. I no longer expect my students to demonstrate a specified level of skill proficiency. Rather, the expectation is utilization of various skills to accomplish the tactics within the game." (Berkowitz 1996)

2. *Think small.* Start with *one* class of your choice, giving a high priority to groups that can work together (Griffin 1996). Because the primary structure of a tactical approach is the small-sided game or game form, you need to feel comfortable teaching many small groups or pairs (Berkowitz 1996). Part of the difficulty in introducing a new teaching process into the classroom is students' discomfort with change (Joyce and Showers 1995). Trying a new teaching approach for you is trying a new learning approach for your students, so it is change for all of you. By choosing one class you have begun to build a safe environment to explore an alternative approach to games teaching and learning.

3. *Pick your favorite sport.* Select the game you feel most comfortable with, which for us translates into a strong content knowledge. This strategy provides a way of linking prior knowledge to new information (Stallings 1989). We have had first-hand experience with this, and have also observed and collaborated with preservice and inservice teachers as they grapple with a tactical approach in a game. For us and those teachers a

strong content knowledge made transfer easier. For example, one teacher chose volleyball because she had played competitively at the college level and coached at the high school level. She felt this was her strongest sport, so it was a fit.

4. *Make it yours.* The previous chapters provide you with a model, frameworks, a starting point, and our view of a tactical approach. We recognize that a teaching and learning environment is complex, contextually based, and may require modifications for your school, your students, and you (Griffin 1996). For example, making it yours may require you to change sequence of the tactical problems or levels of tactical complexity. You may need to modify the lessons depending on students' ability levels or the facilities or equipment. We anticipate and encourage you to meet the needs of *your* teaching and learning situation, which is why we advocate *a* tactical approach to games teaching, not *the* tactical approach to games teaching. We understand that any significant innovation, if it is to result in change, requires individual implementers to work out their own meaning (Fullan 1991).

5. *Think gamelike.* Thinking gamelike means considering how you can arrange the skills and tactics for practice within the flow and tempo of the game (Griffin 1996). For example, gamelike practice for volleyball is a triad formation. Figure 11.3 illustrates the triad with a focus on forearm passing. The triad formation involves a minimum of three players fulfilling three roles described as initiator, performer, and target player within each drill (Griffin 1994). If you have more than three players in the drill you can add roles such as collector, feeder, or an additional performer. Triad drills, such as toss-pass to target, serve-serve receive to target, toss-set-hit, pass-set-hit, or any other skill or tactical combinations of the game, simulate the tempo and flow of volleyball. Gamelike drills enhance the quality of practice.

Thinking gamelike increases the likelihood of carryover into the game. Let us again use volleyball and consider drills such as practicing volleyball skill against the wall, partners passing back and forth without the net, using a circle or semicircle to practice skills, or using a shuttle formation to practice skills. These drills provide

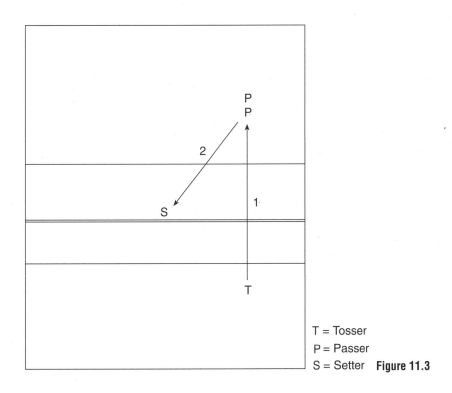

T = Tosser
P = Passer
S = Setter   **Figure 11.3**

many opportunities to practice but clearly have nothing to do with the flow and tempo of a volleyball game. Gamelike practice allows students to develop skills within the context of the game. It also promotes a cooperative learning environment.

6. *Make your lessons reflect a game-practice-game cycle.* Let us start by writing specific lesson plans that reflect a game-practice-game cycle. After determining the tactical problem and lesson focus include the following specifics in your lesson format:

a. *Objective.* The objective relates to the on-the-ball skills and off-the-ball movements you want your students to become aware of to solve a tactical problem. For example, if you are at level I you want your students to understand the value of setting up to attack. The lesson goal will be the on-the-ball skill of forearm pass and the off-the-ball movement of open up.

b. *Initial game.* First, game conditions refer to all the essential components, such as number of students, size of the court or playing area, equipment type (i.e., regulation or modified ball) and modifications (i.e., net height), and specific conditions (i.e., two hits on a side, three passes before a shot). Second, the goal of the game will directly reflect the goal of the lesson. We continue with

the volleyball example in which students are engaged in a small-sided volleyball game. Game conditions are lower net, narrow and short court, modified volleyball, initiating game from a free ball, alternating toss, and rotating after each point. The goal of the game is that teams score a point each time the pass goes to the setter.

c. *Questions.* We have learned that constructing questions presents some difficulty initially. The most important questions are the *what to do* and *how to do it* questions that drive the tactical model. You can simply ask your students, "What was the goal of the game?" and, "How did you accomplish the goal?" You don't have to limit yourself to these types of questions. *Would, should,* and *why* questions will promote students' critical thinking skills. Returning to the volleyball lesson, students gather and the teacher asks questions such as, "Were you able to attack?" "If so why, if not why not?" "What do you need to do to have the opportunity to hit or spike?" "Where must you pass the ball?" "How do you perform the forearm pass?"

d. *Practice task.* Essential elements for quality practice involve (a) running drills on the field or court because this is where games are played, (b) organizing gamelike practice to match the game-playing goal, (c) using specific feedback related to key words, (d) providing goals for practice, and (e) keeping activity compatible with skill levels of players. Going back to the volleyball lesson, students would practice the forearm pass in triads (see chapter 5, level I, lesson 1 for details).

e. *Closing game.* The purpose of the closing game is to reinforce the focus or goal of your lesson and to allow application of practiced skills. The conditions of the game reflect all the essential game components. This game may or may not be different from the initial game you have read about in the specific sport chapters. You can consider it a way of reinforcing the goal of the lesson, perhaps by having students keep track of the number of shots taken in basketball games or number of passes completed in soccer. To finish the volleyball example, students would return to the original game and the original conditions to reinforce the lesson goal. Students could compare the scores of the initial game to the closing game or count the number of successful forearm passes to target.

7. *Plan a unit.* Next consider how you might plan a whole unit. First, consider your goals or objectives. Ask yourself what tactical problems you want your students to solve. Here you have two choices: (a) consult our levels of tactical complexity, or (b) use the tactical problems to organize your unit and develop your own levels. For example, if you are getting ready to teach a volleyball unit you may focus only on the tactical problems of setting up to attack and winning the point. After you have decided on tactical problems, you can consult the levels of tactical complexity to establish the on-the-ball skills and off-the-ball movements appropriate for the level of your students.

Second, what is the length of your unit? The length of your unit should be consistent with your goal. For example, if the duration of your unit is going to be short (8-10 lessons) limit the tactical problems you address in your unit. Using the tactical problems as the organizing feature for the unit provides you with a clear match between length and goals of unit. Limiting the number of tactical problems gives you the opportunity to have depth in your unit. In other words, do a few things well.

Third, organize a block plan that outlines a progression of learning tasks for each day of your unit. A block plan provides you with a view of the big picture and can help keep you focused. Figure 11.4 provides you with an example of a volleyball block plan.

8. *Find company.* We encourage you to learn in a supportive environment, that is, teachers making productive use of peers. Research on training (Joyce and Showers 1995) has documented the benefits of peers helping peers, meaning teachers helping teachers implement innovations. You can then share problems and successes. A collaborative group can give you an opportunity for reflection and problem solving (Stallings, 1989).

A specific strategy for making productive use of peers is the notion of the *coaching of teaching.* That is follow-up help from each other as you implement a new teaching process such as a tactical approach. Peer coaching uses a support community (cohort groups) with feedback procedures to improve or change classroom practice and is not tied to evaluation (Joyce and Showers 1995). Specific outcomes or educational benefits of peer coaching indicated coached teachers (a) practice more, (b) develop more skills, (c) use new strategies more appropriately, (d) have greater long-term retention of skills, (e) are more likely to teach students new skills, and (f) recognize purposes and uses of new skills (Showers 1982, 1984, 1985).

The possible benefits of teachers helping each other are endless. Knowing who to approach, what to ask them for help with, and being sensitive to individual teachers' needs will go a long way in building a strong professional culture. Both preservice and inservice teachers need others to share and confirm small successes and to support each other in taking risks.

REFLECTIONS AND CONCLUSIONS

We believe that a tactical approach enables students to understand games more deeply than a technical approach, to play more effectively, and to appreciate the similarities among games. Again a teacher reflects on her feelings about implementing a tactical approach:

"There have been a number of positive outcomes using this approach. If my goal was to have

Day 1
Introduction to unit
3 v 3 game
  • base position
  • free ball (toss)
Closure
	Day 2
	3 v 3 game
	Setting up to attack
	  • forearm pass (FAP)
	Practice = FAP
	3 v 3 game
	Closure

Day 3
3 v 3 game
Setting up to attack
  • setter open up
Practice = FAP and open up
3 v 3 game
Closure
	Day 4
	3 v 3 game
	Setting up to attack
	  • setter pass to hitter
	Practice = open up and pass to hitter
	3 v 3 game
	Closure

Day 5 3 v 3 game Setting up to attack and winning the point • transition by hitter Practice = pass, open up, and transition 3 v 3 game Closure	Day 6 3 v 3 game Winning the point by attacking the ball Practice = hitting/spiking 3 v 3 game Closure

Day 7
3 v 3 game
Attacking the ball
  • transition to hit/spike
Extend practice
3 v 3 game
Closure
	Day 8
	3 v 3 game
	Review = setting up to attack
	            winning the point by attack
	3 v 3 game
	Closure

Day 9 3 v 3 game Review = setting up to attack winning the point by attack 3 v 3 game Closure	Day 10 3 v 3 tournament Closure

Figure 11.4 Example block plan for volleyball.

students play the game more effectively, then letting them play the game was critical. Because my students have had increasingly more opportunities to play games and solve tactical problems, they seem to have a better understanding of games in general. Technical skill work still occurs but never in isolation, always as it would in the game and mostly as a means to accomplish the tactical problems. Students come in excited, positive, and ready to go because they know they are going to get to play a game of some form. I no longer hear, 'Are we going to play a game today?'" (Berkowitz 1996).

A tactical approach can provide students of all developmental levels with a greater understand-ing of games and improved game performance. Tactical awareness is a developmentally appropriate focus for teaching games (Mitchell, Griffin, and Oslin 1994). This approach also focuses on developmentally appropriate skill acquisition and ensures that students learn skills when they appreciate their value to the game. Then they practice these skills under conditions that enable them to relate skills to game context. The process of teaching for tactical awareness is based on *playing the game,* an enjoyable activity for most students. Physical education programs promote lifetime participation in physical activity as a primary goal. Nevertheless, this goal will only happen if individuals experience enjoyment in physical activity. The identification and assessment of outcomes based on tactical awareness can contribute to progressive gains in game performance, critical thinking, and enjoyment at successive stages of development.

We believe that a tactical approach to games teaching can be more than just a teaching approach. It can be part of a curriculum that reflects a change in the way you think about games teaching. A tactical approach will challenge your core beliefs. We wish to leave you with the challenge of matching content, such as soccer, volleyball, and softball, with a context that helps students make meaning—through playing games!

References

Almond, L. 1986. Reflecting on themes: A games classification. P. 71-72 in *Rethinking games teaching*, edited by R. Thorpe, D. Bunker, and L. Almond. Loughborough: University of Technology.

Berkowitz, R.J. 1996. A practitioner's journey from skill to tactics. *Journal of Physical Education, Recreation and Dance* 67 (4): 44-45.

Booth, K. 1983. An introduction to netball. *Bulletin of Physical Education* 19 (1): 27-31.

Bunker, D., and R. Thorpe. 1982. A model for the teaching of games in secondary schools. *Bulletin of Physical Education* 18 (1): 5-8.

Bunker, D., and R. Thorpe. 1986. Is there a need to reflect on our games teaching? P. 25-34 in *Rethinking games teaching*, edited by R. Thorpe, D. Bunker, and L. Almond. Loughborough: University of Technology.

Burrows, L. 1986. A teacher's reactions. P. 45-52 in *Rethinking games teaching*, edited by R. Thorpe, D. Bunker, and L. Almond. Loughborough: University of Technology.

Doolittle, S., and K. Girard. 1991. A dynamic approach to teaching games in elementary PE. *Journal of Physical Education, Recreation and Dance* 62 (4): 57-62.

French, K.E., and J.R. Thomas. 1987. The relation of knowledge development to children's basketball performance. *Journal of Sport Psychology* 9: 15-32.

Fullan, M.G. 1991. *The new meaning of educational change*. 2d ed. New York: Teachers College Press.

Griffin, L. 1994. Designing drills to make practice more perfect. *Strategies* 8 (3): 19-22.

Griffin, L. 1996. Improving games playing: Teaching net/wall games for understanding. *Journal of Physical Education, Recreation and Dance* 67 (3): 34-37.

Griffin, L., J. Oslin, and S. Mitchell. 1995. Two instructional approaches to teaching net games. *Research Quarterly for Exercise and Sport* 66 (1): Supplement, 65-66.

Jones, D. 1982. Teaching for understanding in tennis. *Bulletin of Physical Education* 18 (1): 29-31.

Joyce, B., and B. Showers. 1995. *Student achievement through staff development*. White Plains, NY: Longman.

Lortie, D.C. 1975. *Schoolteacher: A sociological study*. Chicago: University of Chicago Press.

McPherson, S.L. 1994. The development of sport expertise: Mapping the tactical domain. *Quest* 46: 223-240.

McPherson, S.L. 1995. Expertise in women's collegiate tennis: Development of knowledge and skill. Paper presented at the Annual Conference of the North American Society for the Psychology of Sport and Physical Activity, June, at Monterey, CA.

Mitchell, S.A., L.L. Griffin, and J.L. Oslin. 1994. Tactical awareness as a developmentally appropriate focus for the teaching of games in elementary and secondary physical education. *The Physical Educator* 51 (1): 21-28.

Nisbett, R.E., and L. Ross. 1980. *Human inference: Strategies and shortcomings in social judgment*. Englewood Cliffs, NJ: Prentice Hall.

Pajares, M.F. 1992. Teachers' beliefs and educational research: Cleaning up a messy construct. *Research of Educational Review* 62: 307-332.

Peterman, F.P. 1991. An experienced teacher's emerging constructivist beliefs about teaching and learning. Paper presented at the Annual Meeting of the American Educational Research Association, April, at Chicago.

Pigott, B. 1982. A psychological basis for new trends in games teaching. *Bulletin of Physical Education* 18 (1): 17-22.

Rokeach, M. 1968. *Beliefs, attitudes, and values: A theory of organizational change*. San Francisco: Jossey-Bass.

Showers, B. 1982. *Transfer of training: The contribution of coaching*. Eugene, OR: Center for Educational Policy and Management.

Showers, B. 1984. *Peer coaching: A strategy for facilitating transfer of training*. Eugene, OR: Center for Educational Policy and Management.

Showers, B. 1985. Teachers coaching teachers. *Educational Leadership* 42 (7): 43-49.

Siedentop, D. 1994. *Sport education*. Champaign, IL: Human Kinetics.

Smith, M.D. 1991. Utilizing the games for understanding model at the elementary school level. *The Physical Educator* 48 (3): 184-187.

Spackman, L. 1983. Invasion games: An instructional strategy. *British Journal of Physical Education* 14 (4): 98-99.

Stallings, J.A. 1989. *School achievement effects and staff development: What are critical factors?* Paper presented at American Education Research Association annual meeting.

Thorpe, R., D. Bunker, and L. Almond. 1986. A change in focus for the teaching of games. P. 163-169 in *Sport pedagogy: The 1984 Olympic scientific congress proceedings, volume 6*, edited by M. Piéron and G. Graham. Champaign, IL: Human Kinetics.

Veal, M.L. 1993. The role of assessment and evaluation in secondary physical education: A pedagogical view. P. 93-99 in *Critical crossroads: Middle and secondary school physical education*, edited by J.R. Rink. Reston, VA: NASPE.

Waring, M., and L. Almond. 1995. Games-centered games—A revolutionary or evolutionary alternative for games teaching. *European Physical Education Review* 1 (1): 55-66.

Werner, P., and L. Almond. 1990. Models of games education. *Journal of Physical Education, Recreation and Dance* 61 (4): 23-27.

About the Authors

Linda Griffin

Stephen Mitchell

Judy Oslin

Linda Griffin is an assistant professor at the University of Massachusetts, Amherst. She received her undergraduate degree from Black Hills State University, master's degree from Ithaca College, New York, and her PhD in physical education and teacher education from the Ohio State University. With 20 years of experience as a physical educator and coach, Dr. Griffin has conducted extensive research, published nearly 20 articles and abstracts, and given numerous presentations on the tactical approach. She is a member of both the American Alliance for Health, Physical Education, Recreation and Dance (AAHPERD) and the American Educational Research Association (AERA).

Stephen Mitchell is an assistant professor of sport pedagogy at Kent State University. He received his undergraduate and master's degrees from Loughborough University, England, where the tactical approach was first developed, and earned a PhD in teaching and curriculum at Syracuse University. He has employed a tactical approach throughout 15 years of teaching and coaching at the middle school, high school, and college levels. Dr. Mitchell is a member of AAHPERD and the Ohio Association for Health, Physical Education, Recreation and Dance (OAHPERD).

Judy Oslin is an associate professor of sport pedagogy at Kent State University. She received her undergraduate and master's degrees from Kent State and earned a PhD in sport pedagogy at the Ohio State University. She has 23 years of experience as a physical educator and has coached high school basketball and volleyball for 11 years. An avid slow-pitch softball player, Dr. Oslin has played in 13 national tournaments. She has used the tactical approach throughout the past six years with middle school, high school, and college students. Dr. Oslin is a member of AAHPERD, OAHPERD, and AERA.